THE LIFE OF MUSIC

NICHOLAS KENYON

THE LIFE OF MUSIC

New Adventures in the Western Classical Tradition

YALE UNIVERSITY PRESS
NEW HAVEN AND LONDON

For information about this and other Yale University Press publications, please contact:
U.S. Office: sales.press@yale.edu yalebooks.com
Europe Office: sales@yaleup.co.uk yalebooks.co.uk

Set in Arno Pro by IDSUK (DataConnection) Ltd
Printed in Great Britain by TJ Books, Padstow, Cornwall

Library of Congress Control Number: 2021931489

ISBN 978-0-300-22382-8

A catalogue record for this book is available from the British Library.

10 9 8 7 6 5 4 3 2 1

Contents

CONTENTS

Plates

Plate 7 *Le champion des dames* by Martin le Franc, illuminated manuscript, fifteenth century. Bibliothèque nationale de France, Paris. Granger Historical Picture Archive / Alamy Stock Photo.

Francesco Landini in an illustration from the Squarcialupi Codex, vellum, *c.* 1325–35. Biblioteca Medicea Laurenziana, Florence. Science History Images / Alamy Stock Photo.

Plate 8 Johannes Ockeghem in an illustration from *Chants Royaux sur la Conception, couronnés au puy de Rouen*, vellum, *c.* 1519–26. Bibliothèque nationale de France, Paris. DEA PICTURE LIBRARY / Getty Images.

Plate 9 Title page of Palestrina's *Missa Liber Primus*, woodcut, 1584. Bettman / Getty Images.

The Devil with a Bagpipe by Erhard Schön, engraving, *c.* 1525. Private collection. Granger Historical Picture Archive / Alamy Stock Photo.

Plate 10 *A Concert* by anonymous Italian artist, *c.* 1520s. National Gallery, London. Peter Horree / Alamy Stock Photo.

Queen Elizabeth Dancing with the Earl of Leicester, unattributed, *c.* 1581. The Print Collector / Alamy Stock Photo.

Plate 11 Illustrations from *The Triumph of the Emperor Maximilian I* by Hans Burgkmair the Elder, *c.* 1526. INTERFOTO / Alamy Stock Photo.

Plate 12 Orlande de Lassus (also Orlando de Lasso), illustration from *Sacrae Cantiones* by Hans Mielich, *c.* 1565–70. Bayerische Staatsbibliothek, Munich. Lebrecht Music & Arts / Alamy Stock Photo.

Plate 13 Costume designs by Bernardo Buontalenti for the *intermedi*, Florence, 1589. Victoria and Albert Museum, London. Bridgeman Images.

Louis XIV as Apollo the Sun King by Henri de Gissey, 1653. Pictures Now / Alamy Stock Photo.

Plate 14 *Berenstadt, Cuzzoni and Senesino*, original artist believed to be William Hogarth, engraving, 1725. The Print Collector / Alamy Stock Photo.

Armide at the Palais-Royal by Gabriel de Saint-Aubin, watercolour, 1761. Museum of Fine Arts, Boston. The Picture Art Collection / Alamy Stock Photo.

Plate 15 *The Grand Opera* by Giuseppe de Albertis, eighteenth century. © 2021 Museo Teatrale alla Scala, Milan. Photo Scala, Florence.

Intermezzo by Giuseppe de Albertis, eighteenth century. © 2021 Museo Teatrale alla Scala, Milan. Photo Scala, Florence.

Plate 16 *The Mozart Family* by Johann Nepomuk della Croce, *c.* 1780. Mozart Museum, Salzburg, Austria. Pictorial Press Ltd / Alamy Stock Photo.

Lord Cowper and the Gore Family by Johann Zoffany, 1775. Yale Center for British Art, Paul Mellon Collection, USA. Sepia Times / Universal Images Group via Getty Images.

Plate 17 *Liszt at the Piano* by Josef Danhauser, 1840. Gemäldegalerie, Berlin. Peter Horree / Alamy Stock Photo.

Nicoló Paganini by Daniel Maclise, lithograph, 1831. Hulton Archive / Stringer / Getty Images.

Plate 18 Franz Schubert at a music evening by Moritz von Schwind, *c.* 1820.

The Symphony by Moritz von Schwind, detail, oil on canvas, 1852. Neue Pinakothek, Munich. INTERFOTO / Alamy Stock Photo.

Plate 19 *A Concert in the Year 1846* by Andreas Geiger, coloured lithograph, 1846. Bibliothèque nationale de France, Paris. Pictorial Press Ltd / Alamy Stock Photo.

Brahms at the Piano, illustration after a drawing by Prof. W. von Beckerath, *c.* 1890. World History Archive / Alamy Stock Photo.

Plate 20 Set machinery at Bayreuth, anonymous engraving, *c.* 1876. Set design by Carl Brandt. Richard-Wagner-Museum, Bayreuth. DEA / A. DAGLI ORTI / DeAgostini / Getty Images.

Rhinemaidens photographed during the Bayreuth premiere of Wagner's *Ring* cycle, 1876. Lebrecht Music & Arts / Alamy Stock Photo.

Plate 21 *Italian Theatre*, print published by Charles Motte from lithograph by Eugène Delacroix. agefotostock / Alamy Stock Photo.

The Orchestra of the Opera by Edgar Degas, 1870. Musée d'Orsay, Paris. History and Art Collection / Alamy Stock Photo.

Plate 22 Béla Bartók in Draž, Hungary, *c.* 1907. Apic / Getty Images.

Dancers of the Ballets Russes, 1913. Lebrecht Music & Arts / Alamy Stock Photo.

Plate 23 Silhouette of Gustav Mahler by Otto Böhler, *c.* 1900. Lebrecht Music & Arts / Alamy Stock Photo.

Dmitry Shostakovich photographed during the siege of Leningrad, 1942. Heritage Image Partnership Ltd / Alamy Stock Photo.

Plate 24 Edward Elgar at a recording session, 1914. Science History Images / Alamy Stock Photo.

Vladimir Horowitz at the Concertgebouw, Amsterdam, 1986. BNA Photographic / Alamy Stock Photo.

Plate 25 Janáček's *Moravian Dances* sheet music cover, early twentieth century. Prazska Konzervator, Prague. DEA / A. DAGLI ORTI / DeAgostini / Getty Images.

Debussy's *La mer* score cover, 1905, publisher Durand. Historic Collection / Alamy Stock Photo.

Bartók's *Two Romanian Dances* sheet music cover, 1910, publisher Rozsavolgyi. Lebrecht Music & Arts / Alamy Stock Photo.

Plate 26 Vienna Opera House, early twentieth century. Culture Club / Getty Images.

Place de l'Opéra, early twentieth century. ND / Roger Viollet via Getty Images.

Plate 27 Pierre Boulez Saal, Berlin. Photograph Nicholas Kenyon.

Elbphilharmonie, Hamburg, 2017. Photograph Morris MacMatzen-Pool / Stringer / Getty Images.

Plate 28 Nadia and Lili Boulanger, 1913. Rapp Halour / Alamy Stock Photo.

Imogen Holst at Orford church, Suffolk, *c.* 1950. Photograph Kurt Hutton / Stringer / Hulton Archive / Getty Images.

Sofiya Gubaydulina teaching, Lübeck, 2014. Photograph Olaf Malzahn / dpa picture alliance / Alamy Stock Photo.

Plate 29 Walt Disney, Deems Taylor and Leopold Stokowski, 1940. Courtesy Everett Collection. Everett Collection Inc / Alamy Stock Photo.

Gershwin with Fred Astaire and Ginger Rogers on the set of *Shall We Dance?*, *c.* 1936. RBM Vintage Images / Alamy Stock Photo.

Plate 30 Metropolitan Opera production of *Nixon in China* by John Adams, 2011. Photograph Jack Vartoogian / Getty Images.

Aix-en-Provence Opera Festival production of *Written on Skin* by George Benjamin, 2012. Photograph Boris Horvat / AFP / Getty Images.

Plate 31 Yo-Yo Ma at Red Rocks, 2018. Photograph Andy Cross / The Denver Post / Getty Images.

Sheku Kanneh-Mason and In Harmony, 2019. Photograph Richard Martin-Roberts / Getty Images.

Plate 32 *The Hogboon* by Sir Peter Maxwell Davies, 2016. Photograph © Hugo Glendinning.

BBC Proms at the Royal Albert Hall. Photograph © Chris Christodoulou.

Acknowledgements

This project has been far too long in gestation, and I thank its commissioners Malcolm Gerratt and Robert Baldock, then of Yale University Press, both for originally suggesting it and for their patience in waiting for it. The book was finally completed thanks to the vigorous encouragement of Heather McCallum, the virtuoso support of editor Rachael Lonsdale, and the skilful copy-editing of Richard Mason. Richard Abram read the proofs meticulously. Alison Giles has splendidly assembled the pictures of music in performance. Many have helped along the way with thoughts, comments and advice, including the inspiration of all the musicians across the years who brought this music to life. Although they cannot be blamed for any of the gaps and mistakes which remain, I would like to thank Sally Dunkley, Amanda Holden, Robin Baird-Smith, Richard Wigmore and especially my wife Ghislaine. Through the appalling period of Covid-19, when almost all the evenings and weekends that had been filled with planned performances and events in my full-time occupation at the Barbican suddenly evaporated, she kept me continuously nourished, stimulated and alive. It is one tiny benefit of a dreadful time that at least the book got finished.

N.K.

November 2020

Prelude in a Crisis

Before 2020, this book might have been very different. It would have celebrated the fact that music brings us together in so many diverse ways, that people gathering to make music and listen to music is one of the essential things that makes the art form live for all of us.

How the world changes in an instant! The global pandemic of 2020 turned on its head so much that we had believed about the uniting force of live music, as our survival depended on *not* coming together, on *not* gathering, and on isolating safely away from other people. Large gatherings were banned, concert halls and theatres closed, social interaction kept to a carefully controlled minimum. It was not possible for live music to fulfil its traditional function of a communal experience; instead we had to look for other ways for music to work in our lives.

During the Second World War, at a time of great peril for London, the National Gallery's pictures were removed to safety in Wales. But the music played on: the Gallery mounted concerts by the pianist Myra Hess which drew rapt, dedicated audiences whose challenged lives were for a few minutes enhanced by the music they heard. After the attacks of 9/11 in New York in 2001, concert events both large and small, amateur and professional, around the city, featuring music from Brahms's German Requiem and later John Adams's newly commissioned *On the Transmigration of Souls*, assisted the process of response and renewal. When the sudden death of Diana, Princess of Wales, in 1997 traumatised a nation, there were two moments of music at her funeral in Westminster Abbey that caught the public mood and united everyone in shared emotion: Elton John's performance of his own song 'Candle in the Wind', and John Tavener's hypnotic choral *Song for Athene*, its sounds reaching back across the centuries, sung as the coffin was carried out of the abbey to waiting crowds. The power of music needed no greater proof.

It seems that, no matter how great a crisis, this convening power of music helps us to deal with it. To those who have ever doubted whether the technological innovations of the last century have had a positive or negative effect on musical performance and experience – a frequently heard concern among the purist creators of live music – the situation in 2020 gave the immediate answer: technology became the *only* way for us to interact musically. Within a very short time of venues closing down in many countries, shared experiences were being created through digital exchange. Footage of opera ringing out from Italian balconies, ingenious multi-tracking of distanced individual performers recording five or six parts simultaneously, link-ups across continents of soloists and accompanists, virtual orchestras, virtual choirs, either recorded using social distancing or in individual living rooms and offices: the ability of technology to replicate the illusion of togetherness was being celebrated. That was a decisive change: whatever happens in the future, it is certain that online provision will grow in importance even when the crisis diminishes.

There were those in the past, like the pianist Glenn Gould, who loved so much the control and the isolation that the recording studio offered, that he hoped he would never have to give another public concert. Technology would triumph. This did not turn out to be the case during that period, because there was no imperative to abandon live music-making and the public continued to throng to live events. They saw recordings simply as an addition to live performance, not as a substitute for it, and the thirst for visceral experience remained strong. That story has been reinforced during limited emergence from the pandemic. Starved of live performance for too long, both audiences and artists responded strongly to the reinvention of live music-making. The experience of musicians returning from lockdown to that of playing and singing together again has been overwhelming in its intensity. In an uncertain period of recovery, we can be sure that digital delivery and digital creativity in many forms will continue to complement, rather than replace, the impact of the live gathering.

*

The narrative of this book is informed by two complementary perspectives which have changed the way we relate to music today. The first is our growing understanding that music *is* performance: the act of making music is what makes it live. We need to feel the experience across time of hearing music, performing music and receiving it – in the court or the countryside, the coffee house or the concert hall. The time when music was thought to be essentially notes on a page was a limited period in history. The second point is specific to our age: that through technology, because all music is now available to us instantaneously, musical history has become suddenly simultaneous. Whereas in the past the story was a continuous line of development, from the past through the present to the future, now the instant availability of everything allows us to dip in anywhere, to pick and mix. And because all music is there at the flick of a switch or the click of a mouse button, the story is no longer a simple tale of progress. Our engagement with music today is far from linear, and the new adventures of the classical tradition consist of exploring that new non-linear experience. Across the timeline of Western music there are, however, still moments which mark a seismic shift in musical style, which change the way we hear the world. I call these tipping points, because they face both backwards and forwards, growing out of old practice towards new practice. Those very terms – *prima prattica, seconda prattica* – were used in Italy in the early seventeenth century to define the new language of the baroque as distinct from the language of the Renaissance. The two coexisted and overlapped. That was not the only moment in musical history where a change of practice accumulated to create a tipping moment. Early on in music's life, there was the transformation from an oral culture to one defined by notation, and then the creation of equal-voiced harmonious polyphony from the diverse practices of the Middle Ages. Later in its life music emerged from its role in patronage, the church and the court into the public realm in the early nineteenth century; there was the growth of concert culture and the formation of a canon of accepted works.

And perhaps the most striking of all, there was the twentieth century's moment when composers cast aside the trappings of tonal organisation that had sustained music across centuries, and experimented in many different ways with new approaches to musical language and expression. Each of these tipping points is hugely significant, but none is fixed and final. The experience of Western music is continually being expanded by new works and new interpretations of old works, new understandings of what has been important and significant.

There could be many different perspectives on all this abundant creativity. These are my own personal adventures through the turbulent life of music: I tell this story from the point of view of a listener who has been fortunate enough to encounter over the years a wealth of thrilling, exciting and moving music in the Western tradition as it has developed over centuries. It is necessarily a partial and personal view, for the detailed story of our music is currently being reworked by many scholars, with a greater emphasis on social context, on gender, on race, and on the lives of those (both women and men, amateurs and professionals) who brought the music to life. As in so many areas of our culture, the rapidly evolving focus on identity and representation, in particular issues of gender, sexuality and race, is shifting the balance of thinking towards a more inclusive acknowledgement of the roles of many previously overlooked participants and creators, and the study of music is, rightly, gradually incorporating this. Propelled by movements such as Black Lives Matter, for instance, there is renewed vigour to address the huge undervaluing of the impact of African-American culture and to fully recognise and appreciate Black people's presence in and contribution to music today – a crucial subject which deserves more detailed discussion than we can provide here. All this is vital work in progress, and it is likely to change the shape of our understanding of music in the future.

However, there is one changed perspective here which will immediately be evident, and that is the weight and importance I give to the music of earlier centuries over the more familiar repertory of recent times. This reflects my own enthusiasms and experience, but it also reflects our changing understanding. When I was young, I read a respected *History of Music for Young People* written in 1957 which stated baldly:

People gradually get tired of the older music as it recedes further and further into the past. It no longer makes them feel happy or sad; it ceases to move them . . . composers have come along since who have spoken more clearly and sympathetically . . . they have used richer sounds, bigger orchestras, longer tunes, louder noises, and in doing so they mean more to us.

A chapter was even entitled 'Music Emerges from the Twilight'! Even as a child, loving the music of Byrd and Palestrina in my church choir, I knew this view seemed misguided. It is to the credit of the book's author that when he revised it as *A Short History of Music* a couple of decades later, he omitted that passage and retitled the chapter, writing 'There has been no "twilight", merely unawareness and a lack of opportunity to experience.' That opportunity is now with us in abundance, that unawareness can be corrected, and I want to reflect that perspective to the full.

Inevitably, elsewhere there will be huge gaps in this narrative, but I hope these will stimulate you to explore further. This book can do no more than survey the tip of this huge iceberg of music-making across the ages, serious and frivolous, esoteric and popular, oral and written down, representing the skill of countless generations of performers, instrument-builders, philosophers, composers and creators – and the responses of many different audiences. My ambition here can only be to provide a broad context to enhance your enjoyment of music that has inspired me. Go to the end of the book: after the adventures of a thousand years of music, spool back through the centuries in the opposite direction. Sample any of the 100 great works by 100 great composers in 100 great performances, and see what grips you. These works, just some of the very many that have stood the test of time, in superb performances that express their genius, are signalled through the text by asterisked numbers referring to where they appear in the list.

This book is an encouragement to cast the net as wide as possible in your own listening – and a promise that every piece of music mentioned here across a millennium and more of human creativity is a source of passion, enlightenment and adventure worth exploring and worth spending time on; each will repay many times the effort devoted to enjoying and understanding it.

I

Sound and Notes

Music is nothing until it sounds and is heard. Music lives because it is performed and listened to. Notes written on the page will help us to understand what is meant, what is intended by their creator, but they are not the whole story. Among all the arts, music requires a special degree of involvement and participation from players, singers and listeners. There seems no limit to the varieties of human activity that music can support or accompany, no limit to the range of human emotions that music can capture and express. As John Dryden expressed it in his 1687 *A Song for St Cecilia's Day*, which Handel later set to music: 'What passion cannot music raise and quell?'

We know how much music means to us through people's testimony to the importance of music in their lives. Yet we know all too little about the hidden essence of music – why it works for us, what it expresses, and what makes it such a crucial element in all our lives. Huge progress has been made in understanding the science of our reception of music, how we perceive it and how we remember it. Valuable experiments have explored how we learn music, how we memorise musical notes, and how we make music ourselves. This research explores the issue of what creates musical skill: nature or nurture, talent or practice. But what this science doesn't quite tell us is *why* we like the music we do: is it a question of our character, our upbringing, our memory of the music we have heard since birth (or even before, as we lay in the womb)?

1

It is clear that we have an innate, inbred response to music, which may be instinctive and unreflective, and may lead to a thirst to explore it. Everyone will hear music, some will listen, and some will respond by making music. Shouldn't we just get on with it? Isn't it odd to be writing about music rather than playing and singing it? Many have poured scorn on attempts to elucidate the art of music (various people have claimed the view that writing about music is like dancing around architecture, though I always felt that might not be an entirely fruitless pursuit). For anything so elementally important to us as music, there is always a desire to try and explain, to communicate the excitement. There has always been a thirst for understanding and mediation, for analysis and description.

Old narratives of musical adventures could be singular stories of evolution and advancement, because there appeared to be a single current of history. They tended to establish a narrative from the primitive beginnings of plainsong and folk music to the sophisticated present of the symphony orchestra and opera house. Now, in an age of musical diversity, we value the achievements of the musical past equally alongside those of the present, and this single narrative no longer holds. The vista is different. Rather than walking along a corridor, conscious only of what is immediately behind and focused on moving forwards and what is to be encountered ahead, we are now in the equivalent of an open-plan apartment, where every room is equally accessible to us and we can move about freely; we can step from the present back into past centuries, sideways to distant music of other cultures or forwards to adventurous new music. Rather than seeing musical development as organic but linear, we now appreciate that all musical experiences have the potential to inspire us and feel close to us. This is a radically new understanding of music, and it is a richness of our age.

If we accept that music from a far-off tradition or a past age can be as relevant as music from our own back yard, the question is how this revolution has come about. One answer is immediately clear: it is the technology of recording and broadcasting which over the last hundred years and more has made a huge variety of music from across the centuries available to us in a moment. This has brought about a seismic shift in our perceptions, one that we were arguably very slow to recognise.

2

In previous centuries the only music was live music, what was played or heard: no radio, no discs, no internet. And most of that was the contemporary repertory, the music of the time, or earlier pieces that had been passed down by oral tradition. There was certainly 'old music' preserved: in churches and cathedrals, for example, an ancient repertory was kept alive and renewed by repeated performance. But on the whole, it was the music of the day (and increasingly during the late eighteenth and nineteenth centuries, of the day before yesterday) that was heard in concert halls, eventually helping to create – and, some would say, to fossilise – an accepted canon of the Western tradition. That is how the landmarks of classical music from Beethoven and Brahms onwards acquired their special status in our listening.

Popular music had its own flourishing life, passed down orally and so unrecorded until collections of folk ballads and dance music began to be published, and later researchers such as Béla Bartók and Cecil Sharp began to survey and collect traditional music by transcribing and recording performances in the field. As a result, much of the oral tradition of the past is irrevocably lost to us now. But the oral and the written traditions overlapped: while Mozart's *Figaro* was performed in the opera house, as the composer proudly noted, in the streets of eighteenth-century Vienna they played the opera's hits. As the piano became a common domestic instrument for the middle classes in the nineteenth century, you could acquire transcriptions of orchestral works for piano duet and play them at home. That was a kind of 'reproduction' from the concert experience, through which many learned the central repertory of symphonies and orchestral works.

The technology of recording changed all that. It started as the impulse just to make live performance more widely available. It made stars of individuals: performances by singers like Enrico Caruso could, for the first time, travel beyond the opera houses and concert halls to reach an international audience. One of the first conductors to sense the opportunity of recording as a medium in itself was Leopold Stokowski, who created sonic pictures of great sophistication with his orchestras. He then collaborated with Walt Disney in the creation of one of the modern era's most successful attempts to popularise classical music, the animated film *Fantasia*. Here, masterworks including Dukas's *The Sorcerer's Apprentice*, Schubert's *Ave Maria* and Beethoven's 'Pastoral' Symphony took on new visual identities, some abstract (the graphic opening with Bach's Toccata and Fugue in D minor), some programmatic (the inspired linking of Dukas's Sorcerer with the character of Mickey Mouse) (Plate 29).

Increasingly, recording became key to the careers of conductors and soloists, as it later became crucial to the careers of pop musicians. Old-style 78rpm records, totally unfamiliar to generations today, preserved fine performances and enabled them to be circulated, albeit with the drawback of having to turn over the discs in the middle of symphonies or concertos, and carefully tend the needles that played them. Then from the middle of the twentieth century, in a post-war era which had a strong emphasis on popular education and learning, the growth of the new long-playing (33rpm) record transformed the market. Leading musicians earned significant amounts of money as the public eagerly consumed their work. From the 1950s onwards, in a time of widespread belief in public subsidy and investment as a route to an enlightened education, the arts flourished as never before and were enjoyed by more people from a wider social spectrum. We are still living with the inheritance of that rich and rewarding time (Plate 24).

The period after the Second World War saw a huge growth in musical consumption of all kinds, both as solace and as stimulus; radio and recordings became central to our musical experience; they made music available and accessible to all. But the public did not give up live performance as a consequence. Recording supported a thirst for concert- and opera-going: resources were plentiful, and the record companies were content to look for financial return in the long term on their investments in classical repertory (rather than the immediate commercial rewards demanded more recently). The range of music recorded was very wide, and artists who were supported by the recording industry became equally in demand for live appearances. Instructional material for 'music appreciation' became a part of adult as well as of children's learning. This was a now unfashionably top-down approach to musical education, but it produced a huge and devoted public.

Recording continued to be a generator of enthusiasm for music, and it responded to changing technologies. As the new compact disc succeeded the LP in the 1980s, there was a thirst to re-record huge swathes of the repertory in newly clear and transparent performances, and in a medium not so easily damaged by scratches and clicks. The peak of the recording boom in classical music was marked by the success of the Three Tenors concert in Rome in July 1990, where Plácido Domingo, Luciano Pavarotti and José Carreras came together to perform popular arias and specially arranged medleys. The resulting recording is believed to be the world's best-selling classical CD. 'Nessun dorma' from Puccini's *Turandot* was selected as the theme music for the television broadcasts of the football World Cup that year, reaching many more millions, so it is no surprise that many imitations, by the Three Tenors themselves and by many disciples, followed quickly. The emphasis here on extracts, familiar arias and medleys rather than complete works also followed a trend: not unlike the varied approaches of Classic FM and BBC Radio 3 today, or in the old days, the BBC Light Programme and Third Programme. There have always been offers of highlights and popular numbers for some audiences, alongside the exposure to complete works and adventurous pieces for others, helping to form musical taste and enable listeners to expand their repertory.

However, this flourishing period was soon subject to challenge from the development of new technologies for digital distribution. The music industry was lamentably slow to adapt to the opportunity as online streaming and file-sharing took off, retreating instead into defensiveness and hanging on to outdated business models. The balance of power in the world of musical consumption suddenly shifted, and an alarming amount of material became free to access via file-sharing software such as Napster, which facilitated the sharing of music between users. What was not reckoned in such exchanges was the investment of time, energy and talent by composers. Now we are moving gradually towards a fairer system of recompense for creative artists, but it is a slow process; more artists have begun to retain their own control and originate their own material for distribution. We do not know how the balance of power will shift again; the future is wide open.

*

If music is essentially performance and sound, where does that leave the notes on the page? They are of the greatest importance in mediating between the composer's idea and the performer's actions. But they are not everything we need

5

to know. Over the years, composers have taken very different attitudes to how much of a piece of music needs to be specified in written form. You look at the score of an opera by Monteverdi from the start of the seventeenth century (p. 92) and it is totally empty apart from the vocal line, instrumental bass line and text – which tells you that the priority of the composer was to project the words. You look at the orchestral score of a symphony by Mahler from three centuries later (p. 197) and every detail of how every part is phrased, where it gets louder, softer, faster, slower – all this is indicated (Plate 2). In both cases the performer needs to 'realise' the score, and in both cases, this is a deeply creative act of cooperation with the composer. But the relationship is very different: the simplified instruction would be in the first instance that the performer needs to be inventive, whereas in the second they need to obey. Move on a few more decades, and we reach the avant-garde graphic scores of the 1960s (p. 247); these may look like works of art in themselves, the composer may indicate shapes and some notes, but the idea is to stimulate the imagination of the performer rather than specifying a fixed concept.

The extent and purpose of musical notation has changed over the centuries: it provides a framework for the composer to communicate their intentions, while other aspects are left deliberately open. With plainsong, the repertory could be memorised and passed on through an oral tradition long before a notation was created for the chant. The folk tradition thrives on non-notated transmission, passed from one singer and player to another: this does not necessarily imply any vagueness, but does depend on a close continuity of tradition. As the complexity of music increased, there was a need for notation which conveyed precise details of speed and loudness, the phrasing and articulation of the musical lines, all crowding onto the page in an attempt to be explicit.

That is still only one part of the story. Everything we read about the great performers of the past suggests that even when music existed in written or printed form, they recreated it with freedom and individuality. A nineteenth-century composer-pianist such as Frédéric Chopin or Franz Liszt (p. 172) used *rubato* freely. This is a rhythmic unevenness beyond that portrayed in the score, in order to bring expressive life to the music. For example, while the left hand sustains a steady pace, the right hand of the pianist might take some passages faster or slower, 'stealing' time within the framework of the piece to animate it. Speed varied within a piece even if there was only one tempo marking; the invention of the metronome provided a mechanical measure with which to set tempo. Beethoven and (more reluctantly) Brahms made use of metronome marks to indicate the speed of their movements, but they did not imagine these speeds being inflexibly applied to every bar. Schumann provided metronome marks but then encouraged performers to play faster ('*Schneller!*').

A significant, and potentially negative, aspect of music-making in the last century has been that dependence on a written score has become such a priority both for the training and the work of musicians. In many previous eras, ornamentation and improvisation were expected, and common in performance. Sometimes these elements would be written out, but often they would not be. In baroque opera, the decoration of an aria by a virtuoso singer was expected by the audience, especially in the repeat of the first section which was a regular feature of these arias. We know that Mozart would have assumed that a pianist would improvise or elaborate the solo parts he wrote in a concerto, and that he did this himself: he would certainly have improvised passages and added cadenzas, and some of these he wrote out – but as guides, not as fixed parts of the score. These days we have to use our taste as to what matches Mozartian style: in cadenzas added to Mozart's concertos by later composers from Beethoven to Busoni, they take the music into their own harmonic sound-world, and there is a debate as to how well that fits, or whether it establishes a connection with our time. In the early 1980s, the Russian composer Alfred Schnittke (p. 250) added a strikingly modern cadenza for the adventurous soloist Gidon Kremer to play in Beethoven's Violin Concerto, to consternation from audiences.

Some composers provide detailed information on the type of ornamentation they expected; in publications of seventeenth- and eighteenth-century French keyboard music, for example, there are copious tables of how to realise the signs and symbols which form part of the notation. I particularly like the comment of the French composer Michel de La Barre in the 1710 advertisement of his flute works that 'there are two or three notes which I believe no one knows . . . if those who would like to learn would take the trouble to pass by my home . . . it would give me great pleasure, with no obligation to them, to show them how'. The violin sonatas of Arcangelo Corelli at the start of the eighteenth century (p. 130) were provided with all manner of embellishment by performers, and those elaborations were published in their own right. Composers created their music in very different ways: J. S. Bach's organ preludes and Chopin's piano ballades are probably written-out versions of material that their virtuoso composers improvised in performance. Even music that we think of as fixed, like the opera arias of the nineteenth century, were hugely varied in their delivery by performers: very early recordings show the tremendous liberties that singers took with the written score – liberties that composers such as Verdi clearly expected them to take, even if he resented them (p. 181). He wrote wearily to his publisher, 'Once one had to tolerate the tyranny of the prima donna; now, also, that of the conductor.'

This raised the whole issue of 'interpretation' both by singers and by conductors. We can trace back to Wagner the view that the conductor should not just follow the notes on the page, but should seek to understand them, mould them and deliver them to an audience in an individual way. He considered the unimaginative, slavish adherence to the notes a weakness of the typical German Kapellmeister who could never 'sing a melody, whether his voice was good or bad. Music to them is a mixture of grammar, mathematics, and gymnastic exercises.' Like many artists, Wagner believed that 'the first rule of interpretation is to convey the composer's intention with scrupulous fidelity . . . to transmit his thoughts without any change or loss'; but the question remained how best to achieve this. In one vivid passage, Wagner the conductor imagines the ghost of Beethoven speaking to him about the four-note phrase with dramatic pauses (the 'V for victory' theme, as it became known through its use in wartime) that forms the famous opening of the Fifth Symphony:

My pauses must be long and serious ones. Hold them firmly, terribly. I did not write them in jest or because I was at a loss how to proceed . . . I arrest the waves of the ocean, and the depth must be visible; or I stem the clouds, disperse the mist, and show the pure blue ether and the radiant eye of the sun . . . Ponder them here on the first announcement of the theme. Hold the long E flats firmly after the three short tempestuous quavers . . .

Wagner the interpreter has no doubt what Beethoven the composer is telling him. That, of course, has to be the position of any interpreter, who has to have the absolute conviction that their view of a piece is the right one for that moment in time. The rest of us can balance our views, and choose different interpretations. The performer must deliver.

*

Every music teacher would accept that just observing a text correctly is never going to create a living, breathing performance, yet so many musicians and students (and those who take music examinations) are judged by whether they meet this criterion of accuracy. It may be that our late twentieth-century preoccupation with 'following the composer's intentions' has in this respect been a negative influence. The slogan of going 'back to the original' and the quest for 'pure' editions have been thought to imply a slavish following of the score, whereas that should more readily imply a liberation of the imagination.

We are living with the legacy of a strong traditional line through the Western classical tradition that privileges the notated score as the primary source of music. As we follow the creation of a repertory, we will encounter, by the sixth and seventh centuries, signs called neumes. They were written down, for example in the chant book that survives from St Gall in Switzerland; a text with a symbol, no more than a squiggle, placed above it which shows roughly where it lies in relation to the pitch before or after it. These were probably aids to singing music that had already been learned and memorised. Some chant is then copied with a single red line representing a single note, above and below which the pitches are placed; a yellow or green line for another note was then added. The abbot Odo of Cluny seems to have been the first to assign letters to notes in his *Dialogus de Musica* of 935 AD. It was not until around 1028 that Guido d'Arezzo compiled his now famous *Micrologus* which gave Western music the advanced capability to be written down. The Latin hymn *Ut queant laxis* produced the acrostic (based on the initial letters of each line) for the first notes of the six-note scale *Ut re mi fa sol la*:

> *Ut queant laxis*
> *Re-sonare fibris*
> *Mi-ra gestorum*
> *Fa-muli tuorum,*
> *Sol-ve polluti*
> *La-bii reatum*
> *Sancte Johannes.*

(If that ancient hymn seems vaguely familiar, just say the initial syllables to yourself, substituting *Doh* for the first *Ut*, and you may find yourself singing a famous song from *The Sound of Music*, by which Maria taught the von Trapp children.)

The creation of notation that enabled music to be transmitted by written means is the first big tipping point in Western music: as in all these moments, it was not a sudden change, but a gradual evolution. By the thirteenth century a four-line stave for chant had been developed, and then a five-line stave for polyphony. This has remained astonishingly unchanged across the centuries; indeed, the latter stave became universally used in Western music, with the placing of a clef that shows which notes are represented. The most common clefs, used for instance in most piano music, are the treble clef for the right hand, which curls around the note G on the second line up, and the bass clef for the left hand, which has two dots around the note F in the second line down. You might not recognise these as ornamental versions of the letters G and F, but that is how they originated.

This was not the only way that music was notated. For the lute and guitar, 'tablature' used letters to indicate notes; this was popular in the sixteenth and seventeenth centuries because it helped to indicate the fingerings to be used on the instrument. Some organ music was also written in tablature (including the earliest scores that we believe J. S. Bach wrote out when he was a teenager), sometimes with a mixture of normal notation for the top line and letter notation underneath. The descendant of that today is the normal notational device used for guitars and

for popular song, in which a melody is notated on a stave, while the chord sequence that accompanies it is given as a sequence of letters.

The labels invented by Guido d'Arezzo came back into their own during the
nineteenth century. 'Tonic sol-fa' was a system invented by John Curwen to help
those untrained in notation to learn to sing. The same syllables employed by
Guido (except for *Doh* instead of *Ut,* and the addition of the seventh note, *Te*)
were used to indicate the degrees of the scale; these written syllables replaced the
notes on the stave. This development coincided with the rapid growth of choirs
and choral societies, and the general teaching of singing in schools. It served its
purpose, even managing to indicate rhythms by the spacing of the letters used
to denote the pitch. There have been many other attempts to create alternatives
to conventional notation, but few have succeeded in establishing themselves and
displacing the traditional staves.

However, as modern music has developed new techniques and sounds, so
new notational devices have been invented to communicate them, often of great
ingenuity and visual originality. Graphic notation has proved a fertile source of
invention. Composers combined normal notation and clefs with a graphic layout,
often visually attractive, with cross-cutting patterns of staves and instructions, or
combined staves with graphic lines, pauses, dynamics in seemingly random juxtaposition. John Cage's scores are always exquisitely drawn (p. 245). For music with
limited amounts of freedom, various devices such as boxes of notes are imposed
on conventional staves, indicating where the performers can improvise within
clearly set limits, for example in the superbly crafted orchestral music of Witold
Lutosławski (p. 240), with its controlled areas of improvisation.

At the extreme of contemporary notation are pieces for which the instructions
consist only of texts. Stockhausen's *Setz die Segel zur Sonne* says:

> play a tone for so long
> until you hear its individual vibrations
> hold the tone
> and listen to the tones of the others
> – to all of them together, not to individual ones –

and slowly move your tone

until you arrive at complete harmony

and the whole sound turns to gold

to pure, gently shimmering fire

Some of these instructional notations have other performance elements. La Monte Young's *Composition 1960 No. 5* instructs: 'Turn a butterfly (or any number of butterflies) loose in the performance area. When the composition is over, be sure to allow the butterfly to fly away outside. The composition may be any length but if an unlimited amount of time is available, the doors and windows may be opened before the butterfly is turned loose and the composition may be considered finished when the butterfly flies away.' These verbally notated pieces enjoyed success in the 1960s as composers aimed to strip music back to its barest essentials, but as complexity increased a reversion to conventional notation took place; some of the big orchestral works of recent years have stunningly complex layouts.

The relation between notation and performance is at the heart of our music-making, and has long been a central tension of the Western classical music tradition. A century and more ago, academic study privileged music as a set of texts that had to be analysed in the same way as any other formal literary tradition, with the same editorial rigour. The notes on the page were what mattered. The volumes of collected works on library shelves were what music was. But now you look around, seeing the many sources of music, and the issue is more subtle: we sense how much of what is not written down makes a thrilling performance. What then is the essence of music?

2

Ritual

Tap, tap, tap, tap: the regular beat, knocking on a block of wood, that opens John Adams's minimalist fanfare *Short Ride in a Fast Machine* must be uncannily similar to the elements that first made music in the world. And just as Adams's vividly effective piece becomes more and more complex during its few minutes' length, those percussive sounds from ancient times and remote cultures quickly gained depth and sophistication. There is a common feeling across those experiences: the sense of a rite taking us beyond everyday life into an event that expresses something more than everyday feeling, of art as ritual.

Howard Goodall's 2013 history of music, written as a companion to his illuminating television series *The Story of Music*, claims that 'Not that long ago, music was a rare and feeble whisper in a wilderness of silence.' But surely there never really was silence. There is always something to be heard, which is why the piano piece *4'33"* by John Cage is not just the joke that many like to suppose, but a serious (though also witty) statement about the nature of sound (p. 245). There are no notes written in this supposedly silent piece (which he originally conceived as 'Silent Prayer'), but there is always some noise around the hall, or in the outside environment, to be listened to and attended to; all the piece does is to 'organise' what happens into three movements, limited by time. It focuses our attention, forcing us to concentrate on what we can hear around us.

Recent research suggests that the propensity to concentrate on the musicality of the audible is innate to humankind. Investigations into the complex neurological structure of the human brain suggest, as Henkjan Honing puts it in *The Origins of Musicality*, that the brain is 'hard-wired for music'. We are as tuned into music as we are to language. We start with a natural inclination to musical communication, and, as with language, the basic underlying functions that enable music processing – a combination of many different neural systems which enable us to create, to hear, to reproduce and to memorise music – seem to be present in all normally developing human brains. Some of the sounds that newborn babies make seem closer to music than to language. They use these sounds to communicate, to share, to exchange feelings; they are a natural part of evolution. This is quite a radical discovery. For a long time, music was viewed as a secondary cultural development that needed extensive practice and training to acquire its skills – a view which played into a deep-seated Western view that music was somehow an add-on to life, an unnecessary luxury. The respected cognitive psychologist and linguist Steven Pinker was taken to task by the popular neuroscientist Daniel Levitin for saying as late as 1997 that 'music is auditory cheesecake', while in 1994 Pinker wrote in *The Language Instinct* that 'music is useless . . . music could vanish from our species and the rest of our lifestyle would be virtually unchanged'.

Musicality is increasingly understood as core to our being, a view argued by Levitin and others who have studied music's physiological impact. Making music may have emerged comparatively late in the long lifespan of what we now call *homo sapiens*, but given that music appears in some form in every period and every culture (and emerging evidence suggests that it is also perceived and used by some animals), the consensus now is that, as Honing puts it, 'although there is no widely shared definition of music, the presence of several cross-cultural similarities supports the notion of musicality as a prominent characteristic of humankind'. If we agree that music is elemental to our nature, the question is then: how do we define music? What distinguishes music from other human utterances and activity?

For me, it is anything that moves beyond just sound, something that adds a human touch, a creative dimension, to what already exists around us. I like Leonardo da Vinci's phrase (p. 65) that music is 'a shaping of the invisible'. As soon as sound begins to be organised, it moves from nature to art. All humans and animals breathe and shout, creating noise to communicate; it is a small step from that to making particular noises and sounds in patterns, perhaps to accompany significant rites or ritual events. It is a small step from hitting a stone on a stone accidentally or in anger, or to attract attention, to hitting it rhythmically and for a purpose. It is a small step from tapping two sticks together, perhaps to strike a fire, to make them sound and create a pattern with those taps. It is another step, involving a creative understanding of the possibilities, to empty a bone and puncture it with holes so that when it is blown into it creates differently pitched notes.

Charles Darwin believed that music – more precisely, singing – was used both by emerging humans and our predecessors the gibbon-apes as a part of courtship, expressing emotions 'such as love, jealousy, triumph – and would have served as a challenge to rivals'. Other cultures have used music as a medium for communication with the dead, for initiation rituals, varying its meanings but understanding its power. As a leading scholar in this field Ian Cross has expressed it in *Music, Mind and Evolution*, there seems to be a paradox. On the one hand 'music appears to have no immediate specifiable effects. Music neither ploughs, sows, weaves nor feeds; in itself music ... seems to be inefficacious.' Yet it has some 'universal characteristics – roots in sound and movement, heterogeneity of meaning, a grounding in social interaction and a personalised significance, together with an apparent inefficacy'. We can surely add that just because we cannot measure music's effect on us, this does not mean its effect cannot be profound and indeed crucial: Cross concludes that 'a good case can be made for music, or proto-musical behaviours, as being not only useful but essential for individual cognitive development and in the development of capacities for flexible social interaction'. At root, we need music in order to live a full life.

What music there may have been in the distant past we are unaware of today, because it was not written down. Some have presumed that there was no music until it could be transmitted or transcribed, but from the beginning, music may have been central to life without ever needing to be captured in the way that became a preoccupation for later ages. Others have theorised a startlingly precise starting point; John Frederick Rowbotham in his 1885 history of music

15

memorably suggested that primitive man was originally content with one note (G!), and subsequently progressed to two and three notes. This seems inherently implausible. We cannot say as he did that instrumentally there was a 'drum stage', followed by a 'pipe stage', followed by a 'lyre stage' – that represents a rather limited view of the development of musical genres.

The problem is that the records of how such music came to be in ancient civilisations are tantalisingly elusive. What we do have is a scattering of instruments that have survived to us. What is believed to be a bone flute was discovered in a context linked to human activity near Württemberg in Germany that dates back around 35,000 years. It does not appear so very different from a recorder we would play today. There is an isolated earlier survival from 9,000 years before, a bone with holes that could possibly be a flute-like instrument, or maybe is just the result of animal wear and tear over the centuries. Archaeologists are experimenting with the implications of sounds that can be created from rock formations and flint tools: do they suggest that these were used in some form of music-making? Consider too the famous cave paintings of Lascaux in southwestern France, which depict flutes made of bone and percussion instruments from 17,000 years ago. We cannot be certain what they were used for, but they seem to represent music's use in ritual which is central to many cultures, whether for the worship of gods or the sharing of human emotion. There are certainly common trends in hunter-gatherer societies, where communities meet to express their cohesion and common purpose, using music as a method to do so. There is much still to be discovered here.

Tutankhamen's golden face mask may be the most instantly recognisable find from the magnificent treasures unearthed in the Valley of the Kings by archaeologist Howard Carter a century ago, but to musicians, equally compelling survivals were the bronze and silver trumpets preserved in the tomb, which must have been put there around 1325 BC. They can, just about, be played, though who knows whether their rasping sounds bear a relation to what was originally heard from them. We cannot even be sure whether they were used in a way we would recognise as musical instruments. They were probably used for signalling, in hunt or battle. They do, however, symbolise the importance of such instruments as possessions of the young king that he would want or need in the afterlife.

The many depictions of musical activity recorded in art from the ancient Mediterranean lands are vivid, but it is a continuing puzzle for us what this music sounded like in actuality; many instruments are pictured, but their sounds are irretrievably lost. The Old Testament, especially the Book of Psalms, has vivid depictions of praising the Lord to the sound of wind and percussion instruments accompanied by dancing. It was the sound of trumpets that caused the walls of Jericho to collapse. David cures Saul (as reimagined in a later age in Handel's oratorio *Saul*: p. 120) by singing to the harp. But what did he sing?

Only in recent decades have scholars managed to decode one surviving tablet from around 1200 BC that was discovered in Ugarit in modern Syria, consisting of notation on a Babylonian cuneiform tablet. It is a hymn to the goddess Nikkal, and the music seems to be made of consonant harmonious interludes, thirds and sixths, without discernible rhythm. It is impossible to know how it was performed, though some have tried, creating hypothetical flowing sounds of beauty but no great substance.

References to music increase in landmark ancient Greek works such as Homer's *Iliad* and *Odyssey* from around 800 BC; however uncertain their authorial origins, music is common in both, and it seems likely that in their transmission they were declaimed to the accompaniment of the lyre. We know from Plato in his *Ion* of the emotions roused by the telling of such tales: 'I must frankly confess that at the tale of pity, my eyes filled with tears, and when I speak of horrors, my hair stands on end and my heart throbs . . . I look down upon spectators from the stage and behold the various emotions of pity, wonder, sternness, stamped upon their countenances when I am speaking.' Of larger gatherings of musicians we know all too little, though there is an early account of some 800 performers in 709 BC where Pherekydes of Patrae is described as 'giver of Rhythm', sitting on a high seat and waving a golden staff so that 'the men began in one and the same time', moving 'his stave up and down in equal movements so that all might keep together'. This sounds like the first account we have of a modern conductor.

We know enough to deduce that music played a fundamental role in classical Greece alongside poetry and movement. The idea of performance was central not just to artistic events but to declamation by a politician or a lawyer; sport was

equally treated as a performance event. After 500 BC there are significant theoretical writings on music, and we can only presume from this that the art of music had progressed in practical as well as theoretical ways. The first outstandingly
important Greek theorist was Pythagoras (c. 570–c. 495 BC), who explored the
harmonic ratios that produce musical sounds. He drew attention to and defined
the sound of the octave, one of the most naturally harmonious intervals we can
recognise. The sense of unity given by the sound of the octave is one of the underpinning ideas of all Western music. There is a physical reason for this: the number of vibrations per second that produce the sound is doubled an octave higher,
halved an octave lower. It is one of the fundamental facts about music.

His understanding of the nature of the octave as a musical interval set the
template for much future thinking. As is often the case with important discoveries, myth and legend surround Pythagoras's discovery. The story recorded in
Nicomachus's *Manual of Harmonics* is that Pythagoras passes a blacksmith's shop,
hears differently pitched, harmonious tones coming from the anvils being struck,
goes in to investigate and sees that the hammers and anvils are different sizes, but
all are ratios of each other – twice as big, or two-thirds the size, and so on – and
from this he derived his theory of intervals: the logically derived ratios between
sounds. Although the anvils story is doubtless a myth, the ratios discovered by
Pythagoras do fit with the sounds produced by vibrating lengths of string, which
he is also credited with identifying. Pluck a string exactly half the length of another and it will play a sound exactly an octave higher: the relationship of the
octave is 2:1. Divide the string into thirds and the pitch is raised an octave and
a fifth: the relationship is 3:1. Split it into quarters and you get a double octave:
4:1. An octave plus a fourth is 4:3, and an octave plus a fifth is 3:2, and so on.
(These relationships are derived from the theories of numerical ratios recorded by
Euclid in his *Elements of Geometry* – an important landmark which may also have
influenced architecture: some commentators have suggested that the placing of
columns in Greek temples relates to the theory of musical scales that Pythagoras
developed.)

Pythagoras's concept is known as the harmonic series, and a Pythagorean
scale is constructed using only perfect fifths (tones in the ratio 3:2) and octaves

(2:1). Such a system embodied an important elemental belief of Pythagoras and the Greeks: that the consonances of music reflected the harmony of the cosmos, which in its turn embodied a numerical truth – the planets themselves sounding notes of vibration depending on their orbit and distance, a perfect heavenly music that humans simply had not the capacity to hear. Much later, there would be an attempt to divide the pure octave into twelve equal semitones, the basis of what became known as the well-tempered keyboard (p. 126). But there has always been a slight conflict between the purity of Pythagorean intervals and the compromises of the well-tempered system, and it is actually the unevenness of some of those chromatic intervals that gives our present-day major and minor keys their individual character.

Ancient Greek philosophers began to treat music as a central part of their world view. Around 450–325 BC, Socrates, his pupil Plato and his successor Aristotle all proposed influential thinking about music, advocating its use as an aid to attain both pleasure and the moral good, but also warning against the strong hold that music can take on our inmost souls. The infectious power of music to lead people to lose their sober judgement was clearly a worry for the purity of Greek thought. Plato derived his thinking from Socrates: he developed it into a consistent philosophy that music and art had the purpose of not merely being entertaining, but helping to build a full and harmonious personality, quelling the more extreme human passions: in his famous dialogue from the *Republic* he said that 'when a man abandons himself to music to play upon him and pour into his soul as it were through a funnel of his ears those sweet, soft and dirge-like harmonies . . . when he continues the practice without remission and is spellbound, the effect begins to be that he melts and liquefies till he completely dissolves away his spirit'. Music was therefore admitted to possess immense power, but it was a dangerous power that could corrupt and destroy, so it had to be used judiciously and with care.

Aristotle debated whether music should be classed among the not-so-serious pursuits and be regarded as pleasant, like sleep and heavy drinking; he nevertheless argued in his *Politics* that the young be taught music, 'for the young owing to their nature cannot endure anything not sweetened by pleasure, and music by

19

its nature is a thing that has a pleasant sweetness . . . We all pronounce music to be one of the pleasantest things, whether instrumental or instrumental and vocal together, and that is why people with good reason introduce it at parties and entertainments for its exhilarating effect.' This distinction between music as frivolous pleasure and serious pursuit was one that was to recur many times over the following centuries, a swing of the pendulum that has continued to this day.

The thinking of Aristotle was refined by his pupil Aristoxenus, born about 350 BC. In his *Harmonic Elements* he moves away from the Pythagorean view that music is a reflection of mathematics and celebrates it as an independent art. He was the first theorist to suggest that the ear needs to be trained to appreciate sound precisely. He seems a somewhat stern theorist, but he had a practical approach to musical art; among his many theoretical observations on the science of harmonies and intervals he characterises the different modes and is credited with bringing the elements of Greek music together in a refined and orderly system. Of great interest to us today is the fact that he was the first theorist to write about the audience receiving music, perceiving it via the ear rather than regarding it as a function of numbers.

It is tantalising that with such a wealth of writing about music from the Greeks, so very little of the actual music survives, probably around forty fragments, and that which does survive is either incomplete or difficult to decode. Yet the Greeks wrote so positively about their music that we must presume that its quality was recognised and appreciated. We read of Sakados, who at the Pythian Games of 586 BC played what sounds to us something like a modern suite of programme music called 'Preparation', 'Challenge', 'The Fight', 'Song of Praise' and 'Victory Dance' – pre-echoing by several centuries the concept behind Heinrich Biber's *Battalia*, a seventeenth-century sequence of picture-pieces about war (p. 89).

We also know something of the instruments that the Greeks created and played (Plate 3). Important among these was the aulos, a wind instrument with twin pipes, played with a single or double reed, central to Greek drama, and extensively used in the celebrations around sports as well. Later it became a solo instrument in its own right: there are accounts by Lucian in the second century BC of a player of the aulos called Harmonides who blew his instrument so loudly that he expired on the spot. Then there was the syrinx, a flute-like wind instrument blown without reeds; Debussy paid homage to the name in the title of a work for solo flute. The lyre, associated with the cult of Apollo, accompanied recitation of dramatic poetry or dancing; it was taken up by the Anglo-Saxons and a famous example is in the Sutton Hoo burial ship. The kithara was a lyre-like plucked instrument for professional musicians, played with a plectrum, at first with seven strings, later up to eleven – a distant ancestor of the guitar. Most familiar to us in much bigger guises today is the organ: a pipe instrument controlled by a keyboard and/or pedals, originally built in Alexandria and praised by Pliny the Elder, and used to accompany games. Organists like to claim a great pedigree for their chosen instrument; as Peter Williams wrote in his authoritative survey, 'the organ is an instrument with the longest history of all, with a repertory larger than that of any other instrument and with a magnificence beyond any other musical invention from the Greeks to the present day'.

We search among the remaining fragments for the survival of notated music. Finding it and recognising it is one thing, decoding it quite another. There is a short fragment of a chorus from Euripedes' *Orestes*, but scholars dispute whether the damaged musical notation (which uses letters to indicate the notes) represents the original of 408 BC or a later addition; in any case it can hardly be deciphered. A couple of pieces of Greek music have come down to us from the first century AD: a Delphic hymn discovered incomplete in 1893, and the very short but complete Seikilos epigraph found on a stele in Tralleiss in Asia Minor in 1883. Because this is intact, it can be transcribed and at least hypothetically performed. In a flowing triple-time rhythm, within the range of an octave, the text exhorts us to be radiant while we live, because life's span is short. Perhaps it would have been accompanied by instruments, as contemporary illustrations suggest – though care needs to be taken not to assume that visual depictions are accurate portrayals of reality rather than purely symbolic in meaning. (This is also an issue with many medieval illuminations of music-making by angels and humans, and in later paintings too.)

As the Western world shifted from Greek to Roman culture, and as the Christian church gained in strength when the Roman Empire collapsed in the fifth century, the church inherited much earlier thinking about the role of music, including a strongly moral tone about its enjoyment. The most important early father of the Christian church, St Augustine of Hippo (354–430), who articulated so many influential positions in early church thinking, famously worried about the effect that music had on him. This relates closely to Plato's concern about the dangerous power of music. Augustine acknowledged the positive benefits of music; as he wrote in his *Confessions*, 'When I recall the tears that I shed at the song of the Church in the first days of my recovered faith, and even now as I am moved by the things that are sung – when chanted with fluent voice and completely appropriate melody – I acknowledge the great benefit of this practice.' But he was equally concerned about perverting his devotions by the performance itself distracting him from the text it was expressing: 'Yet when it happens that I am moved more by the song than by what is sung, I confess sinning grievously, at which time I wish not to have heard the music.' This both expresses an awareness of the value of music, and of the importance in the religious context of the texts being paramount; the beauty of the music should not overcome the communication of the liturgical text and its meaning, a common theme of debates around sacred music across the centuries (which is why plainsong and Palestrina have always been preferred by the Catholic church to the excesses of the baroque, or the Masses of Mozart, which Igor Stravinsky described as 'those rococo-operatic sweets of sin').

The most important link between the Greek theorists and the new world of Christian music-making is the imposing but enigmatic figure of Boethius, born about 480 and executed in 524 on charges of treason. Powerful as an intellectual in his day, Boethius established a major reputation as a theorist which had a long-lasting influence on the medieval world. His treatise *De institutione musica*, bringing together theories of music and mathematics, is perhaps the most famous of his works, repeatedly copied and passed down to his successors, though not printed until as late as 1491. His characterisation of music as a liberal art was influential and long-lasting. He inherited the concept that music could affect our behaviour, either ennobling or corrupting our character: as he wrote in *De institutione musica*, 'nothing is more characteristic of human nature than to be soothed by sweet modes and stirred up by their opposites'. He agreed with Plato that 'the soul of the universe is united by musical concord'. He unpicked further than his predecessors the different kinds of music that provoked differing responses. The first was the music of the universe, *musica mundana*, the relationships of the planets, and the rhythm of the annual seasons, which are beyond our hearing. Then there was *musica humana*, our own music which reconciles the different parts of our nature: 'what else joins together the parts of the soul itself, which in the opinion of Aristotle is a joining together of rational and irrational?' Finally there was *musica instrumentalis*, music produced by instruments: 'this is produced by tension, as in strings, or by blowing, as in the tibiae or in those instruments activated by water, or by some kind of percussion, as in instruments which are struck upon certain bronze concavities, by which means various sounds are produced'. Boethius's noble conclusion was that 'every art, and every discipline as well, has by nature a more honourable character than a handicraft, which is produced by the hand and labour of a craftsman' – that is, that music is more than just a technical skill. 'He is a musician who on reflection has taken to himself the science of singing, not by the servitude of his work but by the rule of contemplation.' Thus, music was elevated into a high art beyond mere craftsmanship (Plate 4).

These theorists may seem remote to us today, but they demonstrate the continuing importance of music in thinking about the human condition. As the Christian tradition developed, St Isidore of Seville (*c.* 560–636) was the theorist who gathered together a wealth of reflections and definitions in his *Etymologiae*, a veritable medieval database. For him, music was not just a science but the exercise of the imagination. Isidore's view was that 'when something is debated in reliable discussion, it is a discipline; when something is treated fancifully and imaginatively, it bears the name of art'. His analysis describes the scientific aspects of intervals, modes and instruments, and he also devotes attention to the live aspects of performance, which was the model for later thinking. He followed earlier theorists in linking music back to the harmony of the heavens ('For the very universe, it is said, is held together by a certain harmony of sounds') and by dividing music into three parts, but placed himself in the line of St Augustine in referring to harmonic music, by which he meant singing, organic music produced by blowing, and rhythmic music 'produced by the impulse of the fingers'. Isidore wrote that 'music moves the feelings and changes the emotions', but he also believed that 'unless sounds are remembered by man, they perish, for they cannot be written down': an important prelude to the first major tipping point in Western music, the arrival of notation. In implying that he was not aware of the earliest musical notations, Isidore represents the quest for a system that would capture those sounds in more permanent form.

Isidore attempts a more humanistic view when summarising 'what music can do'. 'Music composes distraught minds, as may be read of David, who freed Saul from the unclean spirit by the art of melody. The very beasts also, even serpents, birds and dolphins, music incites to listen to her melody. But every word we speak, every pulsation of our veins, is related by musical rhythms to the powers of harmony.' Some believe that Isidore showed the kind of spirit that the originators of opera tried to recapture at the dawn of the Renaissance. His alliance of music with the imagination opened the way to music's role in the future and led to a more open-minded approach to the question of performance and music's role in the liturgy of the church.

In the early years of Christianity, especially around the eastern Mediterranean, elements were adopted both from Greek culture and from Jewish tradition. From the long tussles which resulted in the split between the Eastern and Western church at the end of the fourth century, centres of liturgical life developed in Byzantium and Rome, both spreading their cultural traditions and developing the varied Orthodox and Roman liturgies. What became known as Gregorian chant formed the bedrock of the Roman musical tradition as it spread around Europe. While much of this was initially transmitted orally, and secular music, dance music and folk music continued to be shared in this way, there was, through the work of the monastic communities of the West, an eventual move towards notated music. We are at the first tipping point of the Western tradition, on the threshold of written-down Western music which begins a long – though arguably partial – history of the art form, and transforms our ability to understand the music of the past and its performance through direct contact with its sources.

3

Chant

When we hum a tune to ourselves, in the street or doing the washing-up or in the shower, we are on our own: there is one single line of music for us to experience. We may imagine an orchestra in support of our song, but these days, when every video or advertisement we see is underpinned by pulsating harmony and rhythm, that is a highly unusual way to experience music. Yet it is the way that a whole culture of musical life occurred in the medieval Catholic church. Chanting as an idea may conjure up for us a noisy football match or the hypnotic repetitions of a cult, but it is also what forms one of the longest lasting musical repertories in our civilisation. Just one example: an evocative moment of the liturgy of the Christian church's year is the moment of Christ's passage from death to resurrection as Easter Sunday begins. In the past, this was celebrated with a dramatic transition, from a church in total darkness, to the lighting of a single paschal candle, and then that light spreading from candle to candle to illuminate the whole church with the celebration of new life. The discovery by the disciples of Christ's empty tomb is a moment marked by a line of plainsong that has always remained in my ears from my choirboy days. It is an antiphon from the story in St Mark's Gospel, a short, mostly stepwise chant, concentrated in its simplicity and purity: *Et valde mane una sabbatorum veniunt ad monumentum orto iam sole, Alleluia* ('And early in the morning on the Sabbath, they came to the tomb before the sun had risen, Alleluia').

There is nothing unique about that particular chant compared with the hundreds of antiphons that survive for the Catholic liturgy, but it has a totally memorable melodic shape and flow, and sums up for me the nature of the plainsong repertory. Plainsong achieves something special in music: there is a very elemental feeling in the sound of that single line of music. Even a traditional folk song tends to have supporting chords or percussion; plainsong, however, is an isolated melody that has the sole function of expressing a liturgical text. Yet this can be as expressive and as meaningful as any of the more complex forms of the Western tradition from Beethoven's symphonies to Wagner's operas, and through its performance it is possible to feel a direct link with past centuries that is as real as experiencing an ancient building or an old manuscript.

Plainsong was a continually evolving tradition, always subject to change and development, but it is based on a structure of performance that has remained fundamentally unchanged for centuries, in spite of liturgical and ecclesiastical revolutions. The liturgy of the Roman Catholic Mass has inspired countless composers over many centuries in a number of different forms and idioms – it must surely be the collection of texts most often set by Western composers – so that whether or not we count ourselves as religious, it is a central part of our musical heritage. The unchanging Latin texts of the Ordinary of the Mass recited or sung at certain points underpin the sequence: *Kyrie eleison* (those words are actually Greek, Lord have mercy), *Gloria in excelsis Deo* (Glory be to God on high), *Credo in unum Deum* (I believe in one God), *Sanctus* and *Benedictus* (Holy, holy . . . Blessed is he who comes in the name of the Lord), *Agnus Dei* (Lamb of God, who takest away the sins of the world, have mercy on us). Then interleaved with those chants there are the 'Proper' chants which change for individual Sundays and feast days: the Introit at the start of the Mass, Gradual and Alleluia between the readings, Offertory as the bread and wine is prepared, and Communion when the eucharist is distributed. The plainsong settings of these Proper texts tend to be more elaborate than the Ordinary, with extended melismas (groups of notes) on syllables of the text, except in the Sequences. These tend to have a single note-per-syllable melodic and poetic structure, as in the most famous example from the Requiem Mass, *Dies irae, dies illa* (Day of wrath) (*100), which has been used across the centuries.

Few areas of musical scholarship have been so contested as the origin, history and performance of the plainchant repertory, and this is partly a natural result of the continued use of that repertory in the liturgy of the church. The chants were extensively codified in their modern revival in the late nineteenth century by the Benedictine monks of Solesmes in northwestern France. The achievement of these monk-scholars was far-reaching, and it recreated the chant in a distinctive cultural milieu (as can be heard on the many mellifluous, flowing performances on their own recordings in the warm acoustic at Solesmes, and with the distinctively French pronunciation of the language). In the book which brings together the commonly used chants, called the *Liber usualis*, styles in the Ordinary of the Mass can vary from the early ascetic Mass X, based on the old scales at one extreme, to the much later, more florid and almost tonal construction of the melodic Mass VIII. Before the earliest notated examples in the tenth century, this music was passed on by oral tradition through the monastic communities that used it, and we can tell it acquired a definite character because the earliest notations are similar in melody and shape. With the greater acceptance of Gregorian chant traditions in the eleventh and twelfth centuries, melodies came to be written down, and even without the staff notation that was later developed, melodies could be expressed with some precision. The tipping point from oral transmission to written transmission had been passed, and a new discipline which would dominate the future of so much Western music was formed.

Perhaps because of the central importance of the chant in the Western church, the creation of this music was surrounded by myth. One tradition attributed all its composition to the single person of Gregory the Great (who was Pope between 590 and 604). Later legendary stories and illustrations show the music being directly dictated to Gregory from heaven above. Although an inspiring spiritual leader, Gregory the Great had nothing to do with the writing or even the organisation of the chant that bears his name. Many popes from the fifth to seventh centuries were involved in its organisation, and it is believed that the body of what is today called Gregorian chant, properly established from around the year 800 onwards, originated during the period after Charlemagne's reign as emperor (800–814).

More at issue, and still controversial, is the extent to which Rome was the fount of all such chant, or whether the flow of its evolution was not from Italy to the rest of Europe, but from France to Italy. In the modern revival of chant there has been a wish to believe that the Roman chant is the oldest and purest form, and that later more elaborate versions are in some way corruptions that have to be pared back. There is an anecdote of the Emperor Charlemagne instructing his singers to 'drink from the fountain of St Gregory, not from the far-off rivulets which you have undoubtedly corrupted'. But this story may reflect the increasingly centralising and controlling place of Rome in the Catholic church, rather than the more subtle exchange of cultures which created the chant repertory.

Ironically it was France which provided the impetus for the modern revival of the chant, through the work of the community at the abbey of Solesmes. The approach of the Solesmes monks to editing and presenting the chant received support and endorsement from the popes of the day, notably Pius X in his encyclical *Motu proprio* of 1903, in which he declared that plainsong was the most perfect kind of liturgical music, and wrote that it 'has been happily restored to its original perfection and purity by recent study'. That laid the groundwork for the domination of church usage of Gregorian chant by the editions of Solesmes, which were scrupulously prepared and edited, and beautifully produced.

However, we would now judge it to be just one view of the chant. When the great Dominican historian Dom David Knowles describes the chant as 'majestic, spiritual, austere beyond all other forms of art', we should beware of projecting onto it our contemporary aspirations, matching for example the present grey stone of medieval cathedrals that would actually in their time have been highly decorated. Recent scholarly thinking about the rhythms of Gregorian chant have produced a very different sound-world, using long and short notes and sharper rhythms, which has found favour with some scholars and performers such as John Blackley and his Schola Antiqua. However, the popular concept of plainsong as meditative and restrained remains: in recent times, compilations of chant sung by Spanish monks from the monastery of Santo Domingo de Silos have been marketed as the answer to stress, offering an easy panacea of calm – a telling example of music finding a use far from its original purpose (in this case, to express precisely the texts of the liturgy and be part of a defined ritual). By such means music flies free of its original purpose and surroundings, acquiring new life.

England developed its own distinctive tradition of plainsong and liturgical ritual. The Sarum Rite, developed in the thirteenth century at Salisbury Cathedral, was the most outstanding of these local rites. As Christmas Eve gave way to Christmas Day, a special Mass was chanted called the *Missa in gallicantu*, the Mass at cockcrow, which had *Kyries* with added texts called tropes, and other features with a florid plainsong Gradual and Alleluia, and a hymn-like Sequence. The complex picture developed too in other traditions. Tropes of the eleventh century survive from Chartres Cathedral in France – the *Kyrie* in particular had added texts, but also the Introit was given extra words to deepen the relevance of the words to the liturgical events of the day. The more important the feast, the more richly it was embellished.

It is notable that though we do not know the names of any of the early composers of chant, we do know the name of one outstanding woman who has become today one of the remarkable names in the early history of music. Hildegard of Bingen (1098–1179) was an abbess who became a Benedictine at the age of fourteen and founded her own community of nuns at Rupertsberg, building a new chapel in 1152. She was regarded as a mystic, so at a time when the authority of a woman would have been widely questioned, she claimed divine authority for her views. She became an influential figure, her views sought on a wide range of theological issues, making prophecies of her own with a divine mandate that trumped even those of men. Hildegard has proved a fascinating figure to recent generations: there was clearly an overt sensuality and drama to her liturgical acts. A nearby abbess, Tengswich, questioned her about 'strange and irregular practices that you countenance', including singing 'with unbound hair' and dressing in 'white silk veils so long that they touch the floor'. Hildegard had expounded these practices in her mystical treatise *Scivias* (1151), the ceremony to consecrate virgins into the religious life, and when attacked she defended herself strongly. Her own collections of poetry and music are extensive, including the 'Symphony of the Harmony of Celestial Revelations' containing fifty-seven chants, later enlarged to seventy-five pieces. She led a female community in worship and study, and many of her songs are to the Virgin Mary, St Ursula or her own followers, with women playing a vigorous and active role in the stories and poems. She created a remarkable music-drama, the *Ordo virtutum* (*99), which as far as we know is a unique survival from the Middle Ages.

Hildegard is a key figure in the revival of medieval music in our time by such pioneering groups as Sequentia, and in 2012 she was finally canonised – the first composer to be made a saint by the Catholic church. (As we have seen, St Gregory was not the writer of Gregorian chant.) But what about St Cecilia? Is she not regarded as the patron saint of music? She has been celebrated as such across the ages, but this virginal figure from the early third century is in fact only tangentially associated with the art of music. It may even be a mistake that she is thought of as dedicated to music: the story that when she was unwillingly married, she 'sang to God in her heart', actually meant that she was turning away from the music of the celebration and refusing to be part of it (Plate 1). However, her close link with music remained, and it was marked by many festivals and special works written in her honour, from Purcell's *Hail, bright Cecilia!* and Handel's *Ode for St Cecilia's Day*, through to Britten's *Hymn to St Cecilia* whose words by W. H. Auden express the continuing tradition: 'Blessed Cecilia, appear in visions / To all musicians, appear and inspire'.

The legacy of plainsong has similarly been enormous and long-lasting. Generations of Renaissance composers such as Josquin des Prez (p. 68) built their counterpoint around its models; Martin Luther reworked its hymns for his Protestant chorales which were endlessly developed by J. S. Bach (p. 124); and the composers of the classical era including Haydn (in his 'Lamentatione' Symphony No. 26) and Mozart (in his Requiem) in the eighteenth century made use of its melodies. Some of the most famous chants like the *Dies irae* from the Requiem Mass became favourites of the Romantics in symbolising the Day of Judgement; it makes a massive impact at the climax of Hector Berlioz's huge *Symphonie fantastique* (p. 171), while more surprising is its appearance in Sergey Rachmaninov's *Rhapsody on a Theme of Paganini* for piano and orchestra (p. 215). Modern composers from Arthur Honegger to Olivier Messiaen, Peter Maxwell Davies and Oliver Knussen (pp. 233, 237, 241, 256) have used plainsong as a generating force in their music, demonstrating the continuing relevance of its ritual and melody across the centuries.

*

The vast cathedrals of the Gothic era proclaim a colossal belief in the power of God to determine the ways of man, and the desire of men to build monuments worthy of their devotion. How did sound fill those spaces? The choir operated from their stalls usually within the chancel of the church, at the end of the building near the liturgical celebrations of the clergy; those far away from the source of the sound, who filled the large nave of a church or cathedral, could follow at a distance the rituals of the clergy and would relate to the familiar place of music in the liturgy. How much attention was paid, how far sung texts were heard and understood, is a matter of some debate – but it is clear that however partially perceived, music played a fundamental role in these observances and a central part in the everyday life of churchgoers. Not all this music is easy for us to listen to today, when the liturgical and religious context in which it was originally heard has changed so much. In the past it was described even by music historians who loved it as 'petrified': as Alfred Einstein wistfully put it in 1941, 'petrification is the state of all art which no longer affects us, even though it has proved its historical importance'. But things have changed radically since then, especially because of the technological advances which have made this music immediate, not distanced. Although it is unfamiliar, it is worth absorbing as a unique link back to the culture of those times.

The gradual growth in complexity from the one-line chants of plainsong to multi-layered imitative music is the underlying story of the development of what is known as polyphony, music for two or more voices. Polyphony did begin simply, in the ninth century, by the improvised addition of a second part to plainsong chant in order to create the harmony. 'Organum' is the word used to describe this initial type of polyphony, which is recorded in some examples in the *Musica enchiriadis* of around 850–900, very early in the life of the form. The key aspect of this early polyphony is that it was an improvisational practice. You used certain accepted conventions in order to ornament existing material – initially at the

31

interval of a fourth or fifth above the chant, either strictly in parallel, or more freely in parallel. Sometimes the entire parallel organum would be doubled at the octave. The effect is that of a ritual with echo that we can imagine would be highly suited to the large resonant spaces of the churches, abbeys and cathedrals in which these pieces were performed, elaborating but not preventing the communication of the texts.

Early surviving examples are from England: the Winchester Troper organa of around 1000, an extensive collection preserved in two copies in Cambridge and Oxford. They include a diverse range of pieces suitable for liturgical moments when organa could have been sung, applied to the central chants of the Mass, collected in liturgically ordered groups and preserved as complete pieces. Possibly Wulfstan, cantor at Winchester, was responsible for assembling and perhaps composing this repertory; they have been very challenging to understand and recreate. It is revealing that in the surviving manuscripts there are marginal notes showing that the music was performed, and allowing divergences from the written text, perhaps to suit the meaning of the liturgical texts. Theorists of the time spoke highly of the music: 'Truly, delivered with restrained care, which is most proper to it, and attentive management of concords, the sweetness of the song will be most beautiful.' The Winchester scribe describes them as *melliflua, pulcherrima, iocunda*: sweet, beautiful and joyous.

The provision of organum harmonies became ever more flexible and subtle. A French treatise of around 1100 develops the idioms of the Winchester Troper, showing how to compose them with the added voice above the plainsong. Strikingly different from organum in style, a type of rhymed, metrical Latin poem for one or more voices grew up around 1150 in the south of France, known as *conductus*. These sacred vocal compositions probably accompanied the movement of a participant or object during the Mass and are suitably rhythmic, note-against-note pieces – a form that became known as discant. Subjects for *conductus* included the lives of the saints and biblical stories but also moral and political themes, often topical in their subject matter; later the form was applied to almost any serious Latin secular song. Then the school of Saint Martial, preserved in nine manuscripts from France between 1100 and around 1150, introduces another new idea: instead of the two voices moving strictly together, the top voice may elaborate a longer melody, a melisma, over the chant underneath. That underpinning use of the chant became standard in the following years, and the name *cantus firmus* recognises its function, the plainsong acting as the bedrock of the new polyphony. Gradually, a style of increasing complexity was being imagined.

Paris held a central position in the Catholic world through the Middle Ages, and the Cathedral of Notre Dame symbolised that dominance; begun in the 1160s, the building was not completed until two centuries later, but it was a firm declaration of intent on the part of Paris that it was aiming to be a cultural, religious and intellectual centre. Philip II Augustus, who ruled from 1180 to 1223, was an enlightened monarch who nurtured the arts, supported the production of numerous new works, and created an environment of peace within which music could be written. Notre Dame became a European centre of musical innovation, and the home of some of the first religious music whose origins we can identify quite precisely. It was probably on the feast of St Stephen, 26 December 1199, that a great organum for four voices by Pérotin (fl. *c.* 1200) to the text *Sederunt principes* first resounded in the then incomplete cathedral. Along with the organum *Viderunt omnes*, probably written for the Christmas season of 1198, these are the first two known pieces of four-part music in the Western repertory.

A rather later English chronicler of 1280 known as Anonymous IV praised 'an abundance of colours in the art of harmonic music' by Notre Dame's two masters, Léonin and Pérotin. The Notre Dame composers' service books, one probably copied in England, which now reside across Europe in Florence, Wolfenbüttel and Madrid, demonstrate that polyphony had evolved. We gather that Léonin, who flourished around 1160–70, compiled a *Magnus liber* containing thirty-four polyphonic pieces for the Office and fifty-nine for the Mass throughout the year, and that Pérotin had revised and enlarged the organum of Léonin; it is said that both were revered teachers. Attributed to Pérotin, the four-part *Sederunt principes* and *Viderunt omnes* (*97) are landmarks in music's ability to express text and capture emotion. This piece has always been famous to historians, but as realised by modern performers such as David Munrow's Early Music Consort of London on his classic recording *Music of the Gothic Era*, it acquires power and force, the hypnotic repetitive elaboration of the upper parts stretching out the underlying chant to such an extent that a single syllable of chant produces a whole section of dazzling virtuosity from the singers.

A note of caution is needed: we are reliant on a very limited source of a century later for information about these two masters. Were these actually real individuals, among the first composers to whom we can relate directly? Or did they rather represent the accumulation of practice in their time, gathered together to demonstrate the best that Paris had to offer? The miracle is that the music survives and speaks to us directly across the centuries with vivid energy, and the fact that these pieces spread around Europe with speed testifies to their importance.

*

It is an underlying theme of this story that progress does not always take place in a straight line, and the next stage in the development of polyphony may seem like a regression rather than a move forward. In the thirteenth century the organa of Notre Dame, which had culminated in the magnificent four-part settings attributed to Pérotin, were followed by the creation of the smaller-scale motet. As David Munrow summarised it with typical flair, this takes us 'from the monumental to the miniature': short two-part sections (called *clausulae*) were extracted from organa and a new text was added. This new part was called the *motetus*, perhaps because of the addition of the new words (*mots*), and thus the name became applied to the whole composition. Most thirteenth-century motets were three-part compositions, with the parts called tenor, duplum and triplum. While the tenor usually had a text from plainsong, the duplum and the triplum had separate texts. Sometimes these different texts related to the same subject, but often they diverged, and occasionally were even in different languages. These three parts were written as independent lines, often creating clashes between them. The essential difference from later polyphony is that this music was conceived horizontally, with those individual lines the most prominent aspect; later it became the vertical, harmonic aspect of the music that predominated, creating one texture for the listener. Quite how the earlier pieces with their combination of texts were perceived by listeners is a fascinating riddle, to which we do not quite know the answer.

Later thirteenth-century motets are preserved in collections called the Montpellier and Bamberg codices, which contain hundreds of settings typically with the three parts written independently rather than harmoniously, and are mostly anonymous. These motets developed as secular forms too, even though plainsong tenors continued to be used. The theorist Petrus de Cruce (fl. *c.* 1290) developed ways for the upper parts of the motet structure to incorporate fast-changing, rapid note values, and this was an influence on the next generation. Although primarily a theorist, de Cruce was praised as 'that worthy practical musician, who composed so many beautiful and good pieces of mensural polyphony', and this era became known as that of the Ars Antiqua to distinguish it from the later Ars Nova, whose leader was Philippe de Vitry (p. 49).

These musical forms may seem very remote from us now, but they have links to both architecture and science. It has been suggested that the format of the motet, with its slower-moving fundamental part, and increasingly quickly moving upper parts, mirrors directly the structures of the Gothic cathedrals built around the same time, with their large nave arches, and smaller clerestory and triforium arches above them. In measuring time passing in the motet, it has been pointed out that in the late thirteenth century the mechanical clock had just been invented, replacing both the older clocks that operated with water and sand, and the reliance on the sundial. Did this precision give rise to greater exactness and greater precision in performance? How much freedom was there in this very scrupulously articulated music? The instructions of the thirteenth-century French theorist Elias Salomo say: 'let him correct anyone who may embellish his part excessively by whispering a reproach into his ear during performance'. And the instructions of the fourteenth-century French philosopher and mathematician Jean de Muris say: 'let anyone who wishes to indulge in practical music beware that he does exult too much in his voice'. Both therefore encourage restraint, but in a way which suggests there was a habit of free, demonstrative performance. In terms of coordination, the different parts of the motet were independent; whereas singers today are used to performing church music from a score of a whole piece, the practice then was for parts to be written out separately. (By the time of Elizabethan consort music, the parts were sometimes printed on the same page, but with some displayed sideways or upside down so that they could be read by a group of singers gathered around a table.)

The question of whether instruments were involved in the performance of Ars Antiqua polyphony or whether performance was entirely vocal is a vigorously debated subject which has been compellingly discussed by Daniel Leech-Wilkinson in his study *The Modern Invention of Medieval Music*. The scholar and director of Gothic Voices, Christopher Page, who made superb recordings of vocal-only performance, claims that 'the arguments which have been advanced in favour of instrumental participation in sacred music before the fifteenth century are founded upon a mass of misinterpretation'. Nevertheless, as Leech-Wilkinson argues, instrumental participation is so ingrained and so familiar to our understanding of this music – not just in the distant past, but right up to the performances by Munrow's Early Music Consort – that they may be difficult to shift. Writing of these earlier groups, he concludes that 'the remains of their work are scattered all over our view of medieval music and are probably ineradicable from the public perception of a multicoloured Middle Ages. It may be easier if history vindicates them, for we shall probably never remove them.'

4

Minstrels

Secular music of the Middle Ages tends to be hidden under the cloak of sacred music, because for a long time it was passed down by oral rather than written tradition, its poetry more famous than its music. It originated outside the strictly organised framework of church liturgy and was often practised by wandering musicians who travelled from city to city in the search for support and employment; these may be among the first people to have made a living specifically from performing music. 'When I see winter returning,' wrote the trouvère Colin Muset (fl. 1230–60), 'then I must find me a lodging. O that I might discover a generous host who would make no charge, but would offer me pork and beef and mutton, ducks, pheasants and venison . . .' Such was the reality of life for the travelling minstrel, even if exaggerated to gain sympathy.

To judge from the literary references of the time, musical life in medieval England was very strong. Major poems that survive, notably *Beowulf*, may have been sung or declaimed to musical accompaniment, and there are references in the text to the lyre and the harp – the latter the essential instrument of the bard or virtuoso singer, portable and with a few strings, plucked, without the extent or trappings of the modern instrument. Fragmentary references such as that to St Aldhelm addressing his congregation 'in the manner of a minstrel' are suggestive but inconclusive: what did he sound like? St Bede tells the story of the seventh-century poet Caedmon being shamed because he could not play the cithara when it was handed round after a meal, suggesting both the prevalence of the instrument and the expectation that poets would have mastered it. The welsh harp with its associated masters became well known as a genre of its own, and we read of gatherings of bards exchanging songs and poems. Even King Alfred the Great was said to have been a skilled musician who once entered a foreign camp disguised as a minstrel.

The first surviving settings of English words are believed to be three songs by St Godric (*c.* 1065–1170), a reclusive figure (never formally canonised) who after a life at sea led a simple existence as a hermit near Durham, where he was consulted for his wisdom by leaders of the church. The most famous survival of medieval English music comes from the Benedictine abbey of Reading around 1280, and it is one sheet of deceptively simple music. *Sumer is icumen in* is a thoroughly secular hymn to nature (there is also a Latin text underneath, but that seems secondary). In the Wessex dialect of Middle English it joyously proclaims 'Summer has come, loudly sing cuckoo! The seed is growing, the meadow is blooming, woods are newly green, the ewe bleats after her lamb. The cow lows after her calf . . . Sing cuckoo!' The metre is a skipping rhythm. Halfway down the manuscript page on which it is preserved there is an instruction. Although this looks like a unison song, it can be sung by four singers, starting one after the other: it is what we would call a round, in which the same melody can be sung in sequence, sounding against itself (Plate 5).

In France, first in line in the Pied-Piper-like procession of minstrels were the *jongleurs*, musically skilful itinerant entertainers, who made a precarious livelihood picking their way across medieval England and France from around the tenth century. Spurned by the church, they organised themselves in guilds from as early as 1321, and during Lent (a penitential period when they could not perform) they would assemble for meetings to discuss and exchange their material. Petrarch called them 'people of no great wit but with amazing memory – very industrious, and impudent beyond measure'. Their equivalent in Germany were the *Gaukler*. The contemporary musician Guiraut de Calanson laid down the ideal qualities for a minstrel:

[He should be] good at storytelling and rhyming, and acquit himself creditably in trials of skill. Know how to strike drums and cymbals, and to play the hurdy-gurdy. Know how to throw and catch little apples on knives, to imitate birdsong, do card-tricks and be able to jump through four hoops. Know how to play citole and mandolin, know how to handle monochord and the guitar, string a rote with seventeen strings, be proficient on the harp, accompany well on the gigue, so as to enhance the spoken word. Jongleur, you should be able to handle nine instruments (vielle, bagpipe, pipe, harp, hurdy-gurdy, gigue, decachord, psaltery and rote); and when you have mastered these, you will be equipped to deal with every eventuality. And do not neglect the lyre or the cymbals.

The best minstrels were clearly skilled performers and proficient on a wide variety of instruments. The hurdy-gurdy was a complicated machine, powered by a rotating mechanism turned with a handle, and using finger-stopping on the strings, producing a wiry, rustic sound; originally it would have been performed by two players, testing their coordination. The psaltery was a flat instrument with strings of different lengths stretched across, plucked with a quill; it was the ancestor of the dulcimer, and reached Europe in the twelfth century. The ancestry of the citole is not completely clear; a plucked instrument, it may have been the ancestor of the Renaissance cittern, and references suggest it made a sweet sound. The monochord goes right back to ancient Greece and Pythagoras, having been devised as a way of measuring and testing his harmonic theories; as an instrument with only one string, it was not really versatile or usable in performance, but as the monochord developed with more potential some have seen it as the origin of the clavichord. Clearly the main demand made of a minstrel of the time was versatility.

*

The course of true love never did run smooth, and the turbulence of such relationships has been a stimulus to composers of song and opera through the ages. But rarely has one extreme emotion dominated a genre to the extent that frustrated love flourished in the songs of the troubadours. It was in the prosperous areas of southern France during the later twelfth century that the characterful poetry of the troubadours was first found. Using the language of the *langue d'oc*, Provençal, they sang of the passionate but unattainable love for a perfect beloved who was always out of reach. Some 2,600 poems survive, of greatly varied structure and shape. They tell stories, but above all they dramatise emotional states. Some troubadour songs have written music preserved with them; others may have been improvised or declaimed in speech over an improvised musical accompaniment. They do not indicate rhythm, so that is an element which is wide open to interpretation in performance. There were female troubadours, called *trobairitz*, and both male and female poets may well have been influenced by the Moorish culture of Arabic love poetry which came north from Spain. One *canso* with melody survives by the *trobairitz* comtessa called Beatriz de Dia (d. *c.* 1212), who was known to be the wife of Guillaume de Poitiers but in love with Raimbaut d'Orange, about whom 'she made many good songs'.

Another striking variant of the form is the *trobar clus*, a dialogue or debate in music, for example between two troubadours debating the merits of different types of poetry, or between the poet and his love on an aspect of courtly love. The poet Giraut de Bornelh (*c.* 1138–*c.* 1212) wrote of self-reflective singers arguing among themselves about the virtues of their differing songs. Typical of imaginative accounts of musical competitions through the ages, one story tells of a king confining two rival troubadours to separate rooms in his castle and challenging each to come up with a new composition in a day. One was uninspired and produced nothing – until he heard the other practising his new song, learned it by heart, and sang it first to the king, winning the contest.

The later tradition of trouvères came from northern France; they flourished while the art of the troubadours declined. The best known of the trouvères today is Adam de la Halle (*c.* 1245–*c.* 1280s?), author of *Le jeu de Robin et de Marion*, the first French narrative drama. There are sixteen small dance songs and duets, interspersed with spoken dialogue, captured in an illuminated manuscript which preserves melodies and illustrations. It is apparently unique for its time and has a narrative that is easy for us to relate to: the maid Marion is abducted from her lover Robin by the devious knight Sir Aubert, rescued, the lovers are reconciled, and all ends well. Thus it has become the subject of many contemporary versions and stagings which give it the flavour of a modern mini-opera. I vividly recall it being performed in the courtyard of a Dutch castle; following mini-recitals in the small castle rooms for which the audience was divided up, we all came together for *Robin and Marion*, a celebratory climax.

Thibaut, King of Navarre, was a famous trouvère who wrote some sixty songs that have survived, including a famous example of the *jeu-parti* or debate, called *Dame, merci*. Some of these songs are surprisingly modern in their approach to tonality and rhythm, sounding like folk songs of a much later age. Eleanor of Aquitaine's son Richard, who in 1189 became Richard I 'the Lionheart' of England, was himself a trouvère who wrote in Provençal and French. Trouvères worked in the genres of the *chanson de geste* (song of deeds) or the *chanson de toile* (picture song), depicting a lady sitting and pining for her lover. Without the seriousness that underlies the troubadours, the trouvères developed a more popular mode of music-making that was 'light upon the ear', as the eleventh-century trouvère Conon de Béthune wrote, 'for it matters to me that all may learn it and willingly sing it'.

Indeed, there is a much-elaborated story of Richard I's rescue after the Third Crusade, demonstrating the call-and-refrain form of this music. When his fellow trouvère Blondel de Nesle wanted to find where Richard was imprisoned, he went around the outside of castles singing his most famous songs, discovering the right one after the imprisoned king echoed back the refrain. (Later research suggests that it was actually well known where the king was being held, namely Dürnstein Castle.) The tale is testament to the devotion of trouvère to master, and it was turned into an opera in the eighteenth century by Grétry, and much later into a contemporary rock musical by Stephen Oliver and Tim Rice. Richard himself is supposed to have composed in captivity the ballad 'Je nus hons pris': 'no prisoner will ever state his case cleverly, he will put it in a sorrowful way; he can however write a poem to comfort himself'.

The influence of the troubadours and trouvères spread across the continent. In Germany, they formed a model for the *Minnesänger*, a school of poet-musicians. They too were preoccupied by *Minne*, a version of chivalrous love in a very serious mode, and these singers were usually of noble birth. Another stimulus was offered by the beginning of the Crusades. The leading Minnesinger was Walter von der Vogelweide (*c.* 1170–*c.* 1230), an outstanding poet. His *Palâstinalied*, a song of yearning for the Crusades, has survived with its memorable melody, 'Now at last life begins for me, since my sinful eyes behold the Holy Land'. But he also cultivated sensual songs about love which have a distinctly more modern flavour. *Under den Linden*, which uses the melody of a pre-existing trouvère song, is a narrative from a woman's point of view about the linden tree under which two lovers have made their bed: 'What happened there may no one ever know, except he and I and a small bird which can be trusted.' Vogelweide is repeatedly referenced by later authors, and he has become a part of Germany's cultural heritage, notably as an inspiration for the Meistersinger in Wagner's opera, and he is often depicted in statues and illustrations sitting on a rock, lost in contemplative thought. These songs of the troubadours and trouvères have been interpreted in a host of different ways over the years, from the inventive non-Western sounds of Thomas Binkley's Studio der frühen Musik, one of the most important of continental early music groups, who used the inspiration of Arab instruments and traditions to realise this music, to the pioneering English ensemble work of Martin Best and recordings reflecting new research by Ensemble Céladon and others.

A particularly evocative tradition of medieval song flourished in the Iberian Peninsula. As expressed in the Great Mosque of Córdoba, constructed during Muslim rule towards the end of the eighth century and reconfigured after the Reconquista in 1236 as a place of Christian worship, art in medieval Spain was an amazing melting pot of styles and traditions. The experience of the mosque today testifies to a wonderfully rich mingling of different cultures. During the Muslim period, a large number of Eastern-style instruments was introduced to Spain, and a tradition of singing was established with a female singer from the east, Afza, who was brought to court and accompanied herself on the *oud*. Córdoba became a musical centre where the Islamic scholar Al-Farabi, who died in 950, wrote *The Grand Book on Music*, a book of theory which was widely quoted by continental theorists, and a further treatise which discussed the healing powers of music on the soul. But following the reconquest of Andalusia by the Christians, new musical traditions grew up, doubtless influenced both by folk music and by the troubadours who travelled from France to Spain. Many of these songs were in the Provençal language; songs in the Spanish vernacular start in the thirteenth century with a collection by Martin Codax from the Galician town of Vigo on the west coast of Spain, evoking the landscape and the mood of the area, and six of his seven songs have music that can be transcribed.

The magnificent and unusually extensive collection of Spanish religious songs called the *Cantigas de Santa Maria*, written in Galician Portuguese, is much larger; four superbly written and preserved manuscripts comprise over 400 *cantigas*. These are remarkable in their organisation. Some of the *cantigas* may have been composed and performed by King Alfonso X himself. Known as 'El Sabio' (the Learned), Alfonso was a keen patron of the arts and sciences, and he certainly directed the collection of the songs; a central illustration depicts the king surrounded by scribes on one side and performers on the other. Following a prologue, the 400 songs are arranged in groups of ten; nine each tell the story of one miracle and the tenth hymns the Virgin Mary in general terms. The melodies are quite simple, with no large leaps in the phrases, and not many ornamental notes to each syllable, and the rhythmic implications of the songs are generally clear, meaning that a good attempt at performing the songs can be made. The lavish illustrations accompanying each song contain vivid and detailed depictions of music-making, singers and players interacting, sometimes with dancers, indications of which instruments were played together and which separately. These pictures are so precise that some have wondered whether the musicians portrayed are actual portraits; the instruments can certainly be copied and have been reproduced in modern performances (Plate 6).

Questions remain. There are some seventy musicians depicted, playing a variety of instruments: did they actually play together, or are they simply shown together for visual effect, the pairs of instruments juxtaposed because of the shape of the illustrations, like the two duetting bagpipers? The songs consist of one line, yet the illustrations show several instruments taking part; one group depicts six instrumentalists and four dancers accompanying the song. Were they improvising accompaniments, reflecting the practice of the time, or are these illustrations unrelated to the actual performance of the music they accompany? When the evidence that survives is so particular, to what other repertories might the same evidence, the same practices and the same instruments apply? There is still a huge amount of uncertainty in interpreting this kind of evidence of the musical past. Some indication of the variety of approaches to this repertory of the *cantigas* can be heard on the recordings by Jordi Savall's Hespèrion XXI, the Ensemble Gilles Binchois, and other groups such as Alla Francesca and the Ensemble Unicorn of Vienna who use Arab instruments to great effect.

*

This was a time when music resonated throughout society, from the royal courts to the market square, in both aristocratic and popular forms. Geoffrey Chaucer, the great poet of medieval England, wrote in his 'Miller's Tale' about Nicholas, the poor Clerk of Oxenford, 'on which he made a nights melodye / So sweetly that all the chambre song / And *Angelus ad virginem* he song: and after that he song the kings note / Ful often blessed was his merry throte'. We do not know the identity of the 'kings note', but we do know *Angelus ad virginem*, a famous song of the Annunciation, surviving in various forms in different English and French manuscripts. We also know that music played a vital part in the life of the leading British intellectuals such as Robert Grosseteste, Bishop of Lincoln from 1235 and perhaps chancellor of Oxford University:

> He loved much to hear the harp . . .
> Next his chamber, beside his study,
> His harper's chamber was fast the by
> Many times, by nights and days,
> He had solace of notes and lays.

But so little of English music survives alongside the isolated example of *Sumer is icumen in* that we have to build what we know on precious little evidence. Anonymous fourteenth-century chansons show the strong influence of France, and there are motets honouring St Thomas Becket and Edward the Confessor among the precious survivals in Bury St Edmunds, Durham and the Oxford colleges.

The theorist and composer Johannes de Grocheio (*c.* 1255–*c.* 1320) provided an account of the uses of music he experienced in Paris, divided into three broad categories: that of 'civil or simple music, which they call vulgar music'; that of 'composed or regular music by rule, which they call measured music'; and that which is built on these two and to which they are best adapted: 'This is called ecclesiastic and is designed for praising the Creator.' Grocheio was disparaging about the likely appeal of the motet to the masses: 'This sort of song should not be performed before ordinary people because they do not notice its fine points nor enjoy listening to it, but before learned people and those on the lookout for subtleties in the arts.' This anticipates a revealing divide between connoisseurs and 'ordinary' listeners, between those who understand the subtleties of music and those who just hear it. This will be a theme through all accounts of musical reception, from Mozart (who said a similar thing) to the present, but it is perhaps surprising to encounter it so early. There were also very popular anonymous motets based on the street cries of Paris, much in the same way that in a later generation English street cries would be worked into polyphonic compositions: 'Fresh strawberries! Nice blackberries! There is good bread to be found, good clear wine and good meat and fish.'

Nevertheless, Grocheio was no snob, as for him even dance music had its place in a well-ordered society: it 'excites the soul of man to move ornately and makes the soul of the performer and also the soul of the listener pay close attention and frequently turns the soul of the wealthy from depraved thinking'. In some respects, he was an elitist, a supporter of the intellectual class, but he was also working towards an enlightened position where all music should have its proper place in life. A shrewd observer of the cultural scene in Paris in this period believed that epic songs ought to be provided for 'old men, working citizens, and average people so that having heard the miseries and calamities of others, they may more easily bear up under their own, and so go about their tasks more gladly'.

Medieval music was not all high seriousness or lovelorn despair. There was drama, there was bawdiness, there were moments when the world was turned on its head and the rigorous certainties of life were disrupted. One of the most colourful pictures of medieval life is conjured up by vivid reports of the Feast of

Fools, celebrated on 1 January, when the liturgy was parodied, everyone ran riot in church, and children became bishops for a day. It is an alluring picture, but only partly borne out by reality. There were certainly excesses and abuses, and the antics on the Feast of Fools were the subject of repeated condemnations from the authorities over the years. But the origins of the celebration were more to do with the growing practice of liturgical drama, which was an important part of the way that the scriptures were brought to life for congregations. These made immediate and tangible the stories of the Gospels. The most popular were based around the search for Christ, either in the manger at Christmas (*Quem quaeritis in praesepe*) or in the tomb at Easter (*Quem quaeritis in sepulcro*).

The most famous of the liturgical dramas to have been revived in modern times is *The Play of Daniel* (*98); its revival (and rewriting for modern audiences) by Noah Greenberg and the New York Pro Musica in the 1950s was one of the most influential moments in the revival of the music of the past, and with its use of colourful instruments, turned it into a medieval music-drama to which modern audiences could relate. It is certainly the richest and most varied of the dramas that survive. Originally, young clerics of Beauvais Cathedral performed *The Play of Daniel* towards the end of the twelfth century, though the manuscript that preserves it dates from 1230. It is a compelling and varied drama on its own terms, based upon the stories from the Book of Daniel including Belshazzar's Feast and the famous episode in which during the feast writing appears on the wall, 'Mane Techel Phares'. This subject has become immortalised in music through the dramatic oratorio *Belshazzar's Feast* by William Walton, and was the subject of an oratorio by Handel, *Belshazzar*. But the immediacy across the centuries of the original *Play of Daniel* is remarkable, with its processional choruses, use of secular instruments and varied musical styles. It includes plainchant, popular melodies, allusions to trouvère songs, lively dance rhythms, laments and elements from ancient dramas – a remarkable mixture of genres which has led people to call this a medieval proto-opera. Following the multicoloured versions by the New York Pro Musica and others, including a lively one by the Dufay Collective, more ascetic realisations have been made.

Out of such liturgical dramas also emerged one of the most long-lasting musical developments of the medieval period: the carol. Growing from a simple form, the 'circle dance' with a regular refrain, it began a tradition of verse and refrain structures which has flourished to the present day. Most tell stories of the birth of Christ, often featuring the Virgin Mary giving birth, and draw simple moral conclusions for the listeners. A famous early example is the *Coventry Carol* written (or perhaps first written down) in the sixteenth century for one of the liturgical dramas of the time: it tells the story of Herod's order to kill all young children at the time of the birth of Christ, with the lament as refrain 'Lully, lullay, thou little tiny child, Bye bye, lully, lullay'. It was copied out by Robert Croo in Coventry, who ran the city's entertainments, so his manuscript tells us, on 14 March 1534. Carols have now become associated with Christmas, but it was not always so, and other feasts were marked. The verse with refrain has become a long-lasting feature of the carol genre, with many modern variations on the theme; the nineteenth-century carols which feature in so many Christmas services have lent themselves to the provision of extra descant lines and varied harmonies which have created a musical genre in themselves, indissolubly linked to the Anglican service of Nine Lessons and Carols that originated in King's College Cambridge during the First World War. This enduring example of an 'invented tradition', which seems much older than it is, has been reinvented in recent years with the commissioning of fine new carols from a wide range of contemporary composers including Judith Weir and James MacMillan (p. 257).

Another inheritance from the period of the Feast of Fools is the burlesque that features strongly in the notorious collection known as the *Carmina Burana*, compiled probably in the first half of the thirteenth century, around 1230. It is a huge collection of lyric poetry from all sources, in Latin, German and French, the lowly songs of the minstrels and Goliards alongside the most sophisticated products of scholarship and intellectual life. The poems are full of satirical uses of church phrases, parodies verging on blasphemy. It looks as if the intention was to notate music for the whole collection, but this was never completed; we can only reach some certainty on the music here by comparing the notation with that in other manuscripts where the pitches are clearer. The manuscript of *Carmina Burana* was found in 1803 in the monastery of Benediktbeuern in Bavaria, hence its modern title, but this is misleading since the material originated further south in Bavaria; given its racy contents, it is remarkable that the manuscript survived. When the manuscript and its later added loose leaves were bound together, one of the eight illustrations that accompany it was chosen as the frontispiece. Thus the picture of the Wheel of Fortune became famous, much later catching the imagination of the twentieth-century German composer Carl Orff who immediately saw the potential of the collection to form the basis of what he called 'a new work, a stage piece with choruses to be sung and danced, patterned entirely after the illuminations and the poems' (p. 217). From its first staging in Frankfurt in 1937, Orff's *Carmina Burana* quickly became the most popular of all his works, though we know it as a concert work, whose music has found its way into films and television adverts. It has become a firm favourite with choirs and choral societies, in spite of Orff's ambivalent relationship with the Nazi regime.

5

New Arts

Adventures in musical invention rise and fall across time. This is a different articulation of history from that of the tipping points that mark a change in style and practice; it is a reflection of the sense of innovation in a nation's culture and music. Some periods and countries are by nature conservative in outlook, some naturally forward-looking. England in the nineteenth century was unadventurous in its native music, whereas back in the fifteenth century we read that it led the way in Europe with the music of John Dunstaple (see below). History likes to attach labels to artistic trends which are usually more complex than the labels suggest: at the start of the twentieth century 'impressionism' became a catch-all for different styles (p. 227), as several decades later did 'minimalism' (p. 247). But there is good reason for adopting the label of 'new art', Ars Nova, for the innovations of the 1300s, as this title was adopted by the theorists of the day, and it reflected a desire to push forward the art of music beyond its current boundaries.

So much of composers' reputations is based on what survives of their output. Philippe de Vitry (1291–1361) was influential, but very little of his music remains to us. Vitry was lauded in his day as 'the flower and jewel of singers' and 'the finest figure in the entire musical world'. He was regarded as 'learned in all the mathematical disciplines', a diplomat who served three French kings, and he became Bishop of Meaux, an academic and an intellectual. To Vitry we owe the origination of the term Ars Nova in a celebrated fourteenth-century treatise. It complements the *Ars novae musicae* of slightly earlier by Jean de Muris. Ars Nova was originally used to define the French music that followed the Ars Antiqua, but it acquired a wider reference to the general musical style of the fourteenth century beyond France, capturing a new elaboration and eloquence which carried composed music beyond the sacred sphere and into a new realm of feeling that matched the achievements of an age that fostered Dante and Chaucer.

The beginning of the Ars Nova, clearly reflecting its secular origins, is usually said to be the *Roman de Fauvel*, an entertaining and bitter satire attacking church and state, for which Vitry probably composed at least some of the music. It has been attributed to Gervais du Bus but was reissued with extensive musical inserts in a lavish illuminated manuscript of 1316–17. The pieces capture all the prevailing styles of the day, including 34 motets among its lavish collection of 169 pieces. Reflecting the social tensions of the time, this is one of the great satires in music – the tale of Fauvel the horse, who in spite of being an animal, ascends to the highest positions at court, receives the homage of all hypocrites, and reveals their stupidity. His name can be read as an acrostic for Flattery, Avarice, Villainy, Fickleness, Envy and Baseness: all the evils that are destroying the world. It is a marvellous indictment of the corruption of the period, and a precious source speaking to the culture of its time.

The *Roman de Fauvel* inaugurates the period of the Ars Nova of which Guillaume de Machaut (*c.* 1300–77) was the leading representative. Machaut's music and poetry has a central place in the new art of the fourteenth century, partly because it survives, collected and codified in magnificent volumes for which he was himself responsible. These six large and beautifully illustrated collections of his works bear testimony both to his fame and to his strongly developed sense of preserving his own reputation for posterity. He is the link between the trouvères, whose song forms he took into the era of the new art, and the complex compositions of the motet which became the most elevated form of the day. Machaut created a visible contrast between his popular work and his high art, a combination which only a small number of composers in history have successfully managed. At his most esoteric, Machaut wrote deliberately intellectualised music, for instance a rondeau that sounds the same forwards and backwards – and which inspired the twentieth-century composers of twelve-note serial music: Anton Webern (p. 225) used the same construction in his Op. 18. But at other times Machaut was providing direct and simple declamation for poetry which marks him out as much as a writer as he was a composer.

Machaut was probably born near Reims and spent much of his life there, though he travelled widely. He was secretary and companion to Jean de Luxembourg, King of Bohemia, and he was present at the siege of Znaim in Lithuania in December 1328. He then worked for various noble patrons including Jean's daughter Bonne, and later in life fell deeply in love with Peronne d'Armentières, a noblewoman whom he claimed inspired much of his late work. Poetry was as important to Machaut as music; indeed he probably regarded them as indissoluble arts, with music used to heighten poetic speech in the long sagas that he wrote to honour his patrons. Christopher Page has emphasised the importance of Machaut's work as a poet and drawn attention to his description of music as 'artificial poetry'. (Machaut knew Chaucer and influenced him.) *La Remède de Fortune* is the first of the three major stories which places examples of the principal song genres in the tale of a poet who uses music to win the love of a noble lady. He sings to her in a lai, accompanies her in a virelai while she is dancing, and expresses his joy in a rondeau. As a polyphonist, Machaut was able to take popular song forms and give them harmonic complexity as well as melodic attractiveness.

By far the greatest part of Machaut's work is in these secular song forms of the time, the ballade, the virelai, the rondeau and the motet, each with their own characteristics and compositional devices. But Machaut's solitary *Messe de Notre Dame* (*96) has become rather better known than his secular music, partly because settings of the Ordinary of the Mass became such a vital part of Western music in the following centuries, though it is not unified in the way that later Mass settings would be; it is best thought of as a collection of contemporary styles. In bringing together the Kyrie, Gloria, Credo, Sanctus and Agnus Dei by a single composer (as well as adding in his setting the concluding 'Ite missa est'), Machaut's *Messe* inaugurates one of the most influential forms of the succeeding centuries. Other collections had sometimes paired movements of the Ordinary of the Mass together, for example the Gloria with the Credo, or Kyrie with the Agnus Dei. And there had been collections of the Ordinary movements in the Tournai Mass, gathered around 1349 from diverse sources, and the slightly later Mass of Barcelona, also French and also anonymous. But these were not compositions by a single composer.

Machaut's Mass has been a landmark of the early music revival, marking out many different performing styles and approaches to the repertory, with and without instruments and added colour. My own enthusiasm for it was formed in the late 1970s and early 1980s when Andrew Parrott and his Taverner Choir and Consort were revolutionising our approach to the sounds of medieval and later repertory, in the case of Machaut performing and recording his music without the lavish added instruments and percussion that many had thought necessary to make this music work for a modern audience. As with the Ars Antiqua repertory, the voices-only approach was direct and ascetic; it depended on the absolute clarity and skill of a new generation of singers who had emerged from the English cathedral and collegiate traditions. It also matched the scholarly advances in the field and complemented the activities of other pioneering groups including Gothic Voices, directed by Christopher Page. The question remained: was it correct, or was it just a closer reflection of modern taste than the technicolour versions of the previous generation? The alliance between performer–scholars such as Parrott, Christopher Page and David Fallows ensured a radical change of performance practice over a comparatively short period of time in the 1980s, and brought this music much closer to the taste of our times.

For all its artistic and literary advances this was a turbulent time in Europe: the Hundred Years War which dragged on between England and France from 1337 to 1453 was hugely disruptive of trade and the economy, and the Great Plague of 1348–50 was even more destructive. It was particularly divisive for the Catholic church: Pope Clement V had moved the papal court to Avignon in 1309, causing deep antagonisms in the church. And old objections to the elaboration of music in the liturgy began to surface again with the arrival of the Ars Nova. The conservative reaction to the new style was voiced by the theorist Jacobus of Liège in his *Speculum musice* of around 1300, the largest extant medieval musical treatise: 'Wherein does this lasciviousness in singing so greatly please, this excessive refinement, by which, as some think, the words are lost, the harmony of consonances is diminished, perfection is brought low, imperfection is exalted, and measure is confused?' He was backed up by no less an authority than Pope John XXII, who issued a strong denunciation from Avignon in 1324–5, criticising the way that composers 'truncate the melodies with hocket, they deprave them with discantus, sometimes they even stuff them with upper parts made out of secular song'. So Pope John proclaimed that 'We now hasten therefore to banish these methods, and to put them to flight more effectually than heretofore, far from the house of God.' This inclination of the church to repress excessive decoration in music for the liturgy became a constant theme over the centuries, though the effect was often negligible and composers went their own way, writing, as they frequently do, the music they wanted to write.

The greatest composer of this divided time was Guillaume Dufay (or Du Fay) (?1397–1474), who was born near Brussels and died in Cambrai, where he was a canon of the cathedral. He was one of the most widely travelled and admired figures in Europe during this period. His music, perhaps reflecting some of the strictures of the church, is engaging and immediately accessible. Dufay is often linked with Gilles de Bins or Binchois (c. 1400–60), with whom he is depicted in an illustration in the poem *Le champion des dames* from around 1440, Dufay with a small organ and Binchois with a harp (Plate 7). Over two hundred of Dufay's works survive, ranging from short song-like chansons and ballades to sixty rondeaux. Dufay spent time in Italy and also absorbed the English style of consonance in his hymn *Christe redemptor omnium*, dominated by sonorous intervals of the sixth, sounding sweetly and creating a very different atmosphere from the open fifths and fourths of earlier polyphony. He wrote music for all sorts of special occasions, from family weddings for his patrons to grand occasions like the consecration of Brunelleschi's famous dome of Florence Cathedral in March 1436, for which he filled his motet *Nuper rosarum flores* with intricate number symbolism derived directly from the proportions of Brunelleschi's architectural creation.

Dufay confirmed the practice of setting the texts of the Ordinary of the Mass as a cycle and brought it into the mainstream of music – a form that was to remain prominent for centuries, even after the age of religion had passed. In the earliest examples there was no special unity between the movements: the question of how the very different texts of the Mass Ordinary could be unified was answered through the use of common themes in each movement. In a surprising development, these common themes were often drawn from secular sources, perhaps paying homage to other composers, or advertising the composer's own versatility. A well-known example was one of the most famous secular songs, *L'Homme armé*, which forms the basis of Dufay's longest Mass setting. The original song has the words 'The armed man should be feared / Everywhere it has been proclaimed / That each man shall arm himself / With a coat of iron mail. / The armed man should be feared.' Even though it was dubiously regarded by the church authorities, it was not thought strange to use a secular song to underpin the sacred words of the Mass. It was probably the simplicity and adaptability of the melody that made it so attractive to many composers – there are over forty settings, mostly from the second half of the fifteenth century.

Plainsong chants were also used as the basis of a Mass composition: Dufay showed in his last Mass, *Ave regina celorum*, that both the chant underlying the music (sometimes given with its own original text) and the whole polyphonic structure of the motet could be used to create a setting of great beauty and textural clarity. The way Dufay worked out his voice ranges to support the creation of these contrapuntal compositions established the four-part framework which has remained surprisingly constant to the present day. Perhaps this is one of the reasons we can relate so immediately to his settings. These Masses, perhaps especially *Se la face ay pale* (*94), based on his own ballade, are the landmark musical achievements of their time, and I love their combination of sensuality and clarity, drawing the listener into their sacred texts with concentrated skill.

In Italy the Ars Nova took different forms, stimulated by the arrival of musicians from southern France and teachers at the University of Padua. There, Mass movements were written which matched the style of secular songs. In the racy *Decameron* (1348–53) by Boccaccio, *balata* are sung at the end of each day's storytelling by the young men and women escaping from the Black Death and enjoying themselves on the outskirts of Florence. In his introduction to the sequence of stories, Boccaccio tells of the meal served on the first evening, after which 'the tables having been cleared away, the queen commanded that instruments be brought in, for all the ladies knew how to do the round dance ... the queen together with other ladies and two young men chose a carol and struck up a round dance with a slow pace ... when this was finished they began to sing charming and merry songs'.

Although the *balata* was a humble form, it quickly became elevated through the work of Francesco Landini (*c.* 1325–97) and others. Blind since suffering smallpox in his youth, Landini was like Machaut a poet as well as a musician, an organist also skilled on other instruments. Giovanni da Prato's *Il paradiso degli Alberti*, concerning the famous people of Florence, mentions Landini's musical accomplishments alongside his philosophical, ethical and astrological interests, and tells how a select audience was deeply moved by the love songs Landini performed for them. Matteo da Perugia (fl. 1400–16), who was *maestro di cappella* at Milan Cathedral, developed a new complexity which grew out of the Ars Nova. These composers were all intellectual and cosmopolitan figures who saw the writing of music as but one part of their civilising activities, embedded in the culture of their time.

The early fifteenth century produced one of the greatest illuminated manuscript treasures of the period. The Squarcialupi Codex, with its 216 beautifully organised pages, was compiled in Florence. The pieces are grouped by the name of the composer, and each section opens with an elaborately decorated portrait, for instance of Landini playing a small portative organ – a revealing acknowledgement of how important the individual composer and creator was then becoming (Plate 7). Landini has by far the largest number of pieces, at 146; other composers include Bartolino da Padova (37 pieces) and Niccolò da Perugia (36); and the entry for Paolo da Firenze has his portrait, but an intriguing gap of sixteen pages where his works should have been added. These manuscripts bring us as close as possible to understanding the role of composers as increasingly recognised creative figures, at the forefront of intellectual activity, and respected among their peers, earning recognition – and individual portraits.

The Ars Nova's elaboration and richness were already at their height. The next generation of composers wanted to develop its complexity still further. Philippus de Caserta (fl. *c.* 1370), who probably came from the area around

Naples, wanted to achieve a 'subtiliorem modum', a way of composing with greater subtlety, creating what became known as the Ars Subtilior. Pieces of incredible intricacy were composed by Caserta and his associates, such as Johannes Ciconia (c. 1370–1412), who marks the culmination of the motet in the fourteenth century with music of great rhythmic complexity. Another precious manuscript of the period, the Chantilly Codex preserved in France, contains more than 130 pieces, among which is some of the most complex music of the Ars Subtilior period. It includes music by thirty-four composers, the largest number by the little-known Solage (fl. late fourteenth century), from whom ten surviving works are found there. Their rhythmical and notational complexity is daunting; some have seen a parallel with the most advanced modernist compositions, generating music through technical experiment rather than expressive aims. However, performances of this repertory by groups such as Santenay and the Medieval Ensemble of London have revealed its subtleties with clarity.

Near the front of the Chantilly Codex a couple of pieces have been added by Baude Cordier (fl. early fifteenth century) which have become famous in the history of musical notation because they are written in visually striking form. In one, the music is in the form of a heart, expressing both the words of the text, *Belle, bonne, sage* and a play on Cordier's name, while the other, *Tout par compass*, is entirely circular, expressing the form of the music as a canon. Thus music came to look like it sounded, an important moment in the continuing relationship between the text of a work and its intended performance.

*

The place of music in pre-Renaissance societies is made clear by the accounts of many ceremonies in which it was used to support political and religious events, including one occasion which demonstrated the full power of music in the ceremonies of the time. In Burgundy, Philip the Good had inaugurated the Order of the Golden Fleece to celebrate his dynasty and continue the work of the Crusades in rescuing Constantinople. The knights gathered at the Banquet of the Oath of the Pheasant on 17 June 1454, which included music probably by Dufay, Binchois and others (though the composers are not specified in the compendious account of the celebrations in the memoirs of Olivier de la Marche, who designed the event). The chief impression is of the seamless integration of music into the lavish scenic effects:

> three tables laid out, one of medium size, one large and one small. On the medium one there was a church, with windows, very properly made, and a bell that rang and inside four singers who sang and played on an organ . . . On the second table there was a huge pie in which there were twenty-eight living people playing on divers instruments, each when their turn came . . . while on the third table there was a marvellous forest, just like a forest in India . . . three trebles and a tenor sang a very sweet chanson . . . when they had finished a shepherd from the pie played on the bagpipe in a very novel fashion . . . through the doorway of the hall came a horse, wearing a coat of orange silk, and bearing two trumpeters seated back to back, who sounded a fanfare on their trumpets . . . When the horse tableau had passed, the organ in the church began to play very softly, and in the pie a German cornett played in a very strange way . . . next a chanson from the church, and a douçaine with other instruments accompanying it from the pie, and suddenly a very cheerful fanfare from four trumpets . . .

A speculative musical re-creation of this ambitious feast has been attempted by the Ensemble Gilles Binchois with Dominique Vellard, but we may guess it was less impressive without the visual (and culinary) aspects. Philip the Good proved an exceptionally lavish artistic patron, supporting the artists Jan van Eyck and Rogier van der Weyden, whose paintings provide a visual analogy to the music of this period. When Philip died in 1467, his funeral obsequies were marked by all the many instruments that crowd the angelic paintings by Hans Memling and others:

> Pipes, drums, timpani and trumpets
> Lutes, portatives, harps, psalteries
> Horns, bagpipes, sweet symphonies

Chansons on the clavichord

Proportions, sweet prolations

Perfections of longs and breves

Blend your sounds in dissonances of grief . . .

Two years after Philip's death, we know that the Burgundian court employed fourteen singers in different voice ranges. Scholars have gathered important information about the resources of different courts and chapels over the succeeding years: the baptistery in Florence had between twelve and fourteen singers by 1512, Treviso Cathedral in 1527 had two basses, two tenors, three contras and two adults plus four boys for the top parts, while in Rome by 1544 there were twenty-nine singers in the papal chapel. But we have to be careful in assuming that all these voices sang in every service, as they would in a modern choral foundation. The English Gyffard Partbooks of around 1553 indicate that its four-part music is to be sung by 'three men and a child', thus one to a part. The origins of 'choral music', and the expectations in relation to the performing forces expected in later music, continue to be surrounded by a great deal of controversy, since our ideas of choral forces have tended to be formed by the large-scale performances of the nineteenth century and the inherited traditions from those events.

Some conditions for good singing in church were expressed by the theorist and theologian Conrad von Zabern in his treatise *De modo bene cantandi choralem cantum* published in Mainz in 1474. His six requirements were:

1. *Concorditer* (to sing with one spirit and accord)
2. *Mensuraliter* (to sing in proper measure [strictly following the rhythm])
3. *Mediocriter* (to sing in middle range [so that the pitch suits all voice parts])
4. *Differentialiter* (to sing with discrimination [suiting the mood of the liturgy])
5. *Devotionaliter* (to sing with devotion)
6. *Satis urbaniter* (to sing with beauty and refinement [not in rustic style])

Zabern elucidates his conditions with a host of examples from his day, my favourite of which is his observation that 'a particularly striking crudity is that of singing the high notes with a loud tone ... if there is a person who by nature has a heavy, trumpet-like voice, it makes a great disturbance in the whole choral song and appears as though the voices of several oxen were mixed in with the choir'. Therefore he wrote a couplet, *Ut boves in pratis/Sic vos in choro boatis*: as the cattle in the field, so bellow those in the choir. These instructions are perhaps not so different as might be given to good choral singers across time.

*

English music sat somewhat apart from the developments of the Ars Nova, and pursued its own polyphonic style, referred to as discant. This involved, for example, the use of the *cantus firmus* on the top line of a motet alongside the harmonic intervals of the third and the sixth, leading theorists to comment that 'the more imperfect tones that a man sings in the treble, the merrier it is'. The sporadic appearances and long line of anonymous works made in early modern England come to a glorious halt at the very end of the fourteenth century when there is a remarkable survival: the Old Hall Manuscript, containing some 147 compositions of Mass movements, 100 of which have attributions to 24 named composers. This is a sudden advance in our knowledge, and the music itself is well worth hearing for its soaring lines and florid embellishments.

The Old Hall Manuscript – so called because from 1893 to 1973 it belonged to St Edmund's College at Old Hall Green, Hertfordshire, having been presented to it in payment for some school fees – is the only medieval collection of English music for the Mass. Some of the pieces are attributed to 'Roy Henry': could these be compositions by King Henry V himself? (According to Christopher Hogwood, there was a remark attributed to Brahms: 'Never criticise the composition of a Royal Highness. You never know who may have written it.') Although the question of royal involvement remains inconclusive, the life story of the most frequently included composer, Leonel Power (d. 1445), suggests that the manuscript was compiled while he was in the service of Thomas, Duke of Clarence (brother of Henry V), then passed into the king's household after Clarence's death in 1421, where composers added their own works to the volume. The sound of all this music tells a gradual story of a move from the clear textures of the English medieval idioms towards the complexities of the later motets. There are some quite simple pieces here, among which John Cooke's (c. 1385–c. 1442) three-part *Stella coeli* (Star of Heaven) is memorable, but there is also hair-raising intricacy in some of the more obscure music, notably by the little-known Pycard (fl. c. 1410) who writes complex canonic treatments of the Gloria and Sanctus. It is striking that only a handful of the pieces, including some added to the manuscript later, have been found in continental manuscripts: England went its own way. The music of the Old Hall Manuscript has been beautifully realised in performances and recordings by the Hilliard Ensemble.

All this activity took place against the ferment of continuing English–French wars, which culminated in the famous Battle of Agincourt on 25 October 1415 when Henry V defeated the French. The victory was celebrated at the time in the Agincourt Carol, with its memorable melody, woven into the score that William Walton (p. 220) later wrote for Laurence Olivier's film of Shakespeare's *Henry V*. Subsequent military engagements in what became known as the Hundred Years War were less positive for the English, and eventually the French won back much of their land. Under Philip the Good, France made a determined effort to build back its pre-eminence, and music played a vital role in signalling those efforts. When Philip married his third wife Isabella of Portugal in 1430, one observer noted that 'at least a hundred and twenty silver trumpets' greeted her arrival, while the singers at the ceremony were 'the very best in the art of music one could possibly find anywhere'.

During this period the Duke of Bedford spent much time ruling in France on behalf of the English king, and among the musicians he employed was the composer John Dunstaple, also called Dunstable (c. 1390–1453). Dunstaple thus became well known and influential in France, and his harmonious style of composition, using intervals of the third and sixth, became regarded as a typical English style (*95). There is some evidence that the period featuring Dunstaple is one of the few times that England has actually led the continent in musical style: that seems to be the meaning of a single highly flattering reference by the French poet

Martin le Franc which praised the '*contenance angloise*'. In his massive 24,000-verse poem *Le champion des dames*, written for Philip the Good in 1440–2, le Franc claimed that the composers of the new generation 'have a new practice of making lively consonance both in loud and soft music / in feigning, in rests and in mutations / they took on the guise of the English and follow Dunstaple / and thereby a marvellous pleasingness / makes their music joyous and remarkable'. The poem also praises the French composers Dufay and Binchois and confirms Dunstaple's influence on them and their contemporaries.

There certainly was at this time a trend towards harmonious movement, as demonstrated in Dunstaple's sweet-sounding three-part pieces, some of which are Mass movements or other liturgical antiphons. The theorist and composer Johannes Tinctoris (*c.* 1435–1511) praised Dunstaple and his up-to-date followers, with whom he seems to have been on good personal terms, in his *Liber de arte contrapuncti*, dismissing 'older composers who wrote more dissonances than consonances'. Tinctoris was an advocate of all that was modern in music, and like le Franc he links together Dufay, Binchois and Dunstaple as originators and teachers of the new generation: 'Nearly all the works of these men exhale such sweetness that in my opinion they are to be considered most suitable, not only for men and for heroes, but even for the immortal gods.' Tinctoris's new rules of counterpoint set strict rules for when dissonant notes could be introduced into a composition.

This and many other elements of Renaissance musical theory were codified much later by Gioseffo Zarlino (?1517–90) in his large-scale treatise about the foundations of harmony, *Le Istitutioni harmoniche*, written in 1558. Zarlino has been described by Oliver Strunk as 'easily the most influential personality in the history of musical theory from Aristoxenus to Rameau' because he brought ancient thinking about proportion and numbers into the modern Renaissance musical world; he clarifies the harmonic series, explains major and minor scales and modes, and argues for the acceptance of the third and sixth as harmonious intervals. His highly original thinking is demonstrated by his description of a radical design for a harpsichord which has nineteen notes to the octave instead of the normal twelve. Apparently, one was built and was seen by the traveller and historian Charles Burney, but fortunately for us, it did not catch on.

It is ironic that the reign of Henry VIII, which saw the attack on Catholic liturgical and cultural traditions in the Reformation, was a time of great musical activity in which the king himself played a leading role. He was trained as a musician, played the organ, lute and virginals, composed, and employed a wide variety of English and continental players to travel with the court. We read of him entertaining an ambassador with 'amusements of every description, the chief of which was the instrumental music of his chaplain . . . which lasted four consecutive hours'. Henry's own music is not remarkable, but his collection of decorated keyboards and other instruments (of which a list survives in the British Library) is lavish.

A great deal of earlier religious music was destroyed during the English Reformation, which makes the survivals we have all the more precious. Bookending the fifteenth century in England, matching the importance of the Old Hall Manuscript at the start of the century, is the Eton Choirbook at the end – another miraculous survival of a body of music that sheds light on a whole period of musical development during which the material was collected. It originated at Eton College near Windsor during the reign of Henry VII, and so displays the pre-Reformation spirituality of England at its height. These well-endowed choral foundations such as Eton, New College and Christ Church, Oxford, enlarged both the size of choirs and their technical skills, delighting in sonority for its own sake. The cult of the Virgin Mary was then prominent, and votive antiphons to the Blessed Virgin fill this remarkable collection. As the statutes directed, every evening at Vespers the students of the college were to process into the chapel and sing a votive antiphon 'as well as they know how'. From the evidence of the motets contained in the book their skills must have been considerable since the music enlarges the vocal range in a spectacular way, with the high voices rising in melismas and decorative phrases in passages of long-sustained glory. The sonority of this music is amazing: it speaks of an intense spirituality, a Catholic homage to the Virgin Mary which was to be radically challenged in the years of the Reformation. The elaborate setting of the hymn *Stabat mater* by John Browne (fl. *c.* 1480–1505) is a masterpiece that cannot fail to move the listener who understands the Marian devotion of the time, and can be heard as a foreshadowing of settings of this text by composers as diverse as Pergolesi in the eighteenth century, Szymanowski in the twentieth and James MacMillan in the twenty-first. The elaborate idiom of the Eton Choirbook has been well captured in a series of recordings by the Choir of Christ Church Cathedral, Oxford, under Stephen Darlington.

In the wake of the Eton Choirbook, a new generation of English composers flourished around the beginning of the sixteenth century. Robert Fayrfax (1464–1521) was accounted 'the prime musician of the nation' and left more music than any other English composer of his time. His contribution to the development of the cyclical Mass is important; following his rapid rise through the court of Henry VII, he was in a good position to impress the new king, Henry VIII, and with the composer William Cornysh Jnr met Francis I at the Field of the Cloth of Gold in 1520. Among Fayrfax's twenty-nine surviving works there are some beautiful and not over-elaborate settings which rely more on rhythmic subtlety than on adventurous harmony. John Taverner (c. 1490–1545) worked briefly at what is now Christ Church, Oxford, at that time called Cardinal College under the sway of Cardinal Wolsey. Taverner is considered the leader of pre-Reformation composition in England; his florid motets and Masses make an enduring impression, with their long overlapping phrases which seem destined never to end. His glorious Missa 'Gloria Tibi Trinitas' is a festal setting that stands between the exuberance of the Eton Choirbook and the more restrained polyphony of the next generation. It has pride of place at the start of a volume of Masses including four by Fayrfax and is illustrated by illuminated letters perhaps depicting the composer.

Taverner's career is surrounded by myth and rumour. He was said to have become a Protestant agent, and the martyrologist John Foxe claimed a generation later that he 'repented him very much that he made songs to popish ditties in the time of his blindness', though there is no evidence for this. It seems more likely that Taverner retired from Cardinal College and led a quiet and prosperous retirement. His possible political involvement with Thomas Cromwell and the Dissolution of the Monasteries, which has been disproved by scholars, did become the subject of a compelling twentieth-century opera by Peter Maxwell Davies, Taverner. John Sheppard (c. 1515–58) and Christopher Tye (c. 1505–c. 1573) both worked at the Chapel Royal. Sheppard's substantial Media vita is one of the most beautifully extended sequences of the time, while Tye wrote original, even eccentric consort music for viols. Like Taverner, both Tye and Sheppard used secular melody as well as plainsong as the basis of their sacred compositions, and all three composers wrote Masses on the traditional folk melody *The Western Wind*; these three fine pieces may well have been conceived together and are all well worth hearing.

As the Reformation took hold in England, there was a desire for intelligible settings that could be understood by all: the musical pendulum swung again, as so often across the centuries, between elaboration and simplicity. The need for the words to be clearly expressed led to a desire for a restrained style which would eliminate decoration for its own sake, and instead would be devoted to projecting the texts. The words which were communicated in the *Western Wind* Masses were those of the liturgy, but the song underlying them was anything but sacred in its original text:

> Western wind when will thou blow,
> The small rain down can rain.
> Christ, if my love were in my arms
> And I in my bed again!

6

Craftsmen

Creating music is a science as well as an art. It requires mastery of a craft, and the ability to use that craft rigorously to realise the highest artistic ambitions. There are many aspects to it: the study of counterpoint, the making of musical instruments, the practice of playing and singing, the memorising of music. Especially in the Renaissance, these skills were expected not just of musicians themselves, but of the all-round civilised courtier.

We regard Leonardo da Vinci (1452–1519) as a great visual artist, and a great inventor, but not primarily as a great musician. Yet he was a prolific inventor of musical instruments, a student of acoustics and the properties of sound, and he accorded music the highest place among the arts after painting. In his world, music was firmly integrated with the other pursuits and accomplishments of life. Leonardo was invited to the court of the Duke of Milan principally because he sang divinely, improvising his own accompaniment on the *lira da braccio*. Giorgio Vasari tells us that 'Leonardo brought there the instrument he had built with his own hands, made largely of silver but in the shape of a horse skull – a bizarre, new thing – so that the sound would have the greatest sonority.' Vasari also notes that Leonardo used music to amuse the model for his *Mona Lisa* while he painted her portrait. After nearly two decades in Milan, Leonardo moved to Paris in the service of the King of France. There he studied the origins of both human and instrumental sound, and he sketched ideas for newly mechanical versions of instruments, which anticipated later developments by centuries. He attempted to combine instruments, for instance his cross between a violin and an organ, the *viola organista*, or a bell operated by a keyboard to create different pitches. As a producer of pageants, he created wild fantasy instruments, but these were not, according to the leading expert on Leonardo and music, Emanuel Winternitz, 'merely diverting devices for performing magic tricks; instead they are system-atic efforts by Leonardo to realise some basic aims.' Endlessly curious about everything he experienced, Leonardo is a shining example of someone who unit-ed the philosophical and the practical aspects of the art form, exploring both the purpose of why music existed and the craftsmanship of making music. As noted earlier, Leonardo described music as 'a shaping of the invisible' – a potent phrase placing him in the long tradition of the Greek philosophers, reminding us of the centrality of music at this time, in both spiritual and secular spheres.

The place of music in the civilised life was articulated by Baldassare Castiglione who wrote in his justly famous *Il cortegiano* (1528) that 'I am not satisfied with our courtier unless he is also a musician and unless as well as understanding and being able to read music he can play several instruments'. In the form of his reported dis-cussions by the nobility at the court of Urbino in 1507, we learn a great deal about the tastes of the time and the preferred forms of music. In response to the question as to what music is important and when it should be used, there is a disquisition on singing to the accompaniment of the viol which 'seems to me most delightful, which adds to the words a charm and grace that are very admirable'. The nobles insist that a courtier should have some acquaintance with the craft of playing the viols and be able to accompany himself singing. Castiglione mentions the power of music throughout society, in everyday work and play: 'rough toilers of the field under a burning sun often cheat their weariness with crude and rustic song. With music the rude peasant lass, who is up before the day to spin or weave, wards off her drowsiness and makes her toil a pleasure; music is a very cheering pastime for poor sailors after rain, wind, and tempest; a solace to tired pilgrims on their long and weary journey, and often to sorrowing captives in their chains and fetters.' To which we might add today: sufferers from virus, isolation, mental health issues and the many other afflictions of modern society to which music can turn its healing power.

The Renaissance was at root an artistic movement which looked back to ancient Greece and attempted to reinvent it for a new generation. In doing this, like so many imagined reinventions of traditions, they actually created not something old but something profoundly new and important. The exact timing of the move from the Middle Ages to the Renaissance has always been a difficult one to pin down, for it happened gradually in different places and at different moments. But this is nevertheless a tipping point in moving from medieval musical styles to those of harmonious polyphony. What we can say now is that the artistic and musical concepts of the Renaissance have acquired a special immediacy for us today, speaking directly to our present-day sense of balance and clarity, symbolised by the art of Giotto and the architecture of Michelangelo. This stylistic move has been linked to the spread of humanistic thinking which gradually brought together a major confluence of developments, bringing music into the centre of conceptual thinking around poetry and rhetoric, supported by the growth of a bourgeois culture fuelled by the use of the new technology of printing to circulate texts, and to the dramatic impact of the religious struggles and crises of the sixteenth century. This is a new tipping point for music, as the many complex changes observed in the evolution of polyphony gradually gave way to a sonorous and coherent style based on equal-voiced harmony, reflecting the ideal of transparent unity that was to define the Renaissance.

The composers of the fifteenth century have acquired a reputation for advanced complexity which is only partly deserved. Johannes Ockeghem (*c.* 1410–97), who served the French royal court in the middle of the fifteenth century, developed the *cantus firmus* Masses of Dufay. If we search for ingenuity, it can be found in his *Missa prolationum*, where Ockeghem has vocal canons which increase in their intervals through the work, just as in a later century Bach would structure his *Goldberg Variations* around canons of increasing intervals (p. 129). However, Ockeghem has two canons sounding simultaneously, at different rates of speed, a truly virtuosic feat of composition. It was this sort of skill that came to represent an excessive ingenuity, and hence an unproductive era of composition, in a way rather similar to the constructions of the ultra-serial twelve-note composers after the Second World War (p. 236). Yet Ockeghem's music can be expressive and eloquent on its own term; he wrote a touching motet in memory of his contemporary, Binchois, and a sombre Requiem for King Charles VII (*93) (Plate 8).

Jacob Obrecht (1457/8–1505) and Henricus Isaac (*c.* 1450–1517) both studied in the Low Countries and became part of what is now called the Franco-Flemish school of polyphony. They travelled widely – Obrecht died in Italy, and Isaac in Florence working under the patronage of the famous Medici family. Obrecht owed much to Ockeghem, but his use of the *cantus firmus* is often more literal than his predecessor's, and it can often be heard clearly singing at the top of the texture, pure and unornamented, while the expressive polyphony is developed beneath. Isaac was a much more wide-ranging composer, and has left music in many genres, including some 36 Masses (more must have been lost) and 450 motets of varying kinds included in his *Choralis Constantinus*, a collection of pieces for the Proper of the Mass. Probably his best-known single work today is a short secular song with a memorable melody, *Innsbruck, ich muss dich lassen*, which became adapted as a Lutheran chorale that Bach used.

In the changing perspective of history we would now recognise Josquin des Prez (*c.* 1450/5–1521) as one of the greatest composers of his or any other time, and the eloquence and poised beauty of his music as among the most communicative of the whole medieval and Renaissance period. He was, following Machaut, an early example of the composer as a strong personality, widely known and revered, and it makes little sense to undervalue him, as some have done, in comparison with Palestrina. Martin Luther called him 'the master of the notes. They must do as he wills; as for other composers, they have to do as the notes will'; others compared his work to that of Michelangelo in sculpture.

Born near where Dufay had worked in Cambrai, under what is now known to be his family name of Lebloitte, Josquin worked in Aix-en-Provence for the King of Sicily, and in 1489 joined the papal chapel in Rome. In 1503 he was appointed *maestro di cappella* to the Duke of Ferrara, but stayed only a year; it was said that Josquin 'composes when he wants to, and not when he is asked to', a familiar problem linking him to the semi-independent composers of later times. Josquin represented an ideal of his day, bringing music to a new equilibrium after the innovations of Ars Subtilior; indeed, the theorist Henricus Glareanus declared that

Josquin had created an Ars Perfecta. Josquin sums up the achievement of this era of expression, this new world of harmony. There was a humanist tendency at work here, emphasising more than the application of formal rules, and an added desire for expressiveness. This is an elusive quality to pin down, for it is not as if earlier music we have encountered lacks a powerful sense of expression. It is rather that Josquin refines his expressiveness to a noble simplicity, making it a more explicit preoccupation, in particular moulding the texts of his pieces to demonstrate their meaning. You can sense in his music a newly intellectual ability to create and develop musical motifs, sustaining their argument across the texts he sets, which marks him out from his predecessors.

This creates something that is audible in Josquin's music: a directness of communication. You sense that immediately in the Missa 'Pange lingua' (*92) of around 1515, which is based on the plainsong hymn of that title, in praise of the cross of Christ. In the preceding century we might have expected the plainsong melody to form the underlying chant at the base of the texture, over which elaborate decoration was applied. But Josquin does something different: he takes the plainsong melody and uses phrases from it in each part of a four-part texture, creating an imitative pattern based on themes from the plainchant melody. This is very similar to the procedure we will hear later, using the melodic phrases to match the rise and fall of the polyphonic textures, establishing an ideal of harmonic working which remained constant across many years.

There is another central reason why Josquin acquired the place and the reputation he did: he was the first major beneficiary of the age of music printing. Since the invention of the printing press by Johannes Gutenberg in the fifteenth century, the means had existed to disseminate texts by mass reproduction rather than purely by copying: a prime example of the impact of a new technology on the means of production, comparable to the computer or the internet in our age. This development underpinned the advancement of thought in the Renaissance as ideas and philosophies were spread through the newly aspirational cultural classes. The next breakthrough was the printing of music, though this took some time to become widespread. In 1501 Ottaviano Petrucci produced in Venice the first polyphonic collection entirely made from moveable type, so that the notes and the text could be set clearly and elegantly on the framework of the music staves. Pride of place at the start of his first volume was given to Josquin's *Ave Maria, Virgo serena*. Dissemination of music through printing became firmly established through the publication of dances by Pierre Attaingnant in Paris from 1528, followed by Italian printers in the next decade. Josquin's fame was such that many pieces that were not by him were attributed to him in printed editions, presumably because it made the music extremely saleable – a strategy much used later in eighteenth-century publications attributed to Pergolesi and Haydn, and one that has caused scholars many challenges.

Josquin, like Machaut before him, was something of a star in the social world of the time. He made use of *L'Homme armé* as the basis for at least two of his masses. In another Mass, in honour of Ferrara's ruler, the *Missa 'Hercules Dux Ferrarie'*, Josquin assigns the syllables in that title to the vowel sounds of specific notes, creating a melody that is then used as the *cantus firmus* of the Mass, sometimes heard in different voices, sometimes backwards. It is difficult to believe that the composer meant this construction to be consciously perceived, and more likely that it was a hidden symbolism which helps to generate the music. Such ingenuity has been criticised, but it parallels the symbolism that other composers from J. S. Bach (p. 129) to Alban Berg and Olivier Messiaen have employed to animate and organise their compositions. Another superb work by Josquin which should not be missed is the impressive twenty-minute motet *Miserere mei, Deus*, a setting of the penitential Psalm 51, the vocal entries of its chant motto phrase moving up and down the scale to hypnotic effect. He wrote a beautiful lament on Ockeghem's passing, *Nymphes des bois*, with its moving lyrics 'change your voices, so clear and proud, to sharp cries and lamentations'. His range extends from that sad lament to the jovial little part-song about a cricket, *El grillo*, which is pure fun, or the war-song *Scaramella va alla guerra*, both of which show a more popular side to his writing.

The composer who stands alongside Josquin for his fame in the Franco-Flemish school is Antoine Brumel (*c.* 1460–?1512/13), a vigorous and apparently difficult Frenchman who worked in Chartres, then in Geneva and Paris, and was the successor to Obrecht in Ferrara. Commentators of the time praised

Brumel for creating 'a new style of singing, sweet, pleasant, devout and beauti-ful'. In his music the individual wandering lines of polyphony begin to form into the harmonious style that Josquin made famous. Brumel wrote a Requiem which seems to have been one of the first to include a setting of the *Dies irae*, and the famous *Missa 'Et ecce terrae motus'*, for an unusually large ensemble of twelve voices. This impressive piece has become known as the 'Earthquake' Mass after the Easter antiphon on which it is based. It was later performed at Munich around 1570 under the composer Lassus, whose score (with all the names of performers, including himself, written on it) is the surviving source of this great work.

The music of Josquin, Brumel and their contemporaries has benefited hugely from the lucid, transparent performance styles of recent times. The Tallis Schol-ars under Peter Phillips in Britain, who have completed fine recordings of all Jos-quin's Masses in time for the 500th anniversary of his death in 2021, the Ensemble Organum under Marcel Pérès, the Huelgas Ensemble with Paul van Nevel, who have recorded Brumel's 'Earthquake' Mass, and many other vocal ensembles have shown how warm and yet how clear this music can sound. Heard on recordings, it is inevitably remote from its original circumstances of performance in court and chapel, yet this paradoxically serves to accentuate its remarkable ability to com-municate directly across the centuries.

*

Our view of the development of musical style in this period has been highly co-loured by the historians of the past, especially those who wanted to single out and idolise Giovanni Pierluigi da Palestrina (*c.* 1525/6–94) in the Renaissance as a paragon of virtue: to give him a central place, rather as Beethoven acquired for a later symphonic age. We would now recognise that the composers of the genera-tions before Palestrina are equally important, in standing if not in influence. The urge to create a narrative of progress in the arts is compelling, as is the desire to single out great men (and they were too often all men) upon whose shoulders that progress rests. In Sir Charles Villiers Stanford and Cecil Forsyth's 1916 *A History of Music*, quoted scathingly by a later music historian Jack Westrup, there was a wish to highlight the achievement of Palestrina as the paragon of composers in the Renaissance: 'the muddy stream of misplaced ingenuity' had to be dispersed by 'the big tidal-wave which brought Palestrina's galleon up to her anchorage'; the 'frightful mechanical ingenuities of Josquin and his fellow-workers' were so much 'choking masses of bindweed that lay on the foothills leading upwards to the heights of Palestrina'. As Westrup crisply puts it, 'Absurdity could go no further.'

The real background to the virtual canonisation of Palestrina is the growth of the Protestant Reformation, which gathered speed after Martin Luther nailed his ninety-five Theses to the door of the church in Wittenberg in 1517; many of its stern results were antipathetic to music, reviving the old clichéd view of the art as essentially ungodly and decorative, a frivolous lifestyle choice of decadent clergy. Thus there were branches of Protestantism, such as those led by Calvin and Zwingli, which reduced the role of music and banned its extensive use from their services. Calvin admitted the singing of psalms as long as they were sung together by the whole congregation and not elaborated, and some tunes survive today in hymns, such as 'All people that on earth do dwell'.

Luther himself, however, was a serious musician and a modest composer, and he was convinced of music's importance; 'after theology', he wrote, 'I grant music the highest place and the highest honour'. He disagreed with the Catholic church on many theological points, but valued its liturgy; so that whereas other reformers moved to entirely vernacular ceremonies for their observances, Luther maintained some use of Latin in his services. This enabled the polyphonic tradition to be kept alive in larger Lutheran Protestant churches. But that was secondary to the major revolution Luther brought to the liturgy, when in 1525 he published a *Deutsche Messe*, introducing German hymns into the liturgy to substitute for movements of the Ordinary and Proper of the Mass.

The complete change this brought about in the tradition of liturgical music is one whose importance it is hard to overestimate. Luther wrote some memorable melodies (such as *Ein feste Burg*) himself, and others he adapted from the old plainsong hymns and sequences: the Easter hymn *Christ lag in Todesbanden* derived from the Latin sequence melody *Victimae paschali laudes*; the Christmas antiphon *Veni redemptor gentium* became one of the best-known Advent hymns, *Nun komm der Heiden Heiland*; and the Pentecost hymn *Veni creator spiritus* became the hymn to the Holy Spirit *Komm, Gott Schöpfer, Heiliger Geist*. These new chorales provided the bedrock of the sacred repertory in the vernacular language, and were the start of the tradition that would be worked into cantatas, chorale preludes and the Passions of J. S. Bach and his colleagues in the seventeenth and eighteenth centuries.

Soon these simple chorale settings were themselves extended and elaborated, using the phrases as the basis for imitative writing between the parts. But there was an essential down-to-earth quality about the Lutheran chorale that kept it grounded as a repertory of the people. The aim was that it should be inspirational but intelligible. One of the most approachable Lutheran composers is Michael Praetorius (?1571–1621), and this is particularly evident in his lively settings for Christmas, where he worked with Lutheran chorales accompanied by instrumental ensembles to produce varied and attractive sequences. He was devoted to the church and its music throughout his life and was said on his death to have 'often regretted that he never took holy orders'. His very practical guide to the performance practice of the time, *Syntagma Musicum*, is extremely valuable for understanding the way that voices and instruments were used, and especially how they could be combined in varied ensembles to greatest effect (p. 96).

The response of the Catholic church to the Protestant Reformation was a strong movement for reform, which came to a head between 1545 and 1563 at the meetings known as the Council of Trent. Although theology was the battleground of these debates, attention was also paid to the contrast of musical traditions. Protestants desired music that could be understood by the people, mainly sung in their own language, while the Catholic church sought a more elevated and mystical approach to spirituality, expressed in the Latin language. However, there was one strong point of connection between the two viewpoints: in whatever language was used, both wanted a greater intelligibility of the texts that were sung. Through accounts that quickly took on the status of a legend, Palestrina is credited with having averted any general condemnation of music by the Council of Trent. His *Missa Papae Marcelli* (*91) demonstrates how polyphony can be made simple, intelligible and beautiful. The Council confined itself to concluding that the function of music was 'not to give empty pleasure to the ear, but in such a way

73

that the words be clearly understood by all', an aim which the documents we have from Palestrina show him to have fully supported: he claimed to have worked hard 'to adorn the holy sacrifice of the Mass in a new manner'. Palestrina also crafted a strong narrative of papal approval for his work that quickly took hold. The title page of the first collection of his Masses, printed in 1554, has an iconic image of Palestrina kneeling before Pope Julius III with an open score; the Pope is blessing both the composer and the music (Plate 9). (The image is not unique: a similar engraving opens a set of Masses by the Spanish composer Cristóbal de Morales (c. 1500–53), but Palestrina was closer to the centre of papal power.) Palestrina spent his entire career in Rome: he had been born nearby, received his training there, and then came under the patronage of Julius III. He worked at the Cappella Giulia in St Peter's, and then in two major Rome churches, St John Lateran and Santa Maria Maggiore, in the 1550s and 1560s, before returning to St Peter's for the remaining twenty-three years of his life.

The overwhelming feeling we gain from listening to one of Palestrina's Masses is of its inevitability. We are carried along by a supreme logic that links the parts, shapes the phrases, builds to climaxes, and then reaches a natural conclusion, all this dictated by the shape of the words. Palestrina certainly studied the work of Josquin and wrote at least two Masses on the old *L'Homme armé* song, but he soon moved towards a freer style that was not restricted by a *cantus firmus* and developed its own melodic patterns. So in place of strict imitation between the parts which had to be based on the underlying *cantus firmus*, Palestrina's imagination roves more freely and his imitative writing, though still based on the fundamentals of counterpoint, is not bound to an existing melody; instead it creates its own mood of serenity and transcendental peace, but with elements of dramatic word-painting, reflecting the texts of the liturgy faithfully.

What gave Palestrina his immense reputation was the following of Italian church composers who imitated his style in the succeeding generations, combined with the way in which he was held up as an ideal of Catholic liturgical music. Neither of these aspects really captures the quality of his music, with its considerable drama and perfect balance. Palestrina's reputation as the unquestioned leader in the field was certainly partly self-generated: this takes us back to the contrast between Machaut, ensuring his own prominence by collecting his own works, and Ockeghem, who almost disappeared from musical history because his works were not collected and preserved. Through the reputation he established for himself, Palestrina became a symbol for Catholic church music and an ideal of pure composition which was taken up much later by the nineteenth century when minor church composers yearned to recreate simplicity in music. He was admired by no less a figure than Wagner, who arranged his *Stabat mater*. Another inheritance of his work is the approach to the writing of counterpoint that has held good for many centuries: it formed the basis of common practice in conservatoires and universities, and as formulated, for instance, by Johann Joseph Fux (p. 91), it was pervasive in the European tradition from that time forward. Palestrina's music has never faded from the Catholic church repertory in the same way as that of earlier composers. Alongside the performances and recordings by secular ensembles such as Magnificat and Odhecaton, major ecclesiastical choirs have continued to reinterpret his harmonious counterpoint, with the Westminster Cathedral Choir and others maintaining it in their services.

Among Palestrina's leading contemporaries was Tomás Luis de Victoria (1548–1611). Victoria's Spanish passion has always had a special appeal; although he spent twenty years in Rome, where he must have known Palestrina and his music, he returned to Spain around 1587 and composed for the Dowager Empress María works of peerless depth and intensity. Victoria was capable of uplifting, glorious settings such as his motet and Mass *O quam gloriosum*, whose melodic counterpoint rises and falls like Palestrina's, but with arguably more passion. That passion is caught by those choirs who use a direct, throaty continental sound like the Spanish Escolania de Montserrat, and the choir of Westminster Cathedral when under the characterful direction of George Malcolm: they made a distinctively passionate recording of Victoria's *Tenebrae Responsories* in 1959, still worth seeking out. Victoria's Requiem (*86) is one of the most powerful of those setting both the Proper texts and the Ordinary of the Requiem Mass.

Standing alongside Josquin and then Palestrina as the most famous composer of the age was the Flemish Orlande or Roland de Lassus, also Orlando di Lasso (1530/2–94). A great cosmopolitan, he was clearly extremely cultured and intelligent, speaking several languages and writing letters in a bizarre mixture of tongues. He spent much of his life in the well-endowed ducal chapel in the city of Munich (where, then as now, resources for the arts and performers were ample: Plate 12). He composed an enormous amount of vocal music, which was widely taken up. He wrote advanced chromatic music, as in the twelve motets called *Prophetiae Sibyllarum*, deeply emotional polyphony in the twenty sacred madrigals of the *Lagrime di San Pietro* (*88), and universally admired settings of the Psalms of David, including a famous *De profundis*. He responded to sacred texts with fervour but is almost better known as a composer of secular music: here his diverse background shone through, in Italian-style madrigals, French chansons and German chorales that look forward to double-choir music in the Venetian style. In an age of contrasting national cultures, Lassus stands as perhaps the first truly European composer, and his music has been taken up by choirs across Europe.

The musical impact of the Reformation in England, like the political impact, was much more drastic than elsewhere in Europe, because it was driven by Henry VIII's desire to break the dominance of Rome so as to allow him freedom to divorce. This created a period of political and cultural turmoil during the radical swings between Protestant and Catholic observance in the reigns of Henry VIII, Edward VI, Mary and Elizabeth I, each of which had their own liturgical and musical needs. The resulting Dissolution of the Monasteries was an economic act as much as a religious one, and the violence with which it was carried out led to the destruction of much art, including many musical manuscripts in their libraries.

The most successful composers of the time were those who managed to juggle the conflicting demands of their art and the political situation. Thomas Tallis (*c*. 1505–85), a gentleman of the Chapel Royal, surprisingly acquired with his colleague William Byrd a patent from Elizabeth I in 1575 to print and publish music. Their first volume of motets by the two composers to Latin texts was *Cantiones sacrae*, a remarkable publication in the reign of a Protestant monarch. When Tallis died, Byrd wrote a moving tribute to his colleague, 'Ye sacred muses' (echoing Josquin's plaint on the death of Ockeghem). Tallis's religious convictions remain unclear, though he did set the Lamentations of Jeremiah, which were associated with the Catholics' sense of exile at the time. One supreme English creation which should be listened to by every enthusiast for the music of this period is the motet in forty real parts that Tallis created: *Spem in alium nunquam habui* (*90). This astonishing piece was probably written as a response to the forty-part motet *Ecce beatam lucem* by Alessandro Striggio (*c.* 1536/7–92), and might have been sung in the long gallery in Arundel House in London, or in the octagonal hall of Nonsuch Palace in Surrey, where the eight choirs of five voices could be spread around the balconies. It was known that Striggio had also written a forty-part Mass; this was recently rediscovered by Davitt Moroney, and it includes an amazing Agnus Dei in sixty real parts. But Tallis's motet contains the finer music and has become an iconic work since its publication in 1888; an influential performance was conducted at Morley College by the composer Michael Tippett in 1947, and later recorded by him; and it has been frequently revived since.

The younger composer William Byrd (*c.* 1540–1623) was a gentleman of the Chapel Royal, brought up during the reign of the Catholic Queen Mary but living through Elizabeth I's strictly Protestant regime. He survived the latter period perhaps because his music was by then so valued that there was nothing to be gained by persecuting him. Nevertheless, he spent his later years out of the limelight in Essex, housed by recusant families, where he managed to avoid undue attention while steadily and continuously composing both secular and sacred music. Byrd wrote only three Latin Masses, which are impossible to compare for instance with Palestrina's vast output, but they are three of the most precious works in this form, whose concentration and inward-looking beauty mark them out as music of utter integrity. From the ecstatic madrigalian scales of 'Et ascendit in coelum' (He ascended into heaven) in the Credo, to the yearning dissonances of 'Dona nobis pacem' (Grant us peace) in the Agnus Dei of the Mass for Four Voices (*89), Byrd reflects his sacred texts vividly.

We cannot imagine how dangerous it was for Byrd to write this music, and even more to perform it in the recusant households among which he lived. Byrd kept writing more motets, compiling a two-volume *Gradualia* of settings of the Proper texts for the feasts of the year. His choice of texts often shows his beliefs. It is impossible to hear his great motet *Civitas sancti tui* without sensing a spirit of profound regret; the text bemoans the desolation of Jerusalem, and the analogy with strife-torn England is unavoidable. Several of the texts he set seem to have hidden messages of protest coded within them. Byrd's attention to his texts is just one of the marvellously sensitive aspects of his art. In a statement that has implications for any composer, Byrd believed the words came first: 'there is such a profound and hidden power [in sacred words] that to one thinking upon things divine and diligently and earnestly pondering them, all the most appropriate measures occur as if of themselves'. That concept of music flowing through the agency of the composer, rather than being originated by him or her, is a startlingly modern idea that recalls what Stravinsky said in 1961 (though with some rose-tinted memory of his originality) about *The Rite of Spring* (p. 230): 'I had only my ear to help me; I heard and I wrote what I heard. I am the vessel through which *Le Sacre* passed.'

*

One of the finest characteristics of English music through the ages has been its ability to do things extremely well, very late in the life of art forms. There are the twentieth-century Romantic symphonies of Edward Elgar (p. 200), and the baroque viol fantasias of Henry Purcell (p. 100), but the madrigals produced in England around the turn of the seventeenth century are the supreme example, bringing to perfection a form that had been developed and nurtured in Italy from the 1520s under the patronage of the Medici family in Florence. The impetus for this had also been the new emphasis on the qualities of poetic forms and the desire to illustrate this through musical settings which reflected the nuances of the texts. The concept of 'setting a text to music', which we would immediately recognise today, goes back to the freedom with which this form was created in Italy, enabling a fresh response to the changing emotions of the words. We should also allow that the great euphony and sheer musicality of the Italian language assisted, as it has throughout the centuries of that country's music, the natural word-setting of their native texts.

The first book of madrigals published by Jacques Arcadelt (1507–68) in Venice in 1539 was the most widely printed of all madrigal books; it set the trend for line-by-line settings rather than the verse-and-refrain structures encountered earlier. Arcadelt's most famous madrigal is *Il bianco e dolce cigno*, showing the song style at its best. He wrote in four parts with an easy harmoniousness that reflects the text and keeps the music flowing. Some madrigals were light-hearted, while others were passionate settings of texts by Petrarch and others, especially in the Venetian music by Adrian Willaert (*c.* 1490–1562), whose five-part writing brings a rich and sustained sonority to the form.

Willaert ushered in the greatest period of Venetian musical history, when it was at its most adventurous and innovative. He brought the Netherlandish poly-phonic tradition to Italy and became *maestro di cappella* at St Mark's in Venice from 1527. Perhaps inspired by the architecture of the church and the presence of two organs, he developed the existing practice of writing for two separate choirs, and these *cori spezzati* became a firmly established fashion, alternating verses of the psalms between the two sides of the church, then uniting them in the final verse. He is a composer who is remembered partly for his works, partly for his influence, and partly because of his entrepreneurial skill in persuading local pub-lishers to issue his works.

Willaert also showed considerable skill at gathering around him a brilliant group of musicians. He cultivated the extensive local talent, above all Andrea Gabrieli (*c.* 1532/3–85), who came from a suburb of Venice, studied in Germany and returned to become second organist at St Mark's. Andrea's experiments in *cori spezzati* extended to a sixteen-part Gloria for four choirs in 1585. He was equally famous as a teacher; there is a nice anecdote told of a pupil who was complain-ing that he could do no more with the theme that Andrea had given him to de-velop. Andrea took the theme back from him and wrote four or five fugues on the subject, each more beautiful than the last, saying, 'Did you really think you had done everything possible?' His madrigals were for ceremonial occasions, with a grandeur that belies their innocent texts. He is credited with creating the 'socially adaptable' madrigal that was suitable for both professionals and amateurs. His nephew Giovanni is part of the next generation of Italian church music (p. 91).

Willaert's pupil Cipriano de Rore (*c.* 1515/16–65) was the real innovator of the madrigal form. His dramatic madrigals began to explore a whole new lan-guage full of bold gestures and expressive harmonies. In his *O morte, eterno fin* from his fourth book of 1557, the anguished emotions are expressed in angular harmonies; where he sings of the 'haven of blind and wretched mortals' the bass line creeps by chromatic steps. From this period the modern concept of 'word-painting' began to be firmly established. It is difficult to believe how many thousands of madrigals began suddenly to emerge in Italy: prolific composers such as the Flemish Philippe de Monte (1521–1603) wrote many himself, while Luca Marenzio (1553/4–99), who worked in Rome and then travelled to Poland, returning to Rome at the end of his life, seems to have composed some 400–500 madrigals though he lived only to the age of about forty-six.

The most notorious of these madrigalists was Carlo Gesualdo (1566–1613), whose tortuous music has been overshadowed by his sensational biography, as an aristocrat who murdered his first wife and her lover. It is probably better, if less exciting, to regard his music as part of the general late mannerist style of Italian madrigals rather than something brought on by these circumstances. But it is nonetheless extreme in its effects, in its rapid contrasts of agitation and calm, and especially in its harmonic outlandishness which often makes the listener feel completely disorientated. The opening of *Moro, lasso* from the Sixth Book has been identified as totally dissolving tonal language a long time before it happened in the twentieth century. Whether or not the listener can quite manage to love the bizarre shifts and surprises of Gesualdo's music, they are venerated by many, and his idiom was admired by Igor Stravinsky, who recomposed some of his music for modern performance. The climax of *Dolcissima mia vita* (from his Fifth Book of 1611) on the words 'oh to die' marks an extreme in linear chromatic writing (*85).

It is, however, Marenzio who deserves credit as one of the composers who stimulated the late flowering of the madrigal in England, for he contributed the most pieces to the collection *Musica transalpina* published in 1588 by Nicholas Yonge. Encouraged by Alfonso Ferrabosco the Elder (1543–88), who was resident in England, this for the first time introduced Italian madrigals with translated English texts: it opened the eyes of native composers to the possibilities of the form. Over the next twenty years or so the English madrigal became one of the most important genres of the time, the influence of which has continued to the present – partly because of the immediacy and colour of its word-painting, but also because of the practicality of performance of this repertory by amateur groups, who have revived the music over a long period of time, from the later nineteenth and early twentieth centuries when these madrigals first became available in modern editions. The first native successes in the genre were by the theorist and composer Thomas Morley (1557/8–1602), who is equally important for his guide *A Plaine and Easie Introduction to Practicall Musicke* (1597). He published eleven collections in a short period, including such quasi-instrumental settings as 'Now is the month of maying' and 'My bonny lasse shee smyleth' as well as the more vocally conceived 'Aprill is in my mistris face'. His style is generally light, in the tradition of the canzonet. There is a strong contrast between this aspect of madrigal composition, with plenty of 'fa la la's, and the deeply expressive texts set by other composers. Thomas Weelkes (1576–1623) is more serious, and his output includes church music as well as madrigals, though his career seems to have been blighted by a rowdy alcohol-fuelled temperament. Yet he was unequalled at creating dazzling sonorities in five parts in his *Ballets and Madrigals to Five Voyces* of 1598 and then in five and six parts in his 1600 collection. He conjures up a volcano's 'sulphurous fire' in his wonderful large-scale geographical madrigal 'Thule the period of cosmographie'. Classical allusions fill his 'As Vesta was, from Latmos hill descending'. This was music for connoisseurs, which sophisticated amateurs could perform.

More restrained is John Wilbye (1574–1638), whose 'Draw on sweet night' is unforgettably eloquent in its Schubert-like mixing of modes. His beautiful 'Adew, sweet Amarillis' also has an effect which is astonishingly contemporary at the end, the minor-mode music shifting into the major key with a feeling not of cheerfulness but of ineffable sadness. Other lesser-known madrigal composers made small but permanent contributions to the genre, as in the witty 'Faire Phyllis I saw sitting all alone' by John Farmer (*c.* 1570–1601) and the tremendous 'All cre'tures now are merry-minded' by the otherwise little-remembered John Bennet (?1575/80–1614). This is one of the most successful pieces in the collection of twenty-five madrigals assembled by Morley called *The Triumphes of Oriana* (1601), all of which have the same refrain 'Long live fair Oriana!' This collection was presumed to honour Queen Elizabeth I, a homage disputed by some, but certainly expressing a shrewd mixture of marketing and timing that sold copies towards the end of Elizabeth's reign.

Near the end of the madrigal's life in England, two composers famous in other fields made important contributions. Orlando Gibbons (1583–1625) wrote one of the most eloquently simple and touching of all madrigals, 'The silver swanne, who living had no note'. Gibbons was also active in the fields of keyboard music and church music, and his verse anthems (set for soloists and ensemble rather than full choir) are among the very finest, among them the well-known 'This is the record of John' and the less famous but visionary 'See, see, the Word is incarnate' (*84), which is a mini-portrait of the whole life of Christ condensed into a few uplifting minutes. His Chapel Royal colleague Thomas Tomkins (1572–1656), who spent most of his life working at Worcester Cathedral, composed the intensely moving madrigal 'Too much I once lamented', which must have the saddest 'fa la la's in the repertory. The long-lived Tomkins lasted through the English Civil War, and among his sixty-eight keyboard pieces is *A sad pavan for these distracted times* dated 'Febr.14 1649' – a fortnight after the execution of King Charles I.

A vivid sidelight on the central importance of music during this period is provided by the evidence of some of the best-known texts of the time, the plays of William Shakespeare (1564–1616). His dramas are full of music, both referred to and performed. There are songs sung to reveal character or to portray a scene. 'Tell me where is fancy bred' in *The Merchant of Venice*, 'O mistress mine where are you roaming' in *Twelfth Night*, and the extensive collection of songs in *As You Like It*, 'It was a lover and his lass', 'Blow, blow thou winter wind' and 'Under the Greenwood tree', all help to define place and mood and advance the drama. Ophelia's songs in *Hamlet* painfully express her trauma. There are copious directions for instrumental music, with fanfares, battle cries, doom-laden noises and triumphant sounds that Othello refers to as 'the shrill trump, / The spirit-stirring drum, th'ear-piercing fife'. We know all too little of the way this music might have been performed: only two settings by court lutenist Robert Johnson can be associated with the performances of the time. The plays have provided a constant resource for later composers inspired by their poetry, as in Tchaikovsky's Overture *Romeo and Juliet* and Mendelssohn's *Midsummer Night's Dream* Overture and incidental music (p. 168), and settings of the songs themselves by composers across the centuries from Henry Purcell to Gerald Finzi's song cycle *Let Us Garlands Bring*. Then there is a wealth of operas which have adapted the plays themselves for new audiences; not all of these have managed to match the excellence of their texts, but among the most successful are Verdi's *Otello* and *Falstaff* (p. 186) and the recent success *Hamlet* by Brett Dean (1961–), which ingeniously reorders the verse.

The English madrigal vanished as quickly as it began as new fashions took hold of the musical scene at the beginning of the seventeenth century. The outstanding figure of this generation is John Dowland (1563–1626). His life is shadowy. Because of his Catholicism he worked in the service of King Christian IV of Denmark, and he was associated with Sir Robert Cecil, the Secretary of State, for whom he performed various diplomatic tasks. It is also said that he was approached by Rome to plot against Elizabeth I, but this is unproven. When Dowland eventually returned to England, he was passed over for court appointments – which may explain his tetchy comments about musical life in the preface to *A Pilgrimes Solace*, where he complained about criticism from 'younger Professors of the Lute'. His friend Henry Peacham believed that in spite of his often cheerful disposition, he did not advance his own cause well, and 'slipt many opportunities in advancing his fortunes': like many musicians who knew their own worth, he was probably too argumentative for his own good with those who might have employed him.

From his *First Book of Songs or Ayres* (1597), *Second Book of Songs or Ayres* (1600), *Third and Last Book of Songs or Ayres* (1603) and then *A Pilgrimes Solace* (1612), Dowland explored a wide range of emotions but was especially associated with the cultivation of melancholy as a genre, reflected in Robert Burton's pathbreaking *Anatomy of Melancholy*, published in 1621. The long, extended phrases of 'I saw my lady weepe' and 'In darkness let me dwell' have ensured Dowland a permanent place in the history of English song. Some of his most memorable pieces are based on dance music, such as the Galliard, 'Can she excuse my wrongs' (*87) and 'Fine knacks for ladies', in which the words are an added gloss on a fundamentally instrumental style.

Of all his output, Dowland's most influential single piece is the pavan *Lachrimae* which became his song 'Flow my tears', and was turned into a set of seven varied pavans based on the same theme; Dowland called it 'this long and trouble-some worke, wherein I have mixed new songs with olde, grave with light'. Its sober, mournful clarity made it one of the most copied, varied and elaborated pieces of the period. At the heart of Dowland's style was his own instrument, the lute, as a solo and accompanying instrument; indeed he took the lute as a virtuoso solo instru-ment to new heights, as has been recreated in recent times by Julian Bream, Paul O'Dette and Anthony Rooley. With songs that could be sung in madrigalian style in four parts, but also as demonstrative solos with lute accompaniment, Dowland moves us gradually towards the next era of the baroque. Professionalism, demon-strated by virtuoso declamation, was beginning to take root.

7

Professionals

Music continually looks backwards as well as forwards. Some composers work with what they have inherited, creating within an existing tradition; some react against it in the search for new expression. Some artistic revolutions are the accumulation of gradual changes rather than a sudden shift, and then a tipping point takes us across into a new world. The musical change that took place at the start of the seventeenth century can be compared to the earlier change to harmonious, equal-voiced polyphony (p. 69), and the later move away from tonality at the start of the twentieth century (p. 222). From an idiom bound to the past, there was a tipping point in musical evolution, where there was a general acceptance of radical changes in practice. The impetus was a new kind of personal expression that emerged across the arts, a striving to capture the widest range of human emotions: this led inevitably to an increased focus on a single outstanding performer, and gradually to the professionalisation of the musician's role in society.

At its very simplest, the musical baroque represents a move away from the equal-voiced polyphony of the Renaissance to a solo-led style over the newly emerging continuo bass. In place of four or more lines which intertwine on a basis of equality, here the bass line provides a harmonic foundation which supports a single melodic line for voice or instrument. The middle range is completed by the harmonies of a keyboard instrument, or a member of the lute family, which filled out the texture. A practice of virtuoso display had already developed with the art of ornamentation, adding a florid line to the texture of a madrigal or a motet, and particularly with the technique called diminution, the dividing-up of a musical figure or phrase into notes of short values. Both have a similar result of cramming a large number of notes into a brief space of time, to brilliant effect. One technique this new music demanded was the improvised filling-out of the harmonies above the continuo bass line. The essential skill needed here was an understanding of harmony, so that the player could see from the bass line provided what the implications were for the chords above. The change of idiom was more gradual than this implies, but the impetus of the baroque style hastened the arrival of a new class of soloistic performers, both singers and players, who emerged from the ranks of ensembles to take up newly prominent roles.

One impetus behind the growth of both vocal monody and instrumental solo writing was the emergence of the independent, creative musician. Gone, or rather supplanted in fashion, was the discourse on equal terms of the madrigals and the motet. The professional is king – and queen. Famous ensembles of female singers which gave rise to the new professionalism existed in Ferrara and Mantua, as well as famous solo singers in Naples and Florence. As Vincenzo Giustiniani wrote towards the end of the sixteenth century, the ladies of Ferrara and Mantua:

> vied with each other not only in regard to the timbre and training of their voices but also in the design of exquisite passages delivered at opportune points, but not in excess . . . they moderated or increased their voices, loud or soft, heavy or light, according to the demands of the piece they were singing . . . they accompanied the music and the sentiment with appropriate facial expressions, glances and gestures, with no awkward movements of the mouth or hands or body which might not express the feeling of the song.

Music-making at the court of Mantua was lavish and elaborate, including a staging of Guarini's *Il pastor fido* mounted in 1598 for Margaret of Austria (who was on her way to marry Philip III of Spain). Although this was essentially a play, we read that there was heard between every interlude 'most rare musicke of many parts, with divers instruments, accompanied with angelical and delicate voyces, insomuch as it seemed rather a divine than human thing ... that the voices of heaven had intermixed themselves with entire perfection of that of men, and the spirits of this age'.

It was in Italy that this new art took root. Something of the quintessential nature of the baroque, its quirky expressiveness and distinctively personal spirit, can be seen reflected in buildings: the asymmetrical floor plans and imaginative façades of Bernini's Sant'Andrea al Quirinale and Borromini's San Carlo alle Quattro Fontane in Rome, which reflect the new individualism that was about to emerge in dramatic music. Giulio Caccini (1551–1618) in *Le nuove musiche* of 1602 celebrated this change in vocal music, while in instrumental music it was explored by Giovanni Gabrieli (*c.* 1554/7–1612), especially in the posthumous collection *Canzone e sonate* of 1615 which includes a *Sonata con tre violini* – a slow-moving bass line, over which three soloists exchange fragments of material. The violin developed very quickly as a vehicle for the new instrumental art of the baroque. Giovanni Paolo Cima (*c.* 1570–*c.* 1622) published a collection of sacred music in Milan in 1610 which includes, nestling among the big church pieces, six small sonatas. The wide-leaping intervals and sharp, brittle scales proclaim it as a modest but important inauguration of the violinistic style. It is an idiom shared with the very striking sonatas of Dario Castello (fl. 1620s), who described his pieces as 'in the new style which everyone is attempting to observe', and of Biagio Marini (1594–1663), who worked at St Mark's in Venice under Monteverdi (p. 92), and titled his volume *Affetti musicali* – 'musical emotions' – clearly putting personal, individual expression at the centre of his work.

The transformation of the violin into a serious instrument was a very rapid emancipation given its very limited and poor reputation at this time. According to the seventeenth-century English writer Owen Feltham, 'it is a kind of disparagement to be a cunning fiddler. It argues his neglect of better employment and that he has spent much time on a thing unnecessarie.' But that was before the Italian composers raised the art of the violin to a new level, supported by fanciful explanations of its origin such as that of Bernardi's *Ragionamenti musicali* (1581) that 'the violin was invented by Orpheus, son of Apollo and Calliope. The ancient poetess Sappho invented the bow fitted with horse-hair and was the first to use the violin and viola in the way they are used today.' There is a link here to one of the ancestors of the violin, the *lira da braccio*, a larger instrument with seven strings that was used by reciters of poetry to accompany their declamations, including the earliest drama of Orpheus by Angelo Poliziano; it was favoured by Leonardo da Vinci. As the importance and popularity of the violin grew, the increasing complexity of double-stopping, expression marks and new techniques by composers like Marco Uccellini (*c.* 1603/10–80) pushed the range of the violin upwards to reach high notes on the top string. These extremes were developed in the hands of professional players and composers, newly prominent members of the musician class.

Around Europe, the new art of the baroque took hold, in some places more gradually than others. In England, there was a traditional compromise between old and new, as the viol consort maintained its polyphonic tradition, while a 'broken consort' of mixed instruments also became popular for its colouristic variety in the *First Book of Consort Lessons* of 1599 by Thomas Morley; this included the lute, viol and the cittern which had probably developed from the earlier citole (p. 39). Morley provided a well-organised guide in his *A Plaine and Easie Introduction to Practicall Musicke* (1597), suggesting mostly Italian models for composition: 'You must in your music be wavering like the wind, sometimes wanton, sometimes drooping, sometimes grave and staid . . . the more variety you show the better shall you please'. Truly baroque emancipation was slow to develop, though there were individual achievements like that of William Lawes (1602–45), whose Royal Consorts with their dense counterpoint and dark colours use two violins on the top line with a bass viol and organ beneath.

In central Europe, around the Imperial court and Bohemia, the development of the instrumental baroque was carried on with the greatest imagination. Vienna had become a major musical centre at the Imperial court during the reign from 1619 to 1637 of Ferdinand II, whose two passions in life were music and hunting: we can only look with envy at the investments of time and resources that were made to fulfil these twin passions. Leopold I, who reigned from 1658 to 1705 and who was himself a keen musician who composed, oversaw one of the most lavish events of the entire century on 20 July 1668, when the opera *Il pomo d'oro* by Antonio Cesti (1623–69) was performed to celebrate the birthday of Empress Margaret. The demands of these great celebrations were a huge drain on the resources of the court, but they were regarded as a necessary demonstration of power and patronage.

Also at Leopold I's court was the violinist Johann Heinrich Schmelzer (c. 1620/3–80), who was appointed Kapellmeister there just before his death from the plague. A baroque repertory was collected through Schmelzer and developed at Olomouc where the Prince-Bishop collected works that survive in the Kroměříž archive. The importance of collectors and patrons to the dissemination and preservation of the repertory is demonstrated by the ornate folios that Prince-Bishop Liechtenstein acquired through his agent in Vienna and carefully preserved. Full of light-hearted music depicting nature, birds and rural life, these remarkable, touching pieces shed a sidelight on the baroque. Their music sprang out of the Bohemian tradition and the life of the countryside: they are in their way the ancestors of Dvořák and Smetana (p. 206). Also well worth exploring is Schmelzer's collection *Sacro-profanus concentus musicus* (1662), with colourful canzona-like pieces that pit the violin alongside the cornett, bassoon and trombone: this is one of the earliest collections that Nikolaus Harnoncourt memorably recorded with the period instruments of his Concentus Musicus Wien.

The style was taken forward in both lighter and much more serious vein by Heinrich Ignaz Franz von Biber (1644–1704), one of the greatest composers who crosses the line from early to later baroque. Biber worked at Kroměříž and later in Salzburg, and was one of the most original and inventive of violin virtuosi. His music makes demands that are difficult to realise on the modern violin, but now that we have skilled performers on period instruments, we can appreciate quite how ingenious he was. He wrote jovially programmatic pieces like the *Battalia* (*79) of 1673 with depictions of drunken soldiers, fighting and laments, and pictures of a night-watchman and a campanarum of bells.

The work that may be taken as the climax of seventeenth-century baroque violin style is Biber's collection of sixteen Mystery Sonatas which were probably completed around 1676. Each is a meditation on a mystery of the Rosary, and what makes them extraordinary for their time is that each demands a different tuning of the violin strings; instead of the regular tuning used in most violin music, here particular strings have to be raised or lowered in pitch for particular movements, making a recording of these works more feasible than live performance because of the need for constant retuning. There are now excellent complete recordings by violinists such as Andrew Manze and Rachel Podger. From the Annunciation through the stages of Christ's life the vision of these sonatas is original, and they end with the greatest masterstroke: an unaccompanied Passacaglia in G minor for violin of ethereal beauty, based on a four-note descending bass. It is natural to hear this work as an ancestor of J. S. Bach's great Chaconne from his Partita in D minor, based on a similar sequence (p. 125).

Music had to struggle in central Europe against the background of the Thirty Years War which dominated life from 1618 onwards. The German composer and organist Heinrich Schütz (1585–1672) wrote: 'Among the other free arts the noble art of music has not only suffered great decline in our beloved fatherland as a result of the present dangers of war; in many places it has been wholly destroyed, lying amid the ruins and chaos for all to observe.' Schütz was among the leaders of those who restored the arts to their rightful place. For much of his long life he was in the service of the Elector of Dresden, although he seems also to have travelled during this period. In 1627 Schütz wrote the first German opera of which we know, *Dafne*, but it is lost; we can only guess at its style. He had briefly studied in Italy and was able to bring his understanding of the idioms of Gabrieli and Monteverdi to the development of German liturgical music in the baroque, which he did with unparalleled depth; his music is written in an idiom that became increasingly simple as the years went on.

His expressiveness is rather different from that of the Italians. Schütz wrote larger-scale pieces when the musicians were restored, which appeared in his *Symphoniae sacrae* of 1647 and 1650, with splendid polychoral pieces in the style he had learned from Italy, including the dramatic *Saul, Saul, was verfolgst du mich?* These pieces formed the centrepiece of the revivals of his music in modern times by the Heinrich Schütz Choir under Roger Norrington, whose historic concerts in London churches in the 1960s and 1970s rekindled interest in his music. Schütz's three Passion settings of 1665–6 are much simpler, extremely austere, for voices alone, while his two *Historia* that mark the birth (*Christmas Story*) and the death and resurrection of Christ (*Resurrection Story*) feature instrumental parts but the emphasis is on the vocal declamation. Perhaps his most deeply felt achievement is the *Musikalische Exequien* (*82), written on the death of his patron Prince Heinrich Posthumus von Reuss, who specified the texts to be used. Modern ensembles, such as John Eliot Gardiner's Monteverdi Choir and more recently Vox Luminis under Lionel Meunier, have recorded this masterpiece with a fresh approach to its rhetoric.

Thanks to the interaction of Schütz from Germany and the Gabrielis in Italy, there was a blending of national styles with the individual character of the composers. You could not confuse Schütz's inward, eloquent idiom with Gabrieli's Italianate warmth; both have great subtlety but in different ways. The intricate and beautiful church music of Giovanni Gabrieli is memorable, but perhaps his greatest contribution is through the development of tailor-made instrumental parts in his canzonas, carefully worked out in conjunction with his instrumentalists including the cornett player Giovanni Bassano. Gabrieli's *Symphoniae Sacrae II* of 1615 has sonorous motets in twelve, fourteen and nineteen parts for voices and instruments.

Interestingly at this stage in the development of the baroque, Schütz urged younger composers not to write wholly in the new Italian style and not to abandon the principles of old-fashioned counterpoint. That the old traditions were still valued was evidenced by the appointment of Johann Joseph Fux (1660–1741) to the Vienna court, for which he wrote the lavish opera *Costanza e Fortezza* (1723). His music was effective, and he had a deep veneration for the polyphonic school of Palestrina, whose principles he captured in his important treatise *Gradus ad Parnassum* (1725); this exposition of the basis of music's harmonic language and the ways to write counterpoint had a long-lasting influence on composers including Haydn and Mozart. Even in a time of musical revolution, the study of past masters endured, ensuring a continuity in key areas of learning and composition.

*

Few European cities offer such a direct and inspiring link to music in such a concentrated environment as does Venice, where the heritage of musical performance and the buildings for which the music was written can be seen within a very small geographical area. The music of seventeenth-century Venice emerged in a time of upheaval, under the shadow of its clash with Rome, when the Republic was excommunicated in 1605 by Pope Paul V. The descriptions of music-making at the time have a richness and diversity which is difficult to equal. Engravings of the time show the extent to which music permeated every aspect of life, with ensembles in the streets and on the gondolas – even harpsichords were taken aboard – and the crucial presence of musicians in the flourishing *commedia dell'arte*. Apart from St Mark's, the main musical performances of the period took place in the six *scuole grandi*, where the confraternities gathered. They were well-endowed charitable institutions, which provided musicians for the big state processions and occasions, and cultivated music of great refinement in their own churches. The one at San Rocco drew praise from the visitor Thomas Coryat in 1608 that the music was 'so good, delectable, so rare, so admirable, so excellent, that it did even ravish and stupefy all those strangers that had never heard the like'. Coryat, an inveterate and observant traveller, was a lively chronicler of the scene and noted that the musicians included a choir of twenty voices and an ensemble of twenty-four performers consisting of ten trombones, four cornetts, two violas da gamba, one violin and no fewer than seven small organs in a row. One of the singers seemed to him to possess god-like qualities and 'for my own part I can say this, that I was even rapt up with Saint Paul into the third heaven'.

It is small wonder that artists throughout history have been drawn to Venice: it was there that Richard Wagner wrote Act 2 of *Tristan und Isolde*, and it is where Stravinsky is buried. At the heart of the Venetian story is the church of St Mark's, where a succession of great musicians practised, played and composed. One of the very greatest of these was Claudio Monteverdi (1567–1643), who was appointed the church's new *maestro di cappella* in August 1613. Born in Cremona in northern Italy, he studied at the cathedral and then went to the ducal court of the Gonzaga family in Mantua. He established a major reputation through his work there, but considered that he had suffered neglect at the hands of the family, being passed over repeatedly for the post of *maestro di cappella* at the ducal chapel until he was finally appointed in 1601. Monteverdi had used the period to develop his own pioneering approach to harmony and invention in his books of madrigals, which were published to considerable controversy in the 1600s. They were admired for their vivid word-setting and emotional appeal, but attacked by traditionalists for abandoning the strict rules of harmony and counterpoint as formulated in the rules of Fux and Palestrina. Monteverdi answered his critics with his fifth book of madrigals, moving beyond the traditional equal-voice madrigal style and providing a basso continuo part, and thus making them part of the new baroque performance idiom.

In church music Monteverdi is now best remembered for his 1610 collection of music for the Vespers of the Blessed Virgin, which is an astoundingly up-to-date and memorable assembly of psalm settings and vocal motets in the most modern style of the day, and yet includes deeply old-fashioned elements of traditional counterpoint. It is the perfect example of the tipping point between the harmony of the Renaissance and the new age of the baroque. He dedicated the volume to Pope Paul V, going above the heads of his patrons to demonstrate his devotion to the church, and referring to the music as 'these my nocturnal labours' – deliberately alluding to the fact that writing this music was beyond his work for the Gonzagas, and it had been written out of hours. Although associated in performances and recordings with the church of St Mark's, and presented as a single work, the Vespers should probably be regarded as a collection to be drawn on, for the publication of 1610 also includes a complete Mass setting, and an alternative Magnificat. The Mass, which is derived from a motet by Nicolas Gombert, *In illo tempore*, demonstrates Monteverdi's skill in the *prima prattica*, the old-style counterpoint. The Vespers settings on the other hand are a demonstration of the *seconda prattica*, or new style. The same stirring fanfare that opens his opera *Orfeo* opens the Vespers, now in vocal garb, with triumphant voices appealing 'God, make speed to save us'. The intricate choral settings of the psalms alternate with dramatic concertos for solo voice or voices. The echo setting of *Duo seraphim*, with solo voices overlapping in biting dissonances and competing for attention, is thrilling, and at the heart is an instrumental Sonata with a single text line 'Sancta Maria, ora pro nobis'. Here and in the larger Magnificat setting, the instrumental solos are meticulously indicated. The concertos *Nigra sum* and *Pulchra es* are settings of the Song of Songs, normally heard as antiphons; it has been queried whether these movements should be heard as part of the work, but their keys suggest that they are fully integrated into the sequence of movements.

As we look across musical history, there are few collections of music which express the dynamic of their age as powerfully as Monteverdi's Vespers of 1610. Looking backwards and forwards, drawing on old-style vocal counterpoint and modern operatic-style solo declamation, ancient harmoniousness and contemporary dissonance, mingling all these elements with complete confidence, technical wizardry and emotional commitment, Monteverdi balances the centuries in his hands. No wonder that this has become a cornerstone of what we now call the early music revival, performed in numerous competing versions and editions, with or without all the music, with or without plainchant additions, and always compelling audiences with its power. But it is worth recalling that Monteverdi was truly neglected and ignored for centuries until the time of Nadia Boulanger, Walter Goehr and others. In 1964 the twenty-one-year-old John Eliot Gardiner formed his Monteverdi Choir to revive the Vespers in Cambridge, beginning a modern revival of his music.

Monteverdi's vital involvement with the beginnings of opera is described in the next chapter. In Venice he continued to develop the drama of the madrigal. His later books include the sixth book of 1614 and the seventh of 1619, by which time none of the pieces are really madrigals in the traditional sense; they have become solos, duets or trio mini-dramas. There was then a long interval before the publication of his eighth book in 1638, which contains dramatic episodes such as the *Combattimento di Tancredi e Clorinda* with its violent writing for strings in the *stile concitato* (agitated style), and the *Lamento della ninfa*, written as a solo with an accompanying group of three singers. Finally, there was another collection of sacred music, *Selva morale e spirituale* of 1641, including some of his most mature works like the psalm setting *Beatus vir* (*81), using the same dancing material as his secular madrigal *Chiome d'oro*.

Huge amounts of Monteverdi's music, referred to in letters and documents, have not survived. Yet he has acquired a status in musical history which equals those who organised their own legacy through extensive collections, like

Machaut, Palestrina and Josquin. He has even been called by the music historian Leo Schrade 'the creator of modern music'. Perhaps Monteverdi felt that his relatively few published works showed the best of his music, and was content to let their quality speak for him. His many surviving and very colourful letters certainly conjure vividly the strength of his personality and his confidence in his own abilities. He was quick to complain about his treatment by his employers and patrons, quick to argue with those who criticised him, and eloquent in his defence of his own work. His letters bring to life the challenges of a composer in a way that is rare before Mozart's equally sparky correspondence. Monteverdi frequently complains to his employers about his conditions, about money, about being valued for his work. And he provides sidelights into the sources of his inspiration. In one vivid example among many, he expresses his frustration to his librettist Alessandro Striggio (the Younger); for a planned entertainment of *Le nozze di Tetide*, Striggio has provided him with a text that imagines characters who are winds rather than people. Monteverdi objects: 'How, dear sir, if winds do not speak, shall I be able to imitate their speech? And how, by such means, shall I be able to move the passions? Arianna moved us because she was a woman, and Orfeo did the same because he was a man and not a wind . . . I do not know what this will inspire in me'. As it happens, the commission for this work was cancelled, so the issue was never forced, but the text demonstrates Monteverdi's intense desire for his music to be communicative, as is so powerfully demonstrated in his surviving operas, beginning with *Orfeo* (p. 104).

*

'Dancing,' wrote Thoinot Arbeau, possibly sardonically, in *Orchésographie*, his late sixteenth-century study of the form, 'is essential in a well-ordered society, because it allows males and females to mingle and observe one another. How else does a lady choose whom to marry?' The social function of dance provided an impetus for musical development in the Renaissance and baroque period as dancing was a vital part of court entertainment, in which the nobility was expected to participate – quite energetically so, when it came to the more lively, virtuosic dances like the branle and galliard. Royalty too participated; Elizabeth I expected to be literally swept off her feet by her noble attenders (though her participation may have been exaggerated by obsequious reports and pictures: Plate 10).

Music for instruments alone came into its own with the rise of printed publications in the mid-sixteenth century. These first made available an extensive repertory of dances, including those collected in 1530 by the publisher Pierre Attaingnant (*c. 1494–1551/2*). This was followed twenty years later by *Danserye* by Tylman Susato (*c. 1510/15–c. 1570*), which provides a number of instrumental options. As a result it became popular in kickstarting the instrumental early music revival in our time, especially through the performances and recordings of David Munrow and the Early Music Consort of London at the end of the 1960s. Munrow drew on his extensive knowledge of folk instruments from Europe and beyond to supply the models for some of the instruments that had passed out of circulation, with fresh and compelling results.

The most famous publication of the time was *Terpsichore* (1612) by Michael Praetorius, a collection of over 300 instrumental dances (only one volume of eight he planned). This is an effervescent compendium of secular consort music, largely containing arrangements of French dances. Dance music was available both for instrumental consorts of different combinations, or for solo instruments such as the lute or keyboard; indeed dance music would go on to become an important part of the keyboard repertory. By the early baroque, dance forms predominate in keyboard suites, giving a defined character to movements such as the allemande, courante, sarabande and gigue. These suites were not for dancing as such, but they showed the extent to which the spirit of the dance lay behind much music of the time.

The second volume of Praetorius's treatise *Syntagma Musicum* (1614–18), *De Organographica*, is one of the richest sources of illustrations and information about the instruments of the time. His extremely careful observations on the combinations of voices and instruments provide highly practical guides:

A very splendid sound is possible in full choirs if one adds to a bass, from the group of instruments, an ordinary or bass trombone . . . when one employs a full consort in the English manner he should add to them a loud clavicembalo,

two or three lutes, a theorbo, viola bastarda, cittern, bass viol, block or transverse flutes, soft trombone, viola bastarda, and a small discant violin, all very
purely and sweetly tuned together . . . I have found it better to place the capella
or chorus somewhat to the side, and away from the organ and those who are
singing the Concertato parts, so that the vocalists will not be overshadowed
or drowned by the instruments, but each separate group can be clearly heard
and understood . . .

This demonstrates the care and attention with which instrumental and vocal ensembles of the time were gathered and placed – quite as precisely as the balancing
and combining of instruments in the modern symphony orchestra. Praetorius's ensembles aimed at harmonious beauty, in which every line could be heard distinctly.

The recorder became the most popular instrument of the Renaissance and
baroque and was the first to have its own tutor, the *Fontegara*, published by
Sylvestro di Ganassi dal Fontego (1492–c. 1565) in Venice in 1535, exploring a
range from the small soprano recorder to the huge extended great bass recorder.
Ganassi suggested in his preface that recorder players should learn from singers,
for 'be it known that all musical instruments, in comparison to the human voice,
are inferior to it'. Similarly, other instruments were conceived in groups covering
all ranges, rather than as a single instrument. The crumhorn was very popular,
played with a double reed enclosed by a cap, giving an especially reedy sound;
a consort of crumhorns with different ranges could play polyphonic dances
effectively. Similarly, and even more pungent, was the shawm, played with a reed,
which developed into an entire extended family of different sizes; a consort of
several shawms makes a quite brutal noise. At the top end of the texture of these
dances would have been the transverse flute. As with earlier flutes, it was blown
across the hole (rather than directly into it as with the recorder) and was usually
wooden in construction. Lower sounds emerged from the rackett, built from a
long length of tubing folded into a small, chubby container, played with a double reed. Down at the bottom on the bass line might have been the dulcian, also
known as the curtal, played with a double reed, which was developed to replace
the bass shawm, an ancestor of the bassoon.

Instruments used for ceremonial processions and outdoor performances included the sackbut, an early form of trombone with a rather gentle tone, and a small bell; four sizes are shown by Praetorius and they can be seen played on horseback with a range of trumpets in the magnificent engraving by Hans Burgkmair the Elder, *The Triumph of the Emperor Maximilian I* (Plate 11). In this period, the trumpet was made of a tube that was folded to enable variations of length and pitch, and several different versions exist which Praetorius praised as able to achieve most notes of the scale. By contrast the horn was still fairly primitive, based on the development of a traditional hunting instrument with different crooks and pitches, reinforcing the basic harmonies of the scale. One of the most eloquent of Renaissance instruments was the cornett, which until it was revived had to be replaced by the modern trumpet or clarinet in modern performances. With a mouthpiece and seven holes, it is versatile and sounds beautiful, capable of great agility, and probably nearest to the voice in its shaping of phrases. Its bass version was known as the serpent, because of its distinctively winding shape (immortalised by the satirical drawings of the humorist Gerard Hoffnung).

The music of the early baroque, and particularly the emerging world of continuo playing, highlighted two groups of instruments which were central to the realisation of the accompanying of vocal and instrumental music: the plucked instruments of the lute family, and the large range of keyboard instruments. The lute was by now a most sophisticated instrument with plucked strings, the neck bent back, a large rounded back to provide sonority, and the strings arranged in courses of two strings each: the eight-course lute has fifteen strings. There is also a long-necked version which was vertical, often depicted in literature and painting, for instance in works by Caravaggio, which played some of the greatest music of the period by John Dowland and others. Other support instruments in the continuo group were the theorbo and the chittarone, long-necked versions of the lute with extra strings and a lower octave in the chittarone, both used as an instrument to support the voice. Then there was the Spanish version, the vihuela, an ancestor of the modern guitar: among that family of instruments it was the *vihuela de mano* that was closest to what we now recognise as a guitar, with finger-plucked strings.

Among the keyboard instruments, the most important was undoubtedly the harpsichord, played by a keyboard which plucks the strings (rather than striking them as a piano does). The earliest survivor is an Italian instrument from 1521. The harpsichord eventually became the central instrument of the emerging orchestral ensemble, leading and keeping the ensemble together with its percussive edge. And it becomes one of the richest and most important of solo instruments through the Renaissance and baroque periods, leading for example the flourishing of the solo keyboard fantasia in the hands of the great Dutch organist Jan Pieterszoon Sweelinck (1562–1621), who wrote an exceptionally touching set of variations on the folk tune 'Mein junges Leben hat ein End' which reaches a yearning, intense climax. His pupil was the German Samuel Scheidt (1587–1654), who compiled fantasias in his *Tabulatura nova*.

Other keyboard instruments of the period include the spinet, a small keyboard with the strings overlapping so as to save room, useful for domestic circumstances; the regal, a small portable organ using entirely reed stops, so with a very distinctive pungent sound, used as an accompanying instrument; the clavichord, the most intimate of keyboard instruments, in which the keys are used to flexibly vibrate rather than pluck the strings, giving an extra expressivity to the sound; and the virginals, a specific type of keyboard in Flanders, depicted in Jan Vermeer's painting *A Young Woman Standing at the Virginals* – England's Queen Elizabeth I is said by an observer to have played well on the virginals, 'that is for a queene'.

With good reason, the organ in its full flourishing in churches and cathedrals was described as the king of instruments since its range was incomparable and its mechanical possibilities seemingly endless. The first great individual virtuoso of the organ, a true professional of his trade, was Girolamo Frescobaldi (1583–1643), who played at St Peter's to the admiration of many thousands of listeners. The French musician André Maugars heard him in Rome, and noted that Frescobaldi 'displayed a thousand kinds of inventions on his instrument while the organ stuck to the main melody . . . although his printed works give sufficient evidence of his skill, to get a true idea of his deep knowledge, one must hear him improvise toccatas full of admirable refinements and inventions'. His skill seems to have been in his flexibility: he told his listeners in his 1624 *Capricci* that the tempo 'must not be subject to the beat, making it now languid, now quick, and occasionally suspending it in mid-air, according to their affections'. Frescobaldi's music, especially the *Fiori musicali* of 1635, was studied and copied out by J. S. Bach.

Johann Jacob Froberger (1616–67), Frescobaldi's pupil, developed the keyboard toccata with music of programmatic invention, from his *Tombeau de M. Blancrocher*, which at the end descends right down the keyboard to his tomb, to his *Lamentation on the Death of his Imperial Majesty Ferdinand the Third*, which has an evaporating final passage rising high into the treble, as the soul ascends to heaven. Some of his scores feature decorative illustrations. He published *Diverse curiose partite* and helped to create the form of the keyboard suite with dance movements, which was to be so important for all later baroque composers.

The final group of instruments that were prominent were the family of viols. The viol consort of different sizes was a familiar feature of the English scene, and a 'chest of viols' was a frequent possession in a musical household. They came to represent an old-fashioned tradition which took a while to die out even with the arrival and emancipation of the new-fangled violin. The tension was well expressed by the seventeenth-century antiquarian Anthony Wood, who had 'from his most tender years an extraordinary ravishing delight in music'; he reported that gentlemen in private meetings 'play'd three, four and five parts all with viols . . . and they esteemed a violin to be an instrument only belonging to a common fiddler, and could not endure that it should come among them for feare of making their meetings seem to be vain and fiddling.' Yet Henry Purcell wrote viol fantasias of great contrapuntal, equal-voiced distinction during his youth, even as he began to write for the newly emerging violin in his superb trio sonatas. This is another example of the tipping point between the equal-voiced writing of the Renaissance, shading into the drama of the baroque: thus do the periods of musical history overlap and merge in the hands of true genius.

8

Singers

Music has served many and varied purposes over the centuries, and the public celebration of power has always been a prominent motive: proclaiming victories, coronations, wealth or an influential dynastic marriage. At the heart of so many of those celebrations, alongside a display of scenery, instruments, dance and spectacle, is singing.

Such lavish celebration was required by Ferdinando de' Medici, who secured control of the Medici family in dubious, *Macbeth*-like circumstances after his brother Francesco, the Grand Duke of Tuscany, and his wife both mysteriously died in October 1587 while staying the night. Ferdinando inherited the title; to seal his command of the family fortunes, he gave up his cardinalate and forged a marriage with Christina of Lorraine, granddaughter of Catherine de' Medici, dowager Queen consort of France. This heralded a radical shift in the allegiance of the family from Spain to France, and the union thus needed to be very grandly celebrated. Ferdinando planned two weeks of festivities for the wedding in 1589: processions, jousts and sea-battles, with as its climax (in the Medici Theatre of the Uffizi Palace) a play in five acts interspersed with six musical *intermedi* or intermezzos – no mere interludes, but constructions of immense splendour and sumptuousness. Ingenious stage machinery was used to create vivid pictures of ascending and descending clouds, boats that moved, dragons that breathed fire, wonderfully costumed sirens, sea-nymphs and gods. The impression they made was well caught by the chronicler Gadenstedt, who described the beginning of the first *intermedio*:

> As soon as a sign was given, the red curtain was quickly drawn aside, revealing a curtain of blue silk. At the top of this, in the centre, was a woman (Harmony) playing a lute. Sitting in a wonderful gilded chair and swathed in silk like a goddess, she was surrounded by a white cloud. She began to sing beautifully, while still playing the lute, so beautifully in fact that everyone said it was impossible a human voice could be so beautiful. Still singing, she was gradually lowered, so slowly that it could hardly be noted. And no one knew how it was done . . .

Bringing these tableaux to life, there was music of elaboration, grace and beauty which far outstripped the interest of the play, so that it provided the focus of the evening's long and lavish entertainment. These celebrations were but one part of the rich artistic patronage exercised by the Medici family, which has rarely been equalled since.

The *intermedi* used complex symbols to evoke the beauty of celestial harmony. They demonstrated the glory of the newly married couple by placing their marriage in the context of a universal harmony – one that is sometimes disrupted by events but always restored. In the grand final *intermedio* the gods of rhythm and harmony descend from heaven to teach mortals the arts of dance and song. Seven choirs of voices and instruments continue in a magnificent thirty-voiced madrigal, and the whole company unite to praise the wedded couple. The complex production brought together some of the most famous names of the age: the designer Bernardo Buontalenti, whose fantastic costume drawings still survive; the madrigal composer Luca Marenzio and the composer Cristofano Malvezzi; and the virtuosi Giulio Caccini and Jacopo Peri, who would both go on to be influential in the development of opera. Emilio de' Cavalieri, whom we would now call the producer of the show, was a guest from Rome. No expense was spared to make the *intermedi* a dazzling success (Plate 13).

The music of the *intermedi* stands at a point of transition, another example of the tipping point from Renaissance to baroque practice, though we are still firmly on the earlier side of the change. The form is in some ways a precursor of opera, though the dramatic structure and approach to reality here is very different: characters accompany themselves on instruments while singing (though the instruments were disguised as part of the elaborate stage set), and groups of sailors or sea-nymphs seem to include the full range of male and female voices.

The desire of Italian Renaissance thinkers and philosophers to recapture the principles of Greek humanism was the subject of lively debate in Florence towards the end of the sixteenth century. To that extent, opera was born out of the desire by enlightened humanists of the early baroque for a form of expression based on individual declamation which owed little or nothing to the forms of the past. The Camerata of the salon of Count Giovanni de' Bardi I of Florence – a group of cultured artists and humanists who met from 1573 – formed the focal point of these early composers. Bardi was a wealthy amateur who devised court entertainments for the nobility, and brought together some of the most creative minds of the period to work out new forms of expression based loosely on the ideals of ancient Greece. They were extremely conscious of the novelty of what they were doing, but their links back to late Renaissance practice in the *intermedi* and decorated madrigals, drawing on the developing tradition of spoken plays, are clear for all to see and hear.

Giulio Caccini (1551–1618) threw down the gauntlet to history by calling his treatise of 1602 *Le nuove musiche*. His aim was to allow the performer to speak, to tell a story in music, *in armonia favellare*, echoing medieval descriptions of music as poetic speech, and pointing forward to modern concepts of music-drama. Caccini was a typically versatile musician of the time, working at the Medici court, playing the archlute and the violin, singing as a tenor, and debating the philosophy of reviving the music of the ancient Greek past which informed so much of the Florentine Camerata's thinking. He was also skilled in navigating the artistic tussles of the time, holding back his rivals. These included Jacopo Peri (1561–1633), who had been the first to create a musical work to the libretto of Ottavio Rinuccini's *Dafne*, which was performed under the patronage of Jacopo Corsi in his palace in Florence in 1598. Peri (perhaps with some input from Caccini) collaborated on the opera *L'Euridice* of 1600 which was performed in the court festivities around the marriage of Maria de' Medici to Henry IV of France. Caccini also made his own setting of the text, which he rushed to publish separately: clearly they were rivals as well as colleagues.

In the work of Peri and Caccini there was something categorically new: the declamation of solo recitative by dramatic characters, over a continuo bass line. Peri's *L'Euridice* is still a work of modest interest. But a mere seven years later in 1607 there appears a piece which set a gold standard for the future: Monteverdi's *Orfeo* is unquestionably the first important opera and the earliest to have returned firmly to the repertory today after years of neglect. It owes a good deal to Peri in the way the modern recitative is constructed, yet Monteverdi's retelling of the story is full of compelling drama, and the immediacy of his writing – as well as his debt to the past – is evident in its use of madrigal-style choruses and interludes. There is elaborate scoring for pairs of instruments: two violins, a pair of cornettos and a double harp, heard especially in Orfeo's great central invocation 'Possente spirto'. This was sung by the tenor Francesco Rasi, one of the most famous of court singers who acquired widespread fame in Europe and regarded himself as a noble virtuoso (in spite of being involved in a plot to murder his stepmother). Rasi sang elaborate passages and declamations with ease and power, and can be seen as one of the most distinguished of emerging solo singers.

Orfeo was written to be performed at the Mantuan court, not in a theatre but in the rooms which used to belong to 'the most serene Lady of Ferrara', during the Carnival season. Its purpose was to entertain the scholarly bodies including the Accademia degli Invaghiti, of which Monteverdi's patron, Prince Francesco Gonzaga, was the head, and *Orfeo*'s librettist, Alessandro Striggio, was a member. *Orfeo* is a *favola in musica*, a musical tale, and its point was to provide an allegory of music and its power: hence its lavish instrumental forces which make it so unlike the other early operas. It remains astonishingly communicative and affecting, its depiction of Orfeo's emotional challenge as he tries and fails to rescue Euridice as vivid now as it ever was. A fascinating feature of the opera is its drastically different denouements in the printed score and the libretto: the libretto has a negative ending, with Orfeo denounced by the Bacchantes, but in the score there is an upbeat twist whereby he is rescued by his father, the god Apollo, and taken up to heaven where he will see Euridice among the stars.

Monteverdi's next opera, *Arianna* of 1608, is likely to have been much less highly instrumented and more closely linked to the dramas of Peri and Caccini. We cannot be sure, because although the libretto survives, and has been reset in our time by the composer Alexander Goehr (p. 241), there is only one piece of surviving music: Arianna's great solo lament, 'Lasciatemi morire'. This was published separately, as it had become famous for its cathartic effect on audiences. It became highly influential as a model for despairing arias in Italian opera, and was even adapted as a sacred text, the 'Lamento della Madonna'. The scholar Mark Ringer has likened the musical impact on future composers and their idiom of this single piece to the impact of Wagner's Prelude to *Tristan und Isolde* (p. 184). Possibly the score of *Arianna* is still lurking in some dusty Italian archive, waiting to be uncovered?

Court entertainments continued to draw on the traditions of the *intermedi* and ballets rather than the new-fangled opera. A leading exponent of mingling these forms with emerging operatic practice was Caccini's daughter Francesca Caccini (1587–c. 1645) who wrote *La liberazione di Ruggiero*, which probably deserves the title of the first extant opera by a woman. It was based on the famous text of Ariosto's *Orlando furioso*, which became a central source for opera composers including Handel in the next century. The Caccini family was outstandingly gifted: with her sister Settimia and her stepmother Margherita, Francesca Caccini toured as part of the ensemble *Concerto delle Donne* which became famous in Ferrara. Francesca takes her place alongside Barbara Strozzi (1619–77), who was notable for her chamber music and cantatas (*80), as one of the most influential women composers of her time, whose works are only now beginning to be revived and fully valued.

It did not take long for opera to shake off the scholarly and philosophical world of its origins and become a truly popular art form played in the public theatres of Italy. In Venice, the new opera houses became ever more popular and successful, and every year there were new operas to delight the public, and a variety of opera companies appearing in the city to perform them with the stars of the day. The social classes were still firmly separated; the nobility attended in the boxes that ringed the auditorium, which were like private rooms where they could transact business, chat, and probably more, during the performance, while the populace filled the bare benches of the stalls in the centre of the theatre and, as one chronicler described it, 'came nearer to the stage for the singing of their favourite songs'. This all implies a much greater freedom of activity than became evident in the more formalised situations of opera-going in later centuries.

The Teatro San Cassiano opened in Venice in 1637, and saw the premieres of Monteverdi's two late masterpieces, *Il ritorno d'Ulisse* and *L'incoronazione di Poppea*. Monteverdi's understanding of the foibles of human nature is at its greatest in depicting the vanity of Penelope's suitors in *Ulisse*, and equally in conjuring up the disruptive passion of Nero and Poppaea: both these works are boldly contemporary in their preoccupations, which is one reason why they have found such favour in recent revivals. Whether Monteverdi was responsible for the whole of both these operas cannot be easily determined, because the scores that survive are later copies, but they are both compelling psychological dramas whose characterisations communicate vividly. Modern interpreters have adopted very different approaches to realising the music, either taking it as the basis for elaborate written-out scorings for added instruments, or simply relying on the vocal lines provided, supported by continuo instruments. Written-out elaboration was preferred in the early years of the Monteverdi operatic revival by Raymond Leppard in his pioneering performances at Glyndebourne, and then by Nikolaus Harnoncourt, using period instruments in the productions by Jean-Pierre Ponnelle: both of them elaborated Monteverdi's bare scoring. Contemporary taste prefers to take the power of the texts as the driving force of the drama rather than elaborate instrumentation; the realisations by Alan Curtis and Roger Norrington add little to the continuo parts, directing the attention onto the words. It is agonising to imagine the amount of Monteverdi's work that has disappeared; from another opera, *Proserpina rapita*, just one ensemble survives as it was published in a book of Monteverdi's madrigals. His successor in the public theatres in Venice was Pier Francesco Cavalli (1602–76), who performed, and may have contributed to, Monteverdi's works. (Some suggest that he may have written the famous final duet of Monteverdi's *L'incoronazione di Poppea*, 'Pur ti miro', as Monteverdi's autograph score does not survive.) Cavalli's operas are distinctively lighter and frothier than Monteverdi's; amusing, but not as dramatically taut.

The spread of public opera to its original home, Florence, and Milan, Rome and Naples as well as to Vienna led to the creation of the form that was to dominate countless serious baroque operas at the turn of the eighteenth century: the *da capo* aria. Led by poets such as Pietro Metastasio, whose widely performed libretti defined the form, the *da capo* aria challenged a composer's inventive powers. The singer has a formal aria text in three parts: a first section displaying one single emotion, whether rage, love, loss or a pictorial allusion like a storm at sea and a ship coming into harbour; then a contrasting central section, usually simpler in texture, sometimes countering the emotions of the first section, sometimes expanding them; and then a return to the first section (*da capo*, that is, from the beginning), which is the chance for the singer to elaborate the material already sung. There are showy later examples by Antonio Vivaldi (p. 131), but the principle of the *da capo* underlies literally countless operas of the period, including Handel's Italian operas and those of other composers who led successful careers including Alessandro Scarlatti (1660–1725), whose output for Naples and Palermo was huge, but who left little imprint on musical history.

*

Opera quickly became a fertile home for artistic development and innovation across Europe, evolving in very different ways. The arts were central to life at the French court – important in every celebration, every feast, every royal tour. We know that some monarchs have been accomplished musicians, but not many kings were accomplished dancers as was the young Louis XIV, who as a teenager in 1653 danced the role of Apollo the Sun King in *Le ballet de la nuit* and is depicted in his resplendent plumed costume. This gave him his much-used title of 'Le Roi Soleil', the Sun King (Plate 13). His father Louis XIII had himself been a composer who assembled his own group of musicians and 'took pleasure in mingling his voice with theirs, sometimes bringing them back to the notes' (presumably meaning that he both sang and corrected them). While the French court remained in Paris, the magnificent cathedral of Notre Dame and the many surrounding churches of the Île de la Cité formed the centre of ecclesiastical activity, and there were many thriving instrument makers and music publishers around the city. But because of the political troubles of the 1640s, the court escaped to Saint-Germain-en-Laye, and gradually Louis XIV built his centre of power outside the city centre at Versailles. This only increased the splendour of the artistic undertakings he promoted.

The coming together of music, dance, theatre and poetry in the characteristic form of the French court, the *ballet de cour*, prefigures the concept of the unified artwork (*Gesamtkunstwerk*) that in a very different context Wagner was to seek in the nineteenth century (p. 182). It had originated back in 1581 with Balthasar de Beaujoyeulx as 'a unified and continuous dramatic action' and its mix of text and music, dance and drama, endured through the seventeenth century. It was as a dancer that the Florentine composer Jean-Baptiste Lully (1632–87) first came to prominence and ingratiated his way into the French court. Arriving at the age of fourteen, his talent was soon spotted by the king's cousin, for whom he led a string band. He worked first within the tradition of the court ballet, writing music for the *Ballet des Muses* and the *Ballet de Flore*, which gained the approval of the king. Lully built on the forms of the *ballet de cour* and the *comédie-ballet* (most famously *Le Bourgeois Gentilhomme* of 1670), which he perfected with Molière, to create distinctively French operatic forms. With France's notable literary culture, in the work of Pierre Corneille and Jean Racine for instance, French opera was a combination of the spoken word with music, dance and spectacle, in contrast to the through-composed methods of Italian opera. So when attempts to introduce operas by Cavalli to Paris failed to take off, Lully cleverly worked within the French tradition of the play with music, with Molière and then with Philippe Quinault, devising lavish entertainments that would appeal to the French palate. Among many other royal fêtes, in 1674 there were six days of celebrations to mark the king's return from the country and his conquest of Franche-Comté; these included performances of plays with music, chamber music for the king's mistress, water music on the canal, and then a performance of the *Fêtes de l'Amour et de Bacchus* to music by Lully.

Lully acquired a patent from the Académie Royale de Musique in March 1672, giving him authority to veto any sung work by other composers. He was quick to exploit his control over performances at court, working with Quinault to ensure that the *tragédie lyrique* took over as the fashionable form. In an annual succession of operas from 1673 to his death in 1687, Lully set the tone for the French operas of the future; among the finest are *Atys* and *Armide*, whose libretti Quinault derived from mythology. The staging of *Atys* in modern times by William Christie and Les Arts Florissants began an extensive revival of Lully's operas by Christophe Rousset and others. *Atys* starts with a prologue in which Time pays tribute to the glory of Louis XIV, and ends with the titular protagonist, driven mad, stabbing his beloved and then attempting to kill himself, before being transformed into a pine tree. *Armide* (*76) was the last and greatest of these tragedies, with exquisite music including the Act 2 sleep scene with muted strings, and its spectacular close as Armida destroys her palace (Plate 14). Alongside the scenes pushing forward the narrative are divertissements of ballet, airs and choruses. These operas were presented first at court, but then to the public in Paris, and they travelled widely abroad to London, Amsterdam and Rome.

The French court's music-making was based around three groups of musicians: the Chapelle (church), the Chambre (chamber) and the Écurie (ceremonial). Musicians had their primary posts in one of the three groups but seem to have exchanged responsibilities where necessary. Each had their own rules and arrangements, and could fulfil needs in some genres of entertainment separately, but on the greatest occasions the three bodies would combine, which was a rather sophisticated arrangement. Lully did much to professionalise the status of the musicians at court, by organising regular payments for the forty singers of the Chapelle and by forming the musicians of the Chambre into a permanent ensemble, who became known as *Les Vingt-quatre Violons du Roi*. The role of this five-part string ensemble was to play 'when the king commands them ... at certain ceremonies, such as the coronation, entries into cities, marriages and other solemnities'. It had been founded under Louis XIII, but this regularisation of its role marks the beginning of the orchestral ensemble as we know it today. Then came the Écurie, essentially consisting of wind and brass players for outdoor processions and feasts, and run by those who controlled the horses and stables of the king. Alongside the professionalisation of his musicians, Lully imposed strict rules on them, fined them for each hour of missed rehearsals, and apparently refused to tolerate 'women singers suffering from colds for six months of the year, or men who were drunk four times a week'. Lully quickly became canonised as the exemplar of French music, confirmed by his self-inflicted death, the result of a gangrenous wound sustained when he reportedly stabbed himself in the foot with a large conducting stick during a performance of his *Te Deum*. Lully's reputation as the founder of a new school of French music and performance was justified, but it was achieved at the expense of others who might well have claimed as much success.

The composer who suffered most from Lully's monopoly was the equally talented Marc-Antoine Charpentier (1643–1704), who was always fated to take second place to Lully, except perhaps in the church and chapel where his talent was recognised. But his powerful opera *Medée* is the equal of any of Lully's, and his 'biblical tragedy' *David et Jonathas*, set in Latin, is an intense and moving piece. Charpentier had his own patrons, notably the Duchess of Guise, by whom he was given a privileged status, and he went on to work for the Jesuits, which explains the predominance of Masses and oratorios in his output. The *Messe de Minuit* for Christmas is a delightfully fresh setting based on Christmas Noëls, while the *historiae* are oratorios often on non-biblical themes, such as *Caecilia virgo et martyr*. For anyone exploring his music, a tiny gem-like work with which to start is the brief Passion setting *Le reniement de St Pierre* (*78) about Peter's betrayal of Christ, with its piercingly tragic final chorus. Charpentier's best-known work today is the cheerful opening of his *Te Deum*, part of which forms the European Broadcasting Union's signature tune – used, among other things, as the opening music for the Eurovision Song Contest.

In the half-century after Lully's last opera of 1687, many *tragédies lyriques* were performed, but none held the stage. The viol player Marin Marais (1656–1728) wrote the opera *Alcyone*, and his chamber music includes a surprisingly modern programmatic description of *The Bladder-stone Operation*; his viol music was memorably used in the 1991 film *Tous les matins du monde*. *L'Europe galante* by

André Campra (1660–1744) was a new-style 'opera ballet', based not on mythology but on the characteristics of European nations; Campra's noble and sonorous Requiem is a magnificent piece. It was not until 1733 that Lully's operatic successor made his debut. Jean-Philippe Rameau (1683–1764) came to opera late in his composing career, when he was fifty. He gained employment with a wealthy tax collector called La Pouplinière, who supported the staging of his first opera *Hippolyte et Aricie* (*70). It was an immediate success: the aged Campra said, 'My Lord, there is enough music in this opera to make ten of them: this man will eclipse us all.' *Hippolyte et Aricie* seems to spring fully formed with some of the most delectable dance music in the genre, and its strong narrative, powerful choruses and vivid characterisation of the leading roles ensures it has a continual momentum.

It begins a sequence of operas by Rameau which stand alongside Handel's as the most memorable of the first half of the eighteenth century. The music drove forward the innovations of Lully with advanced harmonies, dramatic colour, instrumental invention, extrovert writing for the singers and the orchestra, and high-level drama. To some traditionalists this was thought of as subverting Lully's more classically restrained style, and the operas caused furious arguments as they appeared. For even longer than Handel's operas, Rameau's were thought unrevivable because of the complexity of their style and their unfamiliarity for modern performers. Rameau's operas divide into those that follow the principles of the new-style *tragédie lyrique* and those that revive the spirit of the *opéra-ballet* which pre-dated Lully. None is livelier than *Les indes galantes*, an *opéra-ballet* of 1735 with no connected plot but four acts depicting exotic scenes, with ravishingly lovely music. There are magnificent and serious tragedies including *Castor et Pollux*, *Dardanus* and *Zoroastre*, and at least one comic gem, *Platée*, while among many shorter works *Pygmalion* is a taut, concise masterpiece.

Even those who valued Rameau's dramatic works thought they would be impossible to revive today. 'Strains, never alas to be heard,' lamented Rameau's biographer Cuthbert Girdlestone of the last opera, *Les Boréades*, in his pioneering book from 1957. Yet *Les Boréades*, fully written but abandoned without having been performed when Rameau died in 1764, has been one of the outstanding rediscoveries of modern times. It contains some of Rameau's most adventurous music and most innovative dramatic planning, linking scenes and acts in a new way. The instrumental scoring with clarinets, bassoons and horns, plus a bright piccolo, is wonderful, and if you want one piece that sums up the eloquence of the French eighteenth century it would surely be the *Entrée de Polyhymnie* in Act 4, in which gently descending sequences create an undulating set of suspensions and resolutions. The revival of old instruments has made it possible to perform this music successfully, and groups such as Les Arts Florissants under William Christie have spent many years unlocking the codes and understanding the language of Rameau's music. *Les Boréades* has been heard at Salzburg, *Hippolyte et Aricie* at Glyndebourne, *Castor et Pollux* at the English National Opera – a slow but sure revival. Rameau captures the elegance and poise of a vanished era but also probes deep into the human psyche: for me he has been one of the great neglected figures of operatic history, whose work is finally now being brought back to life.

Rameau's theories of harmony were influential and widely followed, collected in *Traité de l'harmonie* (1722) which became a much-used textbook for teaching purposes. His thinking brought new enlightened methods of investigation and scientific enquiry, following Kepler and Newton, to bear on the age-old issues of the purpose and structure of music. They caused intellectual and political controversy in France, and many of the issues he raised have never been fully solved, but Rameau's work lies at the basis of a great deal of discussion of the theory of harmony over the last two centuries.

The last decades of the seventeenth century were a golden age for French keyboard music rather than for opera. Élisabeth Jacquet de la Guerre (1665–1729) performed on the harpsichord from the age of five, wrote keyboard music and cantatas, and composed the opera *Céphale et Procris* in 1694, the first opera by a Frenchwoman. Louis Couperin (*c.* 1626–61) was an expressive keyboard composer credited with one of the interesting musical innovations of the period: the preludes to his keyboard suites are written in unmeasured notation, that is to say they provide pitches and some sense of phrasing, but without any rhythms, leaving this aspect to the improvisational skills of the player. This is a clear example of deliberate freedom being granted to the performer, in which the notes do not dictate everything about how to play them.

Louis Couperin died early, and his nephew François Couperin 'le Grand' (1668–1733) followed in his footsteps, leaving a substantial body of over 200 pieces of keyboard music organised into four books of twenty-seven *Ordres* (or suites). Rather than naming the pieces after the usual dance forms of the day (Allemande, Courante, Gigue, for example), he preferred to give them fanciful titles, sometimes descriptive like *Les vieux seigneurs* and *Les jeunes seigneurs*, sometimes expressing their character, such as *L'âme-en peine* (The soul in torment), sometimes leaving us to guess at their meaning, for example the especially famous *Les baricades mistérieuses* (The mysterious barricades). They were published between 1713 and 1730, and range from light-hearted character pieces like *Le tic-toc choc* to the tremendous, dark and passionate *La ténébreuse* from the third *Ordre*, or the terrific *Passacaille* in the eighth *Ordre*. There is more than a hint of social criticism concealed within these pieces: not all the portraits are uniformly favourable. Any one of this brilliant collection of *Ordres* is worth exploring, and many of them are not too difficult to play. Among the composers across history who have been fascinated by these pieces and edited or arranged them are Johannes Brahms in the nineteenth century, Richard Strauss in the twentieth and Thomas Adès in the twenty-first. Couperin also made a major contribution to the study of performance with his instructional book *L'art de toucher le clavecin*.

Rameau's books of keyboard music, which were published in the 1720s, are more fully organised into suites than Couperin's. They use dance forms like the Allemande and Courante, but there are also brilliant variations in *Les niais de Sologne*, and vivid illustrative movements in *Les tourbillons* and *Les cyclopes*. These are virtuoso pieces demanding great flair at the keyboard. Utterly different are the tender and restrained pieces such as *L'entretien des muses* with sensually overlapping harmonies. *L'enharmonique*, with its twists of modulation, bears witness to Rameau's status also as a theorist and scholar of harmony. These pieces are designed for the rich sounds of the French harpsichord, and have been revived by George Malcolm, Kenneth Gilbert, Trevor Pinnock and now many others, but they have also been adopted by pianists to great effect, notably Alexandre Tharaud, Stephen Gutman and most recently Víkingur Ólafsson.

The other leading light in the keyboard music of the period is the Italian Domenico Scarlatti (1685–1757) – son of Alessandro (p. 107) – whose contributions to opera pale beside the intense excitement and originality of his keyboard sonatas (*72), some six hundred pieces – many written after he moved to Lisbon and Madrid, echoing the sounds of the guitar and other folk instruments, yet always idiomatically captured on the keyboard to the greatest effect. Scarlatti is supposed to have said that 'as nature had given him ten fingers, and as his instrument had employment for them all, he saw no reason why he should not use them'. A few pieces have been given nicknames, like the 'Cat's Fugue' whose theme was supposedly suggested by a kitten walking across the black keys of the keyboard. Most require a virtuoso performer. These brilliant pieces with their sharply dissonant harmonies and dazzling hand-crossing effects have been valued by keyboard players across the years; leading recordings on the harpsichord are by Scott Ross and Pierre Hantai, while many pianists from Vladimir Horowitz to Yevgeny Sudbin have adopted them effectively, adapting their astringent sonorities to the modern instrument.

*

In London's Whitehall, opposite Horse Guards Parade, you pass a fine classical building: the Banqueting House, designed by Inigo Jones, with an elaborate ceiling decorated by Peter Paul Rubens. Isolated today, it is a splendid survival of the Palace of Whitehall; it was planned to become a centrepiece of a much larger scheme designed by Jones which was never built, and the whole original complex around it burned down in 1698. It was a performance space designed for the court masques of the reign of James I and Charles I. These masques were rather different entertainments from our idea of opera, but were no less sophisticated. Influenced by the ballets of the French court, and distantly linked to the Florentine *intermedi*, they brought together the arts of costume and scenic design, instrumental and vocal music, low comedy and high, for court entertainment. Echoes of the masque tradition can be heard in Shakespeare's plays, notably *The Tempest*, or in the dumbshow performed by the players in *Hamlet*.

English masques featured revels in which the performers might mingle with the audience; all had allegorical messages, conceived by playwrights led by Ben

Jonson and designed with Inigo Jones and colleagues, to prove the association between present state events and past histories. *The Masque of Blackness*, on which they collaborated in 1605, was controversial because the twelve ladies who played the daughters of Niger blackened their faces rather than wearing masks. *The Triumph of Peace* had music by William Lawes and others, involving processions through the city before the masque. Much information survives about *Lord Hay's Masque*, performed in 1607 at the nearby hall of the Palace of Whitehall, which had music by Thomas Campion (1567–1620) played by a consort of twelve (violins with three lutes) and a consort of ten (with wind instruments), 'and to answer both the consorts, as it were in a triangle, six cornetts, and six chapel voices, in a place raised higher in respect of the piercing sound of those instruments'. A feature of these artworks was their miscellaneous nature: the opera planned by William Davenant as *The Siege of Rhodes* included music by several composers. It was outside the same Banqueting House that King Charles I was executed in 1649, coming as one witness put it 'out of the banqueting-house on the scaffold, with the same unconcernedness and motion that he usually had when he entered into it on a masque-night'.

The period of the Commonwealth was not a happy one for English music, though activity was kept alive domestically, as the biographer and amateur musician Roger North recounted in the early eighteenth century: 'when most other good arts languished Musick held up her head, not at Court nor (in the cant of those times) profane Theatres, but in private society, for many chose to fiddle at home'. The restoration of Charles II in 1660 was a cause for great rejoicing; it was also the excuse for a public revival of music and cultural activity that had been frowned upon during the Puritan era. The period saw an expansion in musical life in London, with the formation of some of the world's first public concerts in the 1670s under the aegis of John Banister, and a regular array of music-making in small venues such as coal merchant Thomas Britton's premises in Clerkenwell (p. 137). We can follow this wealth of music-making in sources like the diaries of Samuel Pepys, himself an active amateur musician who wrote and arranged songs, and who studied music theory, albeit without much success. He clearly had many ideas he could not realise himself, for instance asking his Italian servant Cesare

115

Morelli to set Hamlet's soliloquy 'To be or not to be' in recitative. In an eloquent letter, he described music as:

> a science particularly productive of a pleasure that no state of life, publick or private, secular or sacred; no difference of age or season; no temper of mind or condition of health exempt from present anguish; nor, lastly, distinction of quality, renders either improper, untimely, or unentertaining. Witness the universal gusto we see it followed with, wherever to be found, by all whose leisure and purse can bear it.

Pepys had a discriminating approach to singing and the communication of the texts, preferring the solo voice and an understanding of national traditions: 'the better the words are set, the more they take in of the ordinary tone of the country whose language the song speaks'.

I cannot restrain my admiration for the central composer of this era, Henry Purcell (1658/59–95). He became the leading figure in Restoration music, as a church composer working at Westminster Abbey before the accession of William and Mary in 1689, thereafter for the theatre. His emotional depth and technical skill are unrivalled among English composers, and the equal of any musician of the time. Purcell was equally adept at providing songs and interludes for spoken plays in the theatre or anthems for the Chapel Royal. We do not know the stimulus for his superb and moving through-composed opera *Dido and Aeneas* (*77); doubt has been cast on the long-held view that it was written for an all-girls' school in Chelsea, though it was performed there, but it has a unique place in the repertory. Across its hour-long span it is one of the most powerful works of all time, with a fantastic strength and variety of music, with inventive dances and vigorous interludes from the ebullient sailors to the hunting scenes and the final lament of the tragic heroine. Elements of the work are missing, notably the prologue for which a text survives, but that only enhances the sense of forward movement in the drama, which scarcely seems to take breath. The immortal lament for Dido, 'When I am laid in earth', is written over the chromatic descending bass line that had become associated with the form of the lament in Italian opera, and is followed by a touching final chorus. *Dido and Aeneas* has become a benchmark for taut, concentrated music-drama, but it remains a glorious exception in the English music of the time. It has provided a showcase for many distinguished singers from Kirsten Flagstad to Jessye Norman, and in the present early music revival has been recorded by Emma Kirkby and Sarah Connolly.

From adding isolated songs and dances to spoken plays, for instance those of the female dramatist Aphra Behn, Purcell moved to create full-scale works like *King Arthur* and *The Fairy-Queen* in which speech and music combine to create a quite new form of 'semi-opera'. They have suffered from the perception when performed in opera houses that there is too much speech and too little music, whereas they should probably be performed in theatres, as plays with a lavish provision of music. It was the contemporary chronicler Roger North who epitomised the problem with this form, that those who went for the music were annoyed by the play, and vice versa. The music is not generally performed by the characters in the play, making the dislocation more noticeable. Yet there are few musical sequences as satisfying as the set-piece scenes of the Four Seasons in *The Fairy-Queen* or the Frost Scene from *King Arthur*, and the dance music in both works is wildly imaginative and effective. Purcell's scores evoke even the stage directions of these pieces with programmatic skill: *The Fairy-Queen* contains a 'Symphony as the swans come forward'. Equally his vocal lines are memorable and unmatched: few melodies have had a longer life than 'If love's a sweet pleasure' from *The Fairy-Queen* or 'Fairest Isle' from *King Arthur*.

Opera did not flourish after the premature death of Purcell until the arrival in London of George Frideric Handel (1685–1759) and the cultural revolution stimulated by the Hanoverian George I succeeding to the English throne in 1714. The German-born Handel had already displeased George when he was the then Elector of Hanover's Kapellmeister by spending too much time in England instead of fulfilling his duties in Germany. Although the relationship between king and composer is shrouded in some mystery, Handel was evidently reconciled with the monarch when he was commissioned to produce the so-called *Water Music* in 1717, a collection of instrumental music compiled for a journey down the Thames in the royal barge. Although we might now refer to it as a site-specific piece, the music was not especially crafted for performance on water, and was later arranged in various suites for publication.

Handel brought with him another European connection to the capital. He had studied in Italy early in the century, and had worked for Cardinal Ottoboni (p. 130) during which time he learned the arts of the Italian chamber cantata and oratorio that were to sustain him during the rest of his composing career. He also had the opportunity to develop his most characteristic import to our musical culture, the genre of Italian opera. Owing to the vagaries of fashion which have affected our musical taste across the centuries, in the opera house Handel was forgotten and overtaken by later taste. Given how popular his operas now are, it is astonishing to reflect that not a single Handel opera was seen complete on the stage anywhere from 1754, five years before his death, until 1920. That revival took root very slowly in Germany from the 1920s onwards, hampered by the absence of male voices for the roles that would have been sung in Handel's day by well-known castrati (who following their unfortunate operation found fame by singing in a brilliant upper register). These parts were first moved down an octave for bass voices, which often spoiled the balance of the scoring, then began to be taken on by mezzo-sopranos and altos, and later by the revival of the counter-tenor male voice. A series of specialised revivals by such groups as the Handel Opera Society helped to bring the operas back into the repertory before the first popular revivals were staged, including *Julius Caesar* with Janet Baker, conducted by Charles Mackerras, and later *Xerxes* in a brilliant production by Nicholas Hytner, both at the English National Opera.

One major difference between opera in Handel's day and our own is that it used to be the performers who dominated the stage and dictated the terms and conditions of their work. In the present we have great singers who are the stars of their shows, but our concept of operas as fixed texts means they are there to realise a work pretty much as it stands: they are expected to sing what is in the composer's score. For Handel it was very different. He was at the mercy of his singers who could accept or reject what he wrote. Take the case of Giovanni Carestini, the castrato whom Handel brought from Italy in 1733 to be a new star. Carestini was described by the historian Charles Burney as 'tall, beautiful, and majestic. He was a very animated and intelligent actor . . . with a lively and inventive imagination'. But when Handel wanted to present him in his opera *Alcina*, and wrote the beautifully simple aria 'Verdi prati' in Act 3 for him, Carestini sent it back to the composer as 'unfit for him to sing', doubtless because it did not contain enough display and virtuosity. An even more famous castrato was Carlo Broschi, called Farinelli, of whom it was said 'his throat was very flexible, so that he could produce the largest intervals quickly and with the greatest ease and flexibility. Broken passages [that is, arpeggios], as well as all the other runs, provided no difficulty for him, and he was very prolific in his use of the optional ornaments of an adagio.'

These singers had immense power and were commented on in detail by the observers of the day. In his pioneering *General History of Music* of 1789, Burney devoted as much detail to their performances as to the music they sang. Of the famous rival sopranos Francesca Cuzzoni and Faustina Bordoni Hasse he wrote that Cuzzoni's 'native warble enabled her to execute divisions with such facility as to conceal every appearance of difficulty . . . the art of conducting, sustaining, increasing and diminishing her tone by minute degrees, acquired her, among professors, the title of complete mistress of her art'. Hasse on the other hand 'in a manner invented a new kind of singing, by running divisions with a neatness and velocity which astonished all who heard her. She had the art of sustaining a note longer than any other singer, by taking her breath imperceptibly.' Recounting the rivalry between them that became so fierce, Burney concludes, 'What a beautiful mixture it would be, if the excellences of these two angelic beings could be united in a single individual!' (Plate 14)

In baroque opera the expectations of the audience also extended to lavish scenic effects. In the second scene of *Alcina*, for instance, 'lightning flashes, and the mountains crumble; as they disappear the exquisite palace of Alcina can be seen'; and at the climax of the opera 'Ruggiero shatters the urn; immediately the whole scene crashes down and disappears. The ruins are submerged by the sea, which is visible through a vast underground cave, where many boulders are turned into men.' It is no surprise that an admiring observer, the artist and letter-writer Mary Delany, thought that observing *Alcina* in rehearsal with the composer directing proceedings from the keyboard was 'so fine I have not words to describe it . . .

Whilst Mr. Handel was playing his part, I could not help thinking him a necromancer in the midst of his own enchantments.'

Alcina is just one of the Handel operas that have proved themselves highly successful in modern revivals and recordings. A sequence of superbly inventive works was written for the Royal Academy based at the King's Theatre in the 1720s, including *Radamisto*, *Giulio Cesare* and *Rodelinda*. Then, to open his first season at Covent Garden in 1735, using the ballet troupe of Marie Sallé, Handel wrote *Ariodante* (*69), which shares with *Alcina* some brilliant ballet music depicting supernatural events, and has two of the greatest arias he ever wrote, the despairing 'Scherza infida' and the triumphant 'Dopo notte' written for Carestini in the title role and now recorded by many leading singers.

Our tastes change over time, and Handel speaks to us now very directly: in his operas he was a sensualist who revelled in the play of human passions and expressed them with a piercing insight. There is something about the deep penetration with which Handel conjures up elemental feelings – not ambiguous as with Mozart, nor with the sense of struggle that Beethoven captures, but cutting to the heart of a character and an emotion. Handel's operas were driven by the conventions of the day, drawing on Italian libretti which had often been previously set by other composers. When his operatic ventures finally failed in 1741, he turned to oratorio, and these have affected his reputation as a stern moralist because they were composed for a rather different, perhaps more puritanically inclined public. Conceived in English, they represent the creation of a fundamentally new form, dominated by a chorus to a far greater extent than the operas. They owed much to the music Handel heard when he came to England in 1712, especially that of Purcell and his followers. Some of these oratorios have been staged, which suits those that are fundamentally dramatic such as *Semele* and *Saul*. The greater role played by the chorus creates impressive movements, for instance in *Solomon* and *Belshazzar*, the big choral fugues which give these pieces a wholly different character from the operas. While the operas continue to receive wildly varied stagings, the oratorios are lending themselves to contemporary reinterpretation on stage, as in Glyndebourne's superb productions of *Theodora* by Peter Sellars and *Saul* by Barrie Kosky.

Handel's most famous oratorio is, of course, *Messiah*. That remains unique in Handel's output as a story of Christ's life, death and resurrection based on the texts of both the Old and New Testaments, organised by his friend and patron of the arts Charles Jennens. It makes use of several of Handel's early Italian duets, cunningly rewritten for four-part chorus but sounding completely spontaneous. It has proved amazingly adaptable, inflated to massive sizes for communal performance, and reduced down to solo performance by small, expert ensembles. The Hallelujah Chorus is one of the very few pieces of music that has entered the national consciousness in the way achieved by, say, Beethoven's *Ode to Joy* from his Ninth Symphony. *Messiah* is a miracle of Handel's art and of the whole high baroque period; it has provided a touchstone for choral performance over the years, and especially for amateur participation through the nineteenth century. It was performed by all as a communal act of music-making. As the composer Charles Dibdin noted in 1788: 'I have been assured, for a fact, that more than one man in Halifax can take any part in choruses from the *Messiah* and go regularly through the whole oratorio by heart; and indeed the facility with which the common people join together throughout the great part of Yorkshire and Lancashire in every species of choral music is truly astonishing.' There had already been enlargements in performances of Handel's music; the 1784 celebrations of the centenary of his birth (a year early) in Westminster Abbey featured a choir of 275 and an orchestra of 248. Mozart arranged the work, enlarging the orchestra with clarinets at the encouragement of Baron van Swieten. By the time of the Great Handel Commemoration festival in 1859 to mark the centenary of his death, there were 2,765 singers and an orchestra of 460. In time, these large-scale gatherings of amateur choral singers were modified by performances that paid attention to the much smaller-sized forces that Handel originally envisaged. It was due to the increasing reservations of critics, including George Bernard Shaw, that such gargantuan performances fell out of fashion; these days both small-scale accounts with period instruments, and larger performances using instrumental additions provided modestly by Mozart, or later and more extravagantly by the conductor Thomas Beecham, are enjoyed.

*

Economic challenges and the expense of talent in London led Handel's operatic ventures to fail, and he moved his activity from opera to oratorio. Across Europe too the conventions of *opera seria* were beginning to be challenged. Writers and philosophers complained of the artificiality of the libretti of these operas and strove for something simpler and more natural. *La serva padrona* by Giovanni Battista Pergolesi (1710–36) was originally an intermezzo performed between the acts of a more serious opera, but it became a leading example of the new informality which entered opera, in which everyday characters expressing normal human feelings were featured (Plate 15). Pergolesi's serious operas have lasted less well. However, his sacred music, notably the famous *Stabat mater*, with its sequence of sensual duets for soprano and alto, has been widely used in films and popular culture. Music thought to be by Pergolesi formed the basis of Stravinsky's neoclassical ballet *Pulcinella* (p. 231), though much of it was actually by lesser composers, which was probably what enabled Stravinsky to make it so imaginatively his own.

The composer who best grasped the reforming principles and created a new kind of opera from them was Christoph Willibald Gluck (1714–87). He brought together the best of the Italian and French styles and argued for a 'noble simplicity' in reaction to the elaboration and decorativeness of the earlier eighteenth century. In the preface to *Alceste*, which he wrote with librettist Ranieri Calzabigi, he made the case for reform: 'I was determined to abolish all those faults that had stolen into Italian opera through the unwarranted pride of singers and the foolish acquiescence of composers, that had made it tiresome and ludicrous instead of the greatest and most impressive spectacle of modern times. I sought to restore music to its true purpose of expressing the poetry and reinforcing the dramatic situation, without interrupting the action or hampering it with superfluous embellishments.'

The opera which formed this style, *Orfeo ed Euridice*, for which Calzabigi also wrote the libretto, set a new template for music-drama with the unadorned directness of its vocal style. Orfeo was sung by the castrato Gaetano Guadagni, whose role culminates in a moving aria after the loss of Euridice, 'Che farò senza Euridice' which has become famous in its own right and was especially associated with the contralto Kathleen Ferrier: the part was one of her few stage roles before her untimely death. *Orfeo* was so successful that Gluck reworked it for Paris, titled *Orphée et Eurydice*, in French with added ballet, and with a high tenor (familiar from French operas) replacing the castrato in the title role. He later wrote the tragic operas *Iphigénie en Aulide* and *Iphigénie en Tauride*, also for Paris, the latter more popular than the former. *Aulide* was later revived and rewritten by Wagner in Dresden, while *Tauride* was arranged by Richard Strauss. Gluck's music was highly influential on contemporary composers, especially his strong minor-mode music for *Don Juan*, which anticipates the literary period of *Sturm und Drang* (Storm and Stress) (p. 134).

At this point it was clear that there was an operatic revolution in the air: the formal devices of *opera seria*, including the endless repetitions of *da capo* arias, were falling out of favour. What was to replace them was a new humanity expressed through Gluck's simplicity, and in this the key figure was the Italian dramatist Carlo Goldoni (1707–93), whose plays brought together serious and comic characters, and created 'mixed' characters combining elements of both. Goldoni brought a new freshness and human reality to the writing of operatic libretti, and he laid the groundwork for one of the most skilful librettists of the eighteenth century, Lorenzo da Ponte (1749–1838). Through his plays, Goldoni enabled the interaction of different social classes on stage, and that was to stimulate the creation of future miracles of humane dramatic music, in the mature operas of Wolfgang Amadeus Mozart (p. 146).

9

Masters

If you were a devout Lutheran in the German city of Leipzig in the mid-1720s, you would have attended the Sunday service in the imposing church of St Thomas near the centre of the city, or perhaps in the less forbidding church of St Nicholas nearby. You would expect a sober service of hymns, prayers and readings, with accompanying organ music and church music newly composed by the Kapellmeister of the day. It was Martin Luther, himself a musician with a profound sense of tradition (even though he had become branded as a revolutionary since his split with Rome), who had adapted hymn tunes from those of the past, modifying plainsong chants and Latin words to the new demands of the German liturgy (p. 72). You would be ready for a long sermon, a devotional service, and then to return home fortified for the rigours of the week ahead.

You would not have been remotely prepared for the barrage of complex music that greeted you: a cantata of demanding difficulty, performed heroically by the boys and men of the choir, with an organist gesticulating wildly, stamping and beating time to lead the performance. 'God, save us, my children!' one congregation member is supposed to have said at the premiere of one dramatic work. 'It's just as if one were at an opera-comedy.' (There may have been a hint of nostalgia in that remark, since Leipzig's opera house had closed in 1720.) The new cantor, Johann Sebastian Bach (1685–1750), who had arrived from Cöthen in 1723, had not been greeted with much enthusiasm by the city fathers; they had preferred the prolific Christoph Graupner but could not acquire him, so as one member of the committee stated, 'since the best man cannot be obtained, mediocre ones will have to be accepted'. It was not an auspicious start. Yet the new cantor, responsible for the teaching of music at the St Thomas School as well as providing the music at Leipzig's churches, had a thorough musical background and a name which linked him to one of the great musical dynasties of the region. Johann Sebastian had been born in Eisenach, where his father Ambrosius had been a town musician and his family were all involved in the local music-making. Although he had never left the eastern area of the country we today call Germany, Sebastian had travelled to Lüneburg for his education and had visited the great composer Dietrich Buxtehude in Lübeck (the story has it that he had walked for days to make this journey). He had learned from his musical relatives and the organist Georg Böhm, transcribing pieces as a teenager and beginning to compose.

Bach came to Leipzig with experience of writing sacred music and organ music for a variety of situations. At the churches of Mühlhausen and Arnstadt, vocal church music and organ music was to be provided; quite early at Arnstadt he was criticised for the elaborateness of his accompaniments to the chorales. Then at the court of Weimar, where cantatas were written for the court chapel, and later at Cöthen, with some supremely talented instrumentalists at his disposal, Bach wrote solo partitas and sonatas for violin, developing the virtuosity of that instrument further than ever. The famous Chaconne from the Partita in D minor dates from this period, a piece which echoes the music of Heinrich Biber (p. 90), and has been transcribed across the centuries for other forces, for grand piano or large orchestra. Bach played the violin and viola as well as keyboard: he knew exactly what was achievable on those instruments and all others in the ensembles at his disposal, and his scores show him responding to individual players and particular instrumental sonorities.

Bach was determined to show the people of Leipzig what he could do, and for the first few years he did so without respite, creating week after week a sequence of sacred cantatas which demonstrated all his compositional skills and theological understanding: contrapuntal choruses in which you could often hear the melodies of the Lutheran chorales striding across the busy textures; comparatively simple melodic material for the boy trebles of the choir to intone, while the other singers managed the complex lines below, surrounded by instrumental elaboration; then a sequence of solo arias, which for all their eloquence must have tested the skills of their singers and players; finally, a chorale whose melody was known to all, simply presented yet often with unnervingly rich harmonies. Every one of these sacred cantatas was closely related in its text to the liturgy of the day, following the seasons of the liturgical year, linked in its devotional meaning and spiritual benefit; the words were available to all in booklets which could be studied. Slowly you might have become aware that this was one of the richest, deepest collections of sacred music imaginable – a deep treasure trove of great music written for an elevated purpose.

Bach himself would play the organ. Freed for a moment, we may imagine, from the frustrations of struggling with singers and players who he may have felt failed to live up to the technical demands he had placed on them, he was able to perform alone. We can only guess from the written examples left to us how Bach improvised from his profound knowledge of harmony and counterpoint. To hear for the first time the elaborate, pulsating opening of the Fantasia and Fugue in G minor, its arabesques and dramatic harmonic shifts swirling around the church, must have been an unforgettable experience. Then after the emotional depth of its Fantasia, a cheerful Fugue that bubbles around the keyboard with unalloyed delight. Or in a completely different mood, the relentless tread of the A minor Prelude and Fugue (which Liszt later transcribed for piano), powering with repeated patterns through a violin-like sequence, leading to a dancing fugue which in turn ends with crashing chords.

For Bach the keyboard was central to his work, both to his composition and teaching. His earliest essays would have been chorale preludes based on the melodies of the day, and he gradually developed a series of Preludes and Fugues which made full use of all the keys available to him on the keyboard. He wrote that the pieces in his first book of the 48 Preludes and Fugues were 'for the use and profit of the musical youth desirous of learning and for the pastime of those already skilled in this study'. He began to write them for his first son, Wilhelm Friedemann, in the keys most often used at that time, but this was a period where a 'well-tempered' tuning system was beginning to be used which enabled all the major and minor keys to be deployed. Bach's predecessors had already experimented with well-tempered tuning: Johann Pachelbel (1653–1706), who also wrote the famous Canon, a cornerstone of the modern baroque revival, used seventeen different keys in his harpsichord suites of 1683, and in Leipzig J. C. F. Fischer (c. 1656–1746) had written pieces in his *Ariadne musica* in nineteen keys in 1715. Bach extended this to the full twenty-four possible keys, based on scales in the major and minor modes beginning on each note of the keyboard octave, with results that have remained a cornerstone of the keyboard tradition. As Schumann intoned, 'let the Well-Tempered Clavier be your daily bread'. Twentieth-century musicians, including the cellist Pablo Casals, have said how playing some of this music daily is a central musical experience for them.

As Bach's time in Leipzig continued through the 1720s, he became more frustrated with the circumstances of his employment and music-making in the church and school there. Nevertheless he composed two of his very greatest works, the St John Passion of 1724 and the St Matthew Passion of 1727, as well as a St Mark Passion whose music is now lost. These drew on a longer tradition of Lutheran church music, notably that of Heinrich Schütz (p. 90); Bach continued to revise and refine them across many years for subsequent performances. These two great retellings of the Passion story for performance on Good Friday encapsulate Bach's theological approach to the spiritual nature of his task, for they bring together the biblical narrative sung by the Evangelist, the communal chorales in which all join together, and the personal reflections of the individual in the solo arias. The St John Passion setting is shorter and more dramatic, the St Matthew Passion longer and more reflective; both are among the greatest expressions of sacred music across the ages, which seem able to speak to those of any religion or none.

Bach made a famous complaint to the Leipzig town council in 1729 about the inadequacy of the singers coming into the school and available for the church services which he had to supply each Sunday. It appears that changes in the school's selection procedure had left Bach with less control over the vocal standards of those who were chosen. In his irritation with the church authorities, Bach seems to have turned his attention more and more to the secular music-making of the

city, using university students and his own children to create events at Zimmermann's coffee house near the city square. For these 'collegium musicum' concerts Bach created some of his most enjoyable works, such as the four Orchestral
Suites, often drawing on music he had written for Weimar and Cöthen (but which
would not have been heard by audiences in Leipzig). He created a new genre:
the concerto for harpsichord, sometimes drawing on old oboe or violin concertos and sometimes newly written. He found opportunities for his sons to be
keyboard players, notably Wilhelm Friedemann (1710–84) and Carl Philipp
Emanuel (1714–88). They would have featured in his series of concertos for mul-
tiple keyboards with ensemble, sometimes adapting the music of other composers such as Vivaldi, whose Concerto for four violins in B minor (*74) became
a four-harpsichord concerto in A minor. Bach wrote a small number of original
concertos which have now been dated to this period in Leipzig, among them
the Violin Concertos in E major and A minor as well as the immortal Concerto
for two violins in D minor with its utterly serene slow movement that has been
played, and has flourished, in so many different styles across the years: in our
time, in the old tradition by father and son David and Igor Oistrakh or in a new
style by Isabelle Faust and Bernhard Forck.

Bach's own music for ensemble had reached new heights of colour and
originality in the six Brandenburg Concertos written while he was at Cöthen,
so called because they were gathered together and presented to the Margrave
of Brandenburg in 1721; they probably represent a tiny proportion of what he
actually composed, and the rest are lost. They include consciously varied combinations of fascinating instrumental sonorities, with recorders, trumpets, violas,
horns, and in the fifth of the set he writes a huge cadenza for solo harpsichord,
marking that instrument's emancipation into a true soloist. We cannot imagine
who except Bach himself could have played this titanic music; it was certainly not
performed by Brandenburg's ensemble. (Let us not blame them, however; at least
they kept the music safe in the Margrave's library for future generations to enjoy.)

At the same time as taking the secular concerto form to new heights, Bach did
not abandon sacred music. He created the exuberant Christmas Oratorio, six sacred cantatas drawn mainly from the music he had composed for secular cantatas,

to be performed on six days in two churches over the Christmas and New Year period. Increasingly concerned to make an impact outside Leipzig, in 1733 he wrote a superb Kyrie and Gloria, making a 'Missa' or short Mass of great elaboration for the new elector in Dresden, doubtless in the hope of acquiring support and employment there. That hope was disappointed, but the music was not wasted; he later incorporated it into his final masterwork, the collection of music for the Latin Ordinary of the Mass which we know as the Mass in B minor. This magnificent collection of Bach's sacred music complements the collections of his last decade: the keyboard virtuosity of the *Goldberg Variations* (*68), the fugal explorations of *The Art of Fugue*, and the canonic ingenuities of the *Musical Offering*, written as a result of a 1747 visit to the court of Frederick the Great where his son Carl Philipp Emanuel was employed. They sum up a life of extraordinary achievement.

Bach was a true polymath. He never stood still; he was always exploring, always developing. He published some of his work in his collections of keyboard music, the *Clavier-Übung*, including the Six Partitas as the first volume, and dense pieces for organ in volume three. He was also an entrepreneur who had shares in a Leipzig silver mine and who sold his son's music at the autumn fair in the city, while all the time exploring ever greater intricacies of counterpoint and canonic ingenuity by joining a Society of Musical Sciences organised in the city by Lorenz Mizler. The most famous portrait of Bach in old age shows the canon he gave to join the Society, containing just fourteen notes, the number that for Bach spelt the letters of his name (if A=1, B=2, and so on, then BACH=14 and J. S. BACH=41). This, for Bach, showed himself in harmony with the universe and with the world. The canon as displayed in this portrait could also be regarded, as the leading Bach scholar Christoph Wolff recently wrote, as his business card.

For us today, when music is so often a side enthusiasm in our busy lives, it is difficult to imagine how completely it was at the centre of life for Bach and his generation. From his earliest childhood he would have been surrounded by music, and he learned about it – by doing it and thinking about it – every single day. As a practical musician he evidently learned fast, and as a perfectionist he continually improved. One of his earliest biographers, Johann Nikolaus Forkel, speaks with admiration of how constantly he revised his work, making the bad into good, the good into better, and pushing the better towards perfect. Bach always strove for perfection, and would not rest till he felt he had achieved it. So often at odds with his employers and those who criticised the complexity of his music, Bach was a master in tune with the richness of the cosmos.

*

For all his undoubted greatness, Bach contradicts the notion that as a supreme master of his craft he was isolated from all those around him, and floats above them in some different sphere. On the contrary, he learned constantly from his contemporaries, and used their music to his advantage. He absorbed the music of others and turned it to his own ends. The pioneer violin soloist of the baroque was Arcangelo Corelli (1653–1713), and we can be sure that he was one of the composers whose music Bach studied as he based an organ fugue on one of Corelli's pieces.

An outstanding performer, Corelli was one of the musicians kept by the famous Cardinal Ottoboni in Rome to provide entertainment. The German composer Johann Ernst Galliard wrote that 'I never met with any man that suffered his passion to hurry him away so much whilst he was playing on the violin ... his eyes will sometimes turn as red as fire; his countenance will be distorted, his eyeballs roll as if in agony'. Corelli met Handel (p. 118) in Rome, but had difficulty playing Handel's overtures because, as he objected to 'my dear Saxon', 'this music is in the French style, which I do not understand'. In fact Handel's instrumental music reflected a growing cosmopolitanism which crossed national boundaries of style and united them. Corelli's Violin Sonatas Op. 5 (*75), which he dedicated on 1 January 1700, were much circulated and reprinted, and were provided by one publisher with elaborate ornamentation 'with the embellishments marked for the Adagios as Mr Corelli wants them played'. Corelli's innovations came in the form of solo sonatas, and particularly his harmonious trio sonatas, where two violins wind in imitation over a walking bass line.

The larger form of the solo concerto had been pioneered by Giuseppe Torelli (1658–1709) in Bologna, who composed both for violin and for trumpet in the early years of the century. His structures mark out the lines of the form, with clearly delineated passages for the tutti (called ritornello) and the solos (called episodes). More memorable and established in the repertory is Tomaso Albinoni (1671–1750/1). Unfortunately his best-known work today, the Adagio in G minor for strings, was actually crafted by a twentieth-century editor from a fragmentary sketch. (It has now been used in so many films including *Rollerball*, *Gallipoli* and *Flashdance* that a well-known film critic called for it to be banned.) Albinoni's own works, especially those for oboe, have memorable melodies and splendid shapeliness and verve. His Op. 7 of 1715 and Op. 9 of 1722 contain a variety of concertos for oboe solo, two oboes or strings, and the oboist Heinz Holliger did much to revive them for modern audiences. In the general three-movement form of these baroque concertos, the middle movements derive inspiration from the lyrical operatic aria, while the outer movements let the soloist's instrumental virtuosity emerge.

Setting a soloist against an ensemble in this way offered great opportunities to composers. The most famous of them all is Antonio Vivaldi (1678–1741), who grasped the potential in literally hundreds of concertos. The title of one of Vivaldi's concerto sets, *The Contest between Harmony and Invention*, is an apt symbol of the development of a form which came to represent one of the most distinctive aspects of eighteenth-century music, linking baroque and classical eras in a single development across the century. Many of his concertos were written for the girl soloists of the Pietà in Venice, where Vivaldi, priest as well as composer, taught from 1703. The Mendicanti drew their teaching staff from the musical establishment at St Mark's, and the girls were trained exclusively in music, as a result of which Venice's orphanages became special centres of musical skill – a major attraction for both teachers and visitors. We read accounts by the travellers of the time thrilled with the level of musical accomplishment they heard: 'they sing like angels, play the violin, flute, organ, oboe, cello, bassoon . . . I swear nothing is more charming than to see a young and pretty nun, dressed in white, a sprig of pomegranate blossom behind one ear, leading the orchestra and beating time with all the grace and precision imaginable.'

Many of Vivaldi's concertos were written for publication and sale across Europe. One of Bach's employers in Weimar certainly brought back scores for Bach to study, and he arranged some of Vivaldi's concertos for solo organ and harpsi-chord. Among the set Vivaldi published as Op. 8 in 1725 were a group that have been universally famous in the baroque revival, *The Four Seasons*. He wrote many pieces with descriptive titles, like *La tempesta di mare* or *La caccia*, but these four are detailed, specific programme music with a sonnet that stands at the head of each concerto, and descriptive passages that bring each season to life. The trill-ing birds and rustic bagpipes of spring, the heavy heat and cuckoo's call of sum-mer, the sleeping drunkards and hunting horns of autumn, and the chilly frosts and raging storms of winter are all depicted. The effects hark back to the word-painting of the Italian madrigals, and point forward to Beethoven's 'Pastoral' Sym-phony No. 6, but the methods of integrating these programmatic effects into the music are wholly new.

Vivaldi was himself a great virtuoso, and we read of his improvised cadenzas from visitors to Venice, including Johann Friedrich von Uffenbach: 'he placed his fingers but a hair's breadth from the bridge, so that there was barely room for the bow, doing thus on all four strings with imitative passages at incredible speed'. There are published collections based around the violin, including *La cetra* and *La stravaganza*. More varied in instrumentation are some of the many concertos that remained in manuscript until the twentieth century, including many more for violin, but seek out the ones for bassoon (thirty-seven survive) and cello (of which there are twenty-seven) which cultivate the lower registers; all have been very well edited and recorded in recent times in the advancing complete record-ing of his music on the Naïve label. The published collection, *L'estro armonico* Op. 3 has a striking passage in the Larghetto of No. 10 where four different bowings are indicated at the same time; this is the concerto that J. S. Bach adapted for four harpsichords (*74).

The baroque concerto was taken forward by violin virtuosi such as Pietro Antonio Locatelli (1695–1764), who pushed the boundaries of what was possi-ble in terms of range and rapidity on the instrument; an observer of his playing in Amsterdam said, 'He plays with so much Fury upon his Fiddle, that in my humble Opinion, he must wear out some Dozens of them in a year.' Italian composers were of great interest to the German players and composers of the time, including the violinist Johann Georg Pisendel (1687–1755), who studied with Vivaldi in Venice and brought his virtuoso skills to the court of Dresden.

That Dresden court, the seat of the elector, was important to Bach, where he hoped for recognition and an appointment: he would have encountered there one of the most fascinating and original of his contemporaries, Jan Dismas Zelenka (1679–1745), whose highly individual music is being revived today. His chamber music and his settings of the Lamentations of Jeremiah for solo voice and ensemble show his taste for elaborate counterpoint and quirky harmony. Zelenka's large-scale sacred works are now also in the process of being recorded; for an introduction to his distinctive idiom, try his very inventive six trio sonatas for oboes and bassoon (*73), performed by Heinz Holliger and colleagues.

The other composer who was a good colleague of Bach's became far more successful in his day. Georg Philipp Telemann (1681–1767) was a hugely prolific and popular composer of cantatas and concertos, and showed special skill in the varied combination of solo instruments that he used; Bach made a detailed study of their music. Telemann wrote a huge amount of music during his lifetime, his works vastly outnumbering Bach's; his music is always perfectly crafted and extremely attractive (*71). Having studied in Leipzig, and working in Bach's birthplace, Eisenach, he knew Bach and became a godfather to Bach's son Carl Philipp Emanuel, who eventually succeeded him in Hamburg before moving to Berlin.

The middle of the eighteenth century saw many changes in musical style and feeling. Regarded as old fashioned in his time, J. S. Bach nevertheless made attempts at the end of his life to keep up with the latest fashions, and Carl Philipp Emanuel brought his father to the court of Frederick the Great in Berlin, where Johann Sebastian encountered a new and influential keyboard instrument, the fortepiano, whose strings were struck rather than being plucked as on the harpsichord; this is the true forerunner of the modern piano. He wrote a three-part Ricercar in his *Musical Offering* which uses the expressive style of the fortepiano, and even became an agent for selling the instrument in Leipzig.

C. P. E. Bach was a master in the developing world of personal expression and intensity of feeling, and used to the full the expressiveness of the keyboard instruments of his day. He wrote an influential *Essay on the True Art of Playing*

Keyboard Instruments used by Haydn, Beethoven, Clementi and others, which became a widely accepted teaching manual. Although it deals with technique, it is very attentive to the impression that playing must make on its audience, and takes the spirit of individual performance into a new realm:

> A musician cannot move others unless he too is moved. He must of necessity feel all of the affects that he hopes to arouse in his audience, for the revealing of his own humour will simulate a like humour in the audience. In languishing, the performer must languish and grow sad. Thus will the expression of the piece be more clearly perceived by the audience.

From the reports of Charles Burney, it is clear that Carl Philipp Emanuel followed his own precepts, for when he was playing 'he looked like one inspired. His eyes were fixed, his under-lip fell, and drops of effervescence distilled from his countenance.' C. P. E. Bach's improvisatory keyboard fantasias and sonatas had a great effect on Mozart, who declared: 'he is the father, we are the children'.

C. P. E. Bach provides a transitional link between the world of the baroque and the rise of classicism – though the move was not a direct one, but depended on national geography and style. In some places a decorative rococo style predominated, in others a fiercely mannerist idiom. Although it post-dated some of the turbulent minor-mode works, the literary movement of *Sturm und Drang* provided the context for some of the most intense music of the mid-eighteenth century. That great observer of mid-eighteenth-century style, the flautist Johann Joachim Quantz (1697–1773), characterised it well in his treatise *On Playing the Flute*:

> In recent times there are two peoples in particular who have earned considerable esteem through their improvement of musical style; led by their natural proclivities they have each taken different paths to achieve this goal ... the Italian manner of playing is arbitrary, extravagant, artificial, obscure, frequently bold and bizarre, and difficult in execution ... the French manner of playing is slavish, yet modest, distinct, neat and true in execution, easy to imitate, neither profound nor obscure but comprehensible to everyone ...

There have always been such national divergencies in musical taste, but as travel became ever more common and idioms overlapped, a consensus emerged around what is today referred to as the classical style. And as these composers explored new styles in the mid-eighteenth century, there was one form which the emerging masters all used to advance their work: the symphony.

10

Symphonists

The musical format of the symphony has become one of the essential genres of Western music, and a surprisingly long-lasting one; you have only to look at the programmes of concert halls around the world to see how the symphony dominates orchestral offerings. This is partly a reflection of how backward-looking our concerts often are, but it is equally a measure of the staying power of pieces which performers, conductors and audiences alike judge to be great. From Haydn and Mozart, Beethoven and Brahms, to Tchaikovsky and Mahler, Sibelius and Shostakovich, the symphony seems to sweep all before it in popular appeal.

The mid-eighteenth century was a period when the skills of instrumentalists were developing quickly; there was an increasing emphasis on the growth of the group skills which aided the formation of ensembles and orchestras. Instruments themselves were developing too, so that by the middle of the century the string-based ensemble was complemented by woodwind and brass, setting the fundamentals of the varied orchestration which was to dominate symphonic writing. The other element in this mixture is the emergence of the public concert, changing the circumstances of performance and extending it to a new audience. In London there had been small-scale concert events in various 'music-houses' and hostelries in the later seventeenth century (p. 115), but the first moves towards venues specially prepared for music came from John Banister, who as Roger North recorded:

procured a large room in Whitfryars, near the Temple back gate, and made a raised box for the musicians, whose modesty required curtains. The room was rounded with seats and small tables, alehouse fashion. One shilling was the price, and call for what you pleased: there was very good musick, for Banister found means to procure the best hands in town, and some voices to come and perform there, and there wanted no variety of humour.

The next development in London was down to a remarkable character, the 'small coal-man' Thomas Britton in Clerkenwell, who alongside his trade as a purveyor of coal was a collector of rare books, manuscripts and prints described in a subsequent sale as about 'English Divinity, Magick, and Chymistry'. Britton turned the upper floor of his warehouse into a music club which met for nearly forty years. His patrons crowded into a room with a window 'very little bigger than the Bunghole of a Cask', 'where any Body that is willing to take a hearty Sweat, may have the pleasure of hearing many notable Performances in the charming Science of Musick'. The lively chronicler of these events was one Ned Ward who wrote in *The London Spy*, 'Musick and wine are usually held to be such inseparable Companions, that the true Relish of one can never be enjoy'd without the Assistance of the other'. These early concerts were miscellaneous in content and enjoyable social gatherings in nature, and it took a while for them to become codified and respectable. Britton's pioneering concerts were developed by the more prestigious Academy of Ancient Music, and later in the seventeenth century by the Concert of Ancient Music, established by the Earl of Sandwich. This had a distinctly backward-looking impetus, and as such is an important precursor to the establishment of the musical canon in the nineteenth century (p. 164); it existed 'for the purpose of preserving, by means of regular performances, the great works of the older masters, which might otherwise, through the desire of novelty, be allowed to fall into oblivion'.

In Paris the Concerts Spirituels, founded in 1725, began from mid-century to include secular music. In Vienna public concerts first appeared during the 1750s. The belief that these public concerts were a natural consequence of the rise of the middle classes has been subject to some revision over the years; it was not until the first decades of the nineteenth century that the idea took root that the symphonic repertory represented the height of culture (p. 162). But there was an increasing awareness, and in some circles veneration, of older music.

The symphony did not emerge fully formed in the eighteenth century; it grew out of the three-movement structure of the opera overture which became well established through the years of baroque opera – usually consisting of a call-to-action Allegro, a contrasted lyrical slower movement, and a final quick movement sometimes in a dance form. At some point the three-movement form of the opera overture was added to, interpolating an extra movement in the dance form of a minuet. An example of that new form was written by the Viennese composer Georg Matthias Monn (1717–50) on 24 May 1740, and his Symphony in D with flutes and horns has been identified by historians as the first four-movement symphony, though it seems untypical of his output and the piece did not have a wide circulation. More influential was Johann Stamitz (1717–57), who drew on the skills of the musicians at the Mannheim court and developed them to such a degree that they were famously referred to as 'an army of generals, equally fit to plan a battle as to fight it'. Stamitz uses a full battery of orchestral effects, ranging from hushed *pianissimi* to huge crescendos, all aimed at creating brilliant and impressive noise. It was said by the poet and musician C. F. Schubart that 'nowhere in performance were light and shade better marked. Nowhere were the half and whole tints of the orchestral palette more clearly expressed.' Stamitz's symphonies established the four-movement form that became common, and the 'Mannheim crescendo' became a well-known device, picked up a generation later by Rossini in his opera overtures (p. 176).

In outline, the first movements of these early symphonies, such as those by Giovanni Battista Sammartini (1700/1–75), have a parallel in the plan of the emerging keyboard sonata, with a first and second subject moving to a new key, a development section, and a return to the opening material, now back in the home key. These forms are relatively predictable, and perhaps unexciting. But the mould (if it ever consciously existed) was quick to be broken by individual composers, such as in the fascinatingly quirky symphonies by C. P. E. Bach (*66), full of exuberance, sudden dramatic gestures and harmonic jolts, well worth exploring in the recordings by Trevor Pinnock's English Concert and others.

Bach's younger son Johann Christian (1735–82), who was a prolific composer of opera, moved to London and wrote attractive, conventional symphonies following the Mannheim model, including some delightful ones for double orchestra, as well as many keyboard concertos which build on the contrasts of the baroque concerto. The eight-year-old Mozart met him soon after arriving in London in 1764; he heard and learned from his work. As a result of a thirst for the symphony, many hundreds of them were published as the century went on, by composers whom we now regard as minor and forgettable. But some of the choices of history may be arbitrary; among the fine lesser-known composers are those with Bohemian origins, who wrote expressive symphonies with a dark tinge in minor keys, including Johann Baptist Vanhal (1739–1813) and Leopold Koželuch (1747–1818), who worked in Vienna after Mozart. Among the many contemporaries writing concertos, a significant figure was Joseph Bologne, Chevalier de Saint-Georges (1745–99), from Guadeloupe, one of the first mixed-race composers to make an impact with his *symphonies concertantes* Op. 9 of 1777; he was also involved in persuading Haydn to write his symphonies for Paris.

Before our time, Joseph Haydn (1732–1809) tended to be regarded as a mere forerunner of those who came after him: 'the father of the symphony' was the rather patronising phrase. But especially at his place of employment in the country at the palace of Eszterháza, he had, as he put it, the 'need to become original', so he was able to experiment in those works; he then brought his insights to the works written for public consumption in Paris and London. Unusually for the time, Haydn had by the end of the eighteenth century acquired international fame, his music often featuring on the main concert programmes in London and Vienna. Enthusiastic scholarship, excellent performances and recordings have now left us with a dilemma: where to start among the riches of Haydn's numbered 104 symphonies? My suggestion would be to take a very few sample works from each period of his productive life. There are three early colourful programmatic pieces based around the hours of the day: *Le Matin* (No. 6), *Le Midi* (No. 7) and *Le Soir* (No. 8), which feature solos for the orchestral instruments. Among the middle-period works are a magnificent group of so-called *Sturm und Drang* symphonies related, like C. P. E. Bach's symphonies, to the turbulent literary movement of the time, especially *La passione* (No. 49), 'Maria Theresia' (No. 48) and the famous 'Farewell' (No. 45). In the 'Farewell' the composer draws the attention of his employer to the pressures of the performers' lives in the country; they creep offstage during the last movement, gradually reducing the forces so that there are only two violinists left at the close: a witty but polite protest piece that apparently made its point. The greatest of this group is surely the 'Trauer' (No. 44), an impassioned, taut, minor-mode work with a slow movement that Haydn said he wanted played at his funeral (*67). Its spare textures include a minuet in canon and a hard-driven finale.

Later symphonies take us to a set written for Paris, including those nicknamed the 'Bear' (No. 82), the 'Hen' (No. 83) and *La Reine* (No. 85); and finally there are the gloriously mature London symphonies for Haydn's concerts in the capital in 1791, arranged by the impresario Johann Peter Salomon. These feature the 'Surprise' (No. 94), including its famous unexpected fortissimo chord in the slow movement, designed to wake the slumbering listener; the 'Miracle' (No. 96), named after the incident in which a chandelier fell into the audience without injuring anyone, though this is now believed to have occurred on a different occasion; the magnificently mature No. 99 in E flat, perhaps less played because it lacks a nickname; the 'Clock' (No. 101), with its rhythmically ticking slow movement; and the 'Drumroll' (No. 103), which unexpectedly begins with a solo timpani roll. The appearance of Haydn in London caused great excitement: he presided at the keyboard himself for Salomon's concerts, and the *Musical Chronicle* reported that 'never, perhaps was there a richer musical treat. It is not wonderful that to souls capable of being touched by music, Haydn should be an object of homage, and even of idolatry; for like our own Shakespeare, he moves and governs the passions at his will. His new Grand Overture was pronounced by every scientific ear to be a most wonderful composition.' In these symphonies, finishing with the 'London' (No. 104), Haydn achieves a synthesis of counterpoint and melody, of brilliance and subtlety, that sums up the enquiring spirit of the Enlightenment: they breathe the spirit of a composer who had both the good fortune and the ability to be positive about life and its possibilities, supported as he was first by enlightened patronage and then by skilful commercial management. Following the pioneering complete recording of the symphonies under Antal Doráti, and then Ádám Fischer and his Austro-Hungarian Haydn Orchestra, period-instrument performances of all the symphonies have now been assembled into a complete set directed by Christopher Hogwood, Frans Brüggen and Ottavio Dantone.

Haydn listed his own string quartets, in the days before that form acquired such weight, under the catch-all title 'divertimento', and indeed such 'divertimenti a quat-tro' were a popular part of entertainment music, especially for the outdoors. Haydn's Ops. 1, 2 and 3 divertimenti tend to have five movements, including two minuets, all worked with strong unisons, original textures and effects. It would scarcely mat-ter how many instruments played these pieces. It is with his quartets Op. 9 and Op. 17 that Haydn creates the world of the quartet for four solo string instruments that was to prove so rewarding for him and us. In his Op. 20 his full personality emerges. It is revealing that in order to create the special character of the quartet where the four voices are truly equal, Haydn goes back to the baroque and writes finales in the form of fugues. These are often brief but highly effective, and there are dark shad-ows in the F minor Quartet Op. 20 No. 5, a concise but turbulent work.

It was not until almost a decade later that Haydn returned to the form with his Op. 33 quartets which he described as written 'in an entirely new and spe-cial manner'. He often develops a movement from a single theme, showing total economy of musical gesture, as if he is stimulating his imagination by confining it, forcing it to work within limited scope. In the later Op. 50 as well as Op. 33 there are jokes galore, but they are witticisms based on musical arguments, with unexpected pauses and sudden modulations. There are so many gems among the Ops. 54, 55 and 64 sets: one matchless moment comes in the C major Quartet Op. 54 No. 2, where in the course of a partly slow finale, itself a revolutionary idea, the cello rises magically from its very lowest note through, up and over the other parts, a highly original effect. Full maturity is achieved in Ops. 71, 74 and 76, where the folk roots of Haydn's inspiration rub shoulders with newly simple, almost vocal melodies whose harmoniousness looks forward to the new age of the Enlightenment.

There are many highlights too among Haydn's keyboard works, including the fine Sonata in A flat No. 46 with its aching Adagio in D flat and buzzing perpetual motion finale, and the E minor No. 34 with a skipping first movement growing upwards from the bass, before the final mature works which he wrote in London, Nos. 50–52. The superb Variations in F minor are based on two contrasted themes in minor and major which are varied in alternation – quite unlike conventional variations, these develop to a powerfully dissonant climax before evaporating into nothing.

The Masses that Haydn wrote for Prince Nikolaus Esterházy late in life equally show him bringing the musical thinking of a lifetime to bear on the texts. The Mass in D minor, known as the 'Nelson' because news of Lord Nelson's naval victory at the Battle of the Nile arrived as Haydn was writing it, has a magnificent sweep and confidence, and in the Benedictus the sudden call of the trumpets gives a vivid meaning to Haydn's original title 'Missa in angustiis': Mass in time of peril. The succeeding Masses, including the *Theresienmesse*, the *Creation* Mass and the *Harmoniemesse* (his last major work), all include music of serene confidence. Haydn's fame has been more dependent on the immediate success and repeated performances of his two great oratorios, *The Creation* and *The Seasons*, to libretti adapted by Baron van Swieten, the Viennese courtier who supported Mozart; they are immediately accessible, full of brilliant word-painting and sonic effects. Haydn was inspired by the large-scale performances of oratorios by Handel which he heard when he visited London, and we can imagine the effect these works had on the Viennese public when we read the enthusiastic accounts of their reception, and the resounding success that Haydn met with at the end of his productive life. These works are another sign that music is being pushed increasingly into the communal sphere as the eighteenth century moves into the public world of the nineteenth, while through it all Haydn retained to the end his profound commitment to God and his creation of the universe.

*

It was arguably in the small-scale music of the eighteenth century that the full subtlety of the classical style emerged, balancing instrumental skills, dense musical argument and expressive dialogue. Haydn's sonatas and string quartets, Mozart's chamber music and Beethoven's lifetime series of piano sonatas are some of the great peaks of Western music, though they have often been thought of as secondary to the achievements of their big orchestral works. Goethe described the act of playing string quartets as 'four reasonable people conversing', which is an apt way to understand the concept of Enlightenment, the most important context for the emerging musical world of the late eighteenth century. Born of a new humanism that valued the power of reason and the intellect, both in the form of bold controlling despotism as practised by the idealistic Emperor Joseph II (who supported and encouraged Mozart), and in the form of a liberating freedom for the individual, the Enlightenment radically changed ways of thinking and behaving. Free discussion of social and religious issues, so long frowned upon or repressed, was now enabled; for composers, it marked a vital transition from the support of courts and patrons to the far more volatile opinions of the public and the marketplace.

We know that Mozart and Haydn respected each other's work very deeply – who else, we may speculate, understood the work of the other so fully? Mozart dedicated a set of six quartets to Haydn, and it was at a quartet party that Haydn told Mozart's father Leopold how he esteemed his son as the greatest composer known to him. It is an enjoyable idea that, as portrayed in the film *Amadeus*, Wolfgang Amadeus Mozart (1756–91) was a complete innocent, who lived a thoughtless, indulgent life yet produced some of the greatest music ever written. It reinforces so many of the myths about Mozart: the tragic character who died young, who was poor and had to beg for help, who was exploited by those around him and whose music was never really understood. The film provides a stimulating basis for a discussion around the nature of genius: an exploration of the difference between the mere talent and political acceptability shown by Mozart's great rival Antonio Salieri (1750–1825), who wrote decent, effective and well-made music, and the depth and long-lasting power of Mozart's own work.

Mozart knew he was good at what he did. He had been led to believe in his own talent from his earliest years by his father Leopold. Every moment of his prodigious development as a performer and composer was chronicled by the proud parent. Leopold not only helped teach and mould his son, but then exploited him and his sister Nannerl relentlessly, taking them around the cities and courts of

Europe to display their skills in a way that must have left a deep imprint on their personalities (Plate 16). We know, because Leopold was so proud of his achievements, exactly when Mozart began to learn and to compose. We can see, in the musical notebook Leopold kept, the eight minuets that Wolfgang learned to play when he was four. There followed a Scherzo by the composer Georg Christoph Wagenseil that 'was learnt by Wolfgangerl on 24 January 1761', three days before his fifth birthday, 'between 9 and 9.30 in the evening' – you cannot get much more precise than that. Then there were the earliest pieces Wolfgang is supposed to have composed, in the first few months after he turned five, written down (and most likely corrected or improved) by his father.

Mozart developed so fast partly because, like Bach before him, he came from a family of musicians and made music every day. But he was also a genius at learning from what he did. Mozart absorbed other composers' music, whether his father's, or that of Wagenseil, or Johann Christian Bach or later his great friend Michael Haydn (1737–1806), who was Joseph's younger brother and worked in Salzburg; but one senses that Mozart always knew that he could do better and knew how to achieve it. He absorbed music constantly: a famous story which may well be true has him in Rome, listening to the music in the Sistine Chapel, and writing down from memory the supposedly secret embellishments to Gregorio Allegri's (c. 1582–1652) famous chant-based *Miserere* (*83). Mozart was an extremely productive composer and took massive leaps forward in his all-too-brief composing life. It used to be supposed that Mozart composed from pure inspiration, rarely stopping to consider what he wrote, but in fact he sketched ideas for his works, rejected many thoughts, left other ideas incomplete and stored them away in case he needed them in the future.

Mozart engaged with the symphony in no less a continuous fashion through his composing life than did Haydn, in his case transforming the genre from innocent entertainment and effective gesture to deep feeling and subtle argument. Given that some early symphonies that circulated are uncertain in their attribution, it is likely that Mozart wrote nearly fifty symphonies rather than the standard accepted number of forty-one. Recent revivals have revealed the attractiveness of the early symphonies: there are some that burst with life, including No. 14 in D.

The middle-period symphonies take Mozart into maturity: the elegant No. 29 in A and the stormy No. 25 in G minor (used as the title music for *Amadeus*). It is in the next group of symphonies that Mozart's genius fully emerges: the effervescent 'Paris' Symphony No. 31 in D, where we learn from Mozart's letters that the audience burst into applause during the piece, so delighted were they by its effects; the sparkling 'Haffner' No. 35 in D; the 'Linz' No. 36 in C, with its yearning, heart-rending sequences in the finale; and the 'Prague' No. 38 in D which anticipates *Don Giovanni* with its tremendous dark, slow introduction, but moves to an effervescent conclusion.

The great three final symphonies, No. 39 in E flat, No. 40 in G minor and No. 41 in C, were written in an astonishingly short space of time in the summer of 1788. It has sometimes been said that they were never performed in Mozart's lifetime, giving them a romantic aura, but there were occasions on Mozart's final concert tours where they could have been heard. They are resoundingly practical works: the famous G minor Symphony even has two versions, with and without clarinets. Each of these works has its own character, though they are often performed together; indeed the conductor Nikolaus Harnoncourt argued at the end of his life that they formed one 'instrumental oratorio'. No. 39 is the gentlest of the three, with a distinctive wind sonority of clarinets and flutes but no oboes, and (once past the grand introduction) a lilting triple-time first movement. No. 40 has become the most popular of Mozart's symphonies, surely at least partly because it allows for such a wide range of interpretations, its G minor first movement sounding passionate, tragic or indeed graceful in different performances. No. 41, later christened the 'Jupiter', is a peerless symphonic argument that culminates in one of the most remarkable movements, a fugal finale that looks back to the baroque while combining five themes into one stupendous coda at the end. It is rather too easy to regard this as Mozart's conscious symphonic testament; as the writer Hans Keller said of this tendency, 'by all means let us be wise after the event, so long as we are sure we are being wise'. What is perhaps surprising is that Mozart did not go on to write any other symphonies in the tragically short three years that remained to him. After a period when only the most famous later symphonies were widely played and recorded, there are now several complete recordings of all Mozart's symphonies: the pioneering set played on period instruments by Christopher Hogwood and the Academy of Ancient Music launched a fresh approach to the classical repertory, which was followed up by Trevor Pinnock, Nikolaus Harnoncourt and many others.

Opera was the genre to which Mozart continually aspired: success or failure in this area was critical to a composer, and Mozart learned very early the routines of serious opera filled with *da capo* arias that repeat after a middle section. That produced lengthy impressive works like *Mitridate*, written when he was fourteen for performance in Italy, and a success in its time. He developed steadily through a succession of operas including *La finta giardiniera*, written for the carnival period in Munich shortly before he was nineteen, whose variety and flexibility of style marks a great advance. Among these early operas I have a special admiration for *Lucio Silla* (which comes across as both expressive and virtuosic in the recording under Harnoncourt with the combined soprano talents of Cecilia Bartoli, Dawn Upshaw and Edita Gruberová). After some uncompleted projects over the following years, nothing prepares us for the impact of his next opera, *Idomeneo*: a great tragic masterpiece with dark colourings and superb orchestral writing featuring the skills of the wind players. Part of Mozart's genius was to absorb the musical world around him and improve on it; after *Idomeneo* comes a German opera for the German court in Vienna, *Die Entführung aus dem Serail*. This is a *singspiel*, an opera with spoken dialogue rather than recitative (as *Die Zauberflöte* was also to be), inspired by the exotic taste for all things Eastern. The plot revolves around Belmonte's attempt to rescue the virtuous Konstanze from the harem of the Pasha Selim and his grotesque comic servant Osmin. Mozart's music expands audibly; it rises to new heights in the stratospheric writing for the two female leads, Konstanze and Blonde, and plumbs new depths for Osmin. Yet the shape of this opera is still relatively conventional, with its formal arias and short third act to wrap up the action. It is a small step for Mozart, but a huge leap for opera, to the first of the three works he wrote to libretti by Lorenzo da Ponte, *Le Nozze di Figaro* (*65).

Figaro is one of the enduring operas in the repertory, and like its two successors *Don Giovanni* and *Così fan tutte*, it deals with real people in real situations, cutting across the class structure of society in a way that must have seemed truly revolutionary. The play by Beaumarchais on which Da Ponte based *Figaro* is actually more radical; some of its fiercer elements of social criticism were toned down. However, the tensions are still there in the story of a Count who enjoys his rights over his female servants, while neglecting his wife, the Countess. The maid Susanna, who is targeted by the Count, and her love Figaro manage to expose the Count's duplicity on their wedding day. It could be a cruel tale, but Mozart clothes it in music of surpassing beauty and subtlety, writing ensembles that bring together the complexities of the characters in a way rarely matched before or since, and elevating the emotions of betrayal, anger and innocent love onto the highest level of feeling. The arias of this opera, from 'Voi che sapete', the artless paean to love by the pageboy Cherubino, to the Countess's dignified 'Dove sono', are famous pieces on their own, but it is the dramatic sweep of each act, the superb musical planning, and the denouement as the Count is exposed and the Countess uneasily forgives him, that make it one of the greatest operas of all time.

The second Da Ponte opera, *Don Giovanni*, written for Prague where *Figaro* had been a great success, is almost a morality tale, a stern reproach to loose living, as is made clear in the moralistic final ensemble after Giovanni has been dragged down to hell for his sins. Here Mozart achieves something quite different from the human warmth of his other operas; within the context of a comedy (he called the work a *dramma giocoso*) he creates an elemental conflict between the forces of good and evil, expressed in music of the most demonic strength. Mozart's third Da Ponte collaboration, *Così fan tutte*, was for a long time frowned upon because of its dubious moral tone. It is a story of two sisters swapping their lovers through the provocation of the arch-manipulator Don Alfonso. They all demonstrate their infidelity in a way that invariably leaves the listener feeling uncomfortable, but set in a perfectly shaped musical language of seductive sensuality and human warmth.

The story of Mozart's engagement with opera continues right into his final year, with the intertwined composition of two totally different works in 1791, *La Clemenza di Tito*, a commission for the celebrations surrounding the coronation of Leopold II as Emperor of Bohemia, and *Die Zauberflöte* (The Magic Flute), for his friend Emanuel Schikaneder's out-of-town venue the Freyhaustheater, which was started before *Clemenza* and returned to after that was completed. The two works are completely contrasted: *Clemenza* is a noble elevated piece in the tradition of serious opera, which became Mozart's most revered work after his death but then faded from popularity, to be revived in recent times; *Zauberflöte*, with a racy libretto by Schikaneder himself, produces a truly magical score of the utmost sophistication in a popular genre, which has proved itself open to all manner of interpretation and stage ingenuity in the years since it was written. *Clemenza* did not go down well at the emperor's coronation, but *Zauberflöte* was a great commercial success, enjoyed by the crowds who flocked to see it, and which might well have sustained its composer into the next year, had he lived to enjoy it. But ten weeks after the opera opened, Mozart was dead.

Mozart is such a dominating presence in the second half of the eighteenth century that it is easy to ignore the figures who surrounded him and had great success in their day. In the wind-band music of the finale to *Don Giovanni*, Mozart quoted some music including the hugely popular opera *Una cosa rara* by Vicente Martín y Soler (1754–1806) alongside his own *Figaro*. Giuseppe Gazzaniga (1743–1818) had already written an opera on the story of Don Giovanni in 1787. There is a revival of interest today in the best brilliant showpiece arias (though rarely the whole operas) of Niccolò Jommelli (1714–74) from Naples, whom Mozart met; he is credited with having specified new subtleties of shading and dynamics in his scores, moving towards a scenario where the performer was given instructions rather than being granted total freedom. Domenico Cimarosa (1749–1801) wrote the lively *Il matrimonio segreto* which is still performed.

The highlights of Mozart's successful years in Vienna after 1781 are his piano concertos, a genre which he created for himself to play in public. Over the following four years he wrote fifteen of his twenty-seven piano concertos, which he played himself in concerts. We read of Mozart's instrument being transported across the city. It had an unusual pedal attachment, which like an organ pedalboard added notes in the bass register, and which may have helped Mozart's direction of the ensemble. In these concertos Mozart reaches into a new world of expressive virtuosity, developing the form into what has been described as the symphonic concerto. These were the most personal of his creations, full of arias that, as it were, he wrote for himself to sing, symphonies that he wrote for himself to play. Often the solo parts require elaboration and improvisation, while the orchestral parts are superbly crafted for solo wind instruments and strings to create an effect at once intimate and grand. Any of the series of later piano concertos would provide an ideal introduction to Mozart's supreme skill: the tragic, intense Concerto No. 20 in D minor, or the poised and witty Concerto No. 21 in C (its central movement so innovative with its throbbing triplets and aching dissonances on the bassoon), misleadingly known in recent years as the 'Elvira Madigan' for its use in that film. The tremendous Concerto No. 24 in C minor is the darkest of these pieces, while the grandest and most extrovert is the magnificent Concerto No. 25 in C. The final one that sums up so much of Mozart's last period of composition is the B flat Concerto No. 27, with its wistful last movement based on a song he wrote around the same time called 'Longing for Spring'.

Mozart also wrote concertos for the horn, for a colleague Joseph Leutgeb with whom he evidently had a jovial relationship to judge from the sarcastic markings in his autograph scores, and one superb, deeply moving Clarinet Concerto, completed in the last year of his life, which was for his friend Anton Stadler to play on the basset clarinet, an extended instrument with an added lower range. Some of Mozart's finest piano writing occurs in the duets for four hands: the magnificent Sonata in F and the graceful Variations in G are outstanding. Among his single piano movements are his most personal utterances: the Adagio in B minor and the Rondo in A minor are works of deathly resignation and grief, while the Little Gigue in G is so quirky in its darting lines that it seems to anticipate twelve-note writing.

The end of Mozart's brief life continues to be a puzzle. Once he had moved to Vienna in 1781, kicking the shackles of Salzburg away, he had no visible means of support. He was full of hopes that Vienna would be the perfect city for his genius, and for a time he was highly successful. He gave lessons, put on concerts and published his music, until economic circumstances changed and he struggled to make a living. Whether we believe that he was needlessly extravagant or (as some of his early biographers tried to explain it) needlessly generous and often exploited by those around him, it is true that he was finally forced to borrow money from his friends. He might have followed Haydn to London, but instead fell ill. Again, do not believe the story told in the film *Amadeus* that Salieri helped Mozart to write down his Requiem: that is total fantasy. The truth is in fact slightly stranger; the work was commissioned by a nobleman, Count Walsegg, who wanted to pass it off as his own work. Mozart struggled with the composition, leaving numerous sketches on his death; his wife Constanze attempted to have them completed by his pupils in order that the work could be performed (and more importantly to her, paid for). For all its imperfections and in spite of its incompleteness, Mozart's Requiem is one of his most compelling pieces, grounded in the past of baroque music with its use of Handelian fugues and plainchant themes, yet looking forward in a visionary way.

The direct evidence of Mozart's dedicated attitude to his craft and his own compositions can be seen from the catalogue of his works that he began to compile in 1784. Every work has its date, scoring and opening line of music carefully notated. The most touching aspect of this notebook, now preserved in the British Library, is that Mozart wrote its title as 'Thematic Catalogue from 1784 to 1____', clearly intending that it would be used into the future. At the end, after the works he completed before his untimely death in 1791, are pages and pages of blank staves, waiting for the music he would never write.

11

Individuals

The essence of the appeal of nineteenth-century music, which has emerged in the later work of Haydn and Mozart, and will dominate the musical world after Beethoven, is the quest for individual expression. No longer would the role of the composer be to take the common language of the time and to polish it, say something new in it, and thus contribute to the enlightened society of the time. The composer's function would be increasingly to define his or her individuality by creating something new, something previously unthought and unexpressed, and thus reveal their own inner self to the world. And it was in Ludwig van Beethoven (1770–1827) that this search for individuality found its ideal hero, expressed admiringly by the writer and composer E. T. A. Hoffmann, who summed up the feelings of the age by praising Haydn and Mozart as predecessors, but said that it was Beethoven whose music 'opens up to the realm of the monstrous and the immeasurable . . . setting in motion the lever of fear, awe, horror, suffering, and wakens just that infinite longing which is the essence of romanticism'.

Beethoven's career reflects the changing pressures on performers and composers as this transformation took root. He came from a family that served the court of the Elector of Cologne and he played the harpsichord in the court orchestra. His talent as a player quickly became recognised, and after a visit to Vienna in 1787 when he may possibly have met Mozart, he returned to Vienna in 1792 to study with Haydn, still supported by a patron, Prince Lichnowsky, through whom he entered Viennese society. Conscious of his status as a creative artist, Beethoven never suffered fools gladly, and some of his reported comments have an aggressive air, and encapsulate the spirit of changing times. He is supposed to have retorted to one critic of his music, 'I did not write them for you, but for a later age': the new pressure of the possible verdict of posterity was beginning to loom large for composers.

However viewed in the context of changing centuries, it is a big step from the perfectly crafted, wonderfully expressive symphonies of Haydn and Mozart to the explosive nine symphonies by Beethoven. He wrote symphonies in each period of his creative life; the immense variety of the interpretations of these master-works over the decades, by conductors from Wilhelm Furtwängler and Arturo Toscanini via Carlos Kleiber and Herbert von Karajan to Roger Norrington and Simon Rattle, gives us just some idea of their universal appeal. The First Symphony in C, born from Haydnesque models, starts with a dissonant chord and ends with a brilliant scamper; it is a witty and concentrated work, constantly surprising our expectations in each of its four movements. The Second Symphony in D is already on a larger scale, its structures and phrase-lengths extended; the slow introduction springs into the constant action of the first movement, the second movement's Larghetto is more relaxed, and the relentless finale puzzled contemporaries, described by one critic at the time as 'a crass monster, a hideously writhing wounded dragon, that refuses to expire, and though bleeding in the finale, furiously beats about with its tail erect'. Such a reaction speaks of the sheer unfamiliarity of Beethoven's expression, and it is that impact which present-day performances should somehow manage to recreate from music already over two centuries old.

The extraordinary expansion of the Third Symphony in E flat, known as the 'Eroica', is by a long way the biggest symphonic structure heard up to that time. Beethoven here takes the musical argument of the symphony onto a vast canvas, enlarging its emotional scope into an artistic and philosophical statement of great weight. Its first movement alone is unprecedented in its power and length, with a long coda that allows the conflicts of the movement to be resolved. The second movement is a funeral march of deep eloquence whose central fugal section collapses into another long coda, this one totally unresolved. It is left to the energetic scherzo and the more optimistic finale (based on a theme from his music to *The Creatures of Prometheus*) to pull the music to its powerful conclusion. Originally conceived as a homage to Napoleon, Beethoven furiously scratched out that dedication upon learning that Napoleon had proclaimed himself emperor, and the work stands instead as a heroic tribute to the triumph of the human spirit.

The Fourth Symphony in B flat is seemingly smaller but astonishingly pungent, full of rhythmic energy right up to the racing finale. The Fifth Symphony in C minor (*64) starts with the famous four-note unison call (p. 8), which as David Cairns has memorably written 'seems to spring at the audience and seize it by the throat', and ends (after a winding, suspenseful transition to the finale) in a blazing C major. It has become perhaps the most famous symphony in the entire repertory, partly because of its symbolic use in wartime. It certainly pays homage to the libertarian sounds of the French Revolution, especially in its triumphant finale, but it has managed to transcend the specifics of that age and speak across the centuries. Here we feel there is an intense personal drama being narrated as if for the first time, which takes us through deep suffering and uncertainty to final overwhelming triumph: the victory of the individual. Among the many fine interpreters of this Beethoven masterpiece, Carlos Kleiber stands out for his power and precision.

Beethoven's Sixth Symphony, by complete contrast, is the 'Pastoral' in F, an innocently inviting work with which any new listener could start. There are quite precise descriptions of nature at the head of each movement: the first is titled 'Pleasant feelings awakened on arrival in the countryside'; the second is a 'Scene by the brook' – but we quickly realise that the music is about more than mere description: it is about feelings, a response to nature. With his deep love of the countryside, Beethoven has reflected the storms and thunder, country dances and setting sun in a work of the highest symphonic sophistication. With the Seventh Symphony in A we are back on the largest scale with a supremely well-argued work of almost constant positivity: a slow introduction leads to a taut, dance-driven first movement which has great impetus; a second movement Allegretto, based on an almost melody-less tag; a Presto scherzo; and then a fiercely insistent Allegro con brio, with

153

sudden accents, runs of semiquavers, clarion horn-calls and a universal excitement which leads to the final outburst. Richard Wagner described this symphony as 'the apotheosis of the dance'. The Eighth Symphony in F, though on a smaller canvas, combines all the wit, scope and propulsive argument of the earlier symphonies into a concentrated structure that feels at every point as if it might explode. Its opening is sudden, no slow introduction, and its themes are taut and short; the second movement is hardly slow, reminiscent of the ticking mechanism of a clock; the third is for once a minuet rather than a scherzo, while the finale is at once exciting and alarming – racing almost out of control and veering into unexpected keys with frantic unisons, before it is pulled back to the home key of F major.

In his Symphony No. 9 in D minor Beethoven achieves a work which has become iconic in the story of the symphony and of classical music, even though it was for its time entirely untypical for including vocal soloists and a chorus. Within the established four-movement structure he achieves a vision of the world, of the universe and of humanity, which has never been surpassed. It has been interpreted as the composer's autobiography, but its aims are surely bigger than that. The opening Allegro emerges as if out of nowhere and acquires a cosmic energy in its working-out; the Scherzo comes second, too insistent and violent to be thought of as fun; and then the third movement, marked 'Adagio molto cantabile', is a serene set of double variations on two melodies, one a hymn-like theme which sings through the orchestra as it is elaborated by the strings. The finale of the symphony, introduced by recollections of the previous movements, is unique: a complex sequence of musical events that baffled early listeners and is still challenging to us. After the double basses of the orchestra try to imitate a vocal recitative, the sudden appearance of vocal soloists and choir, singing a text by Schiller called 'Ode to Joy', is unexpected and unexplained. Still more, the abrupt sequence of events in this movement is unpredictable, stopping and starting with elements like the Turkish march with grunting bassoon and percussion leading to a choral fugue, a mysterious still passage where the music seems to halt, 'Seid umschlungen, Millionen', and a final huge double fugue. But what shines through is the aspiration: both Schiller's text and the music point towards an ideal world, which can only be glimpsed, in which all men and women are united.

The central melody of the Ode to Joy itself is one of the most famous melodies ever written, simple and flowing, utterly memorable. Ironically, because of both its central place in Beethoven's symphonic output and its aspirational nature, simplified and mangled versions of this melody have been used for countless political and social purposes over the years, some nefarious, some idealistic; it has been used satirically in film (*A Clockwork Orange*) and arranged as the signature tune of the European Union. Leonard Bernstein changed the text into an Ode to Freedom when he conducted it to mark the fall of the Berlin Wall. The freshness and desperately assertive nature of Beethoven's vision never ceases to amaze us: the finale has rightly been described by Richard Wigmore as 'the most overwhelming expression of affirmative idealism in all music'. Here Beethoven claims his central position in the new age of the individual.

Beethoven contributed another great work to the choral tradition, and that is the *Missa Solemnis*, first performed in 1824, a daunting work for performers and listeners alike, stretching the capabilities of his players and singers to their utmost, and bringing the full weight of his symphonic thought to bear on the traditional texts of the Ordinary of the Mass. An earlier Mass setting, the Mass in C of 1807, had been written in response to a request from Haydn's patron Prince Esterházy, perhaps a reaction to the superb series of late Masses which Haydn himself had composed towards the end of his life. A choral work that has benefited from revival in the Beethoven anniversary year of 2020 is the oratorio *Christus am Ölberge* (Christ on the Mount of Olives), with echoes of Mozart's *La Clemenza di Tito* and demanding tenor solos. Not all Beethoven's occasional pieces are on this high level; indeed, dare one suggest he wrote more second-rate music than many great composers?

Beethoven's piano concertos take the existing Mozartian concerto concept of contrast and competition between soloist and orchestra and widen the picture, like moving from small screen to wide screen, with both protagonists working from a common source, sharing material and developing it together. Piano technology was developing fast, and pianos were bigger and more sonorous than before; orchestras were larger, and the scene of action had expanded into larger public concert halls. Beethoven sketched one concerto when he was fourteen, called No. O, but this survives only in a short score. What we now call No. 2 was written next in 1788, though it was subject to constant revision; it sounds influenced more by Haydn than by Mozart, though it has a strong Beethovenian stamp from its opening call to attention onwards. Its central movement is an Adagio which is decorated but then returns to simplicity, and its finale is full of disorientating off-beat rhythms. Beethoven played it in Prague in 1798 alongside the concerto we now know as No. 1, which had been written a few years earlier and subsequently revised.

In view of the tendency to venerate as fixed and final the works of 'great' composers such as Beethoven, which becomes ever more prevalent in the nineteenth century, it is notable how flexible the composer himself was towards the works that he played, for example introducing different cadenzas as he played them. It is difficult to imagine a wittier, more unbuttoned finale than that of the Piano Concerto No. 1 in C, with its syncopated rhythms and the soloist breaking away from the orchestra – it has no equal for sheer exuberance. By contrast the Third Piano Concerto in C minor is more solemn and restrained, proclaiming its emotions on the largest scale. Here Mozart is surely the model, as the key matches that of Mozart's darkest piano concerto and similarly begins in unison. The argument of the first movement is symphonic and taut, the central movement is one of Beethoven's deepest, elaborating an eloquent theme, while the finale uses the wind instruments to great effect.

The Fourth Piano Concerto was the last that Beethoven played himself, and has one of the most original openings of any concerto: the soloist begins alone, the orchestra answers in a different key, and we spend the movement pondering the way in which they can reconcile with each other. In one of his many perceptive remarks, Charles Rosen has observed how Beethoven articulates the first movement, developing from a slow harmonic pulse of two beats in the bar at the start, to the pianist's off-beat accents creating eight quick beats in the bar later on. Beethoven gave the first performance in a concert on 22 December 1808, which seems to have been typical of the circumstances of the time: a huge and sprawling programme, not very fully rehearsed, containing two symphonies, part of the Mass in C, as well as this premiere, and ending with the Choral Fantasy whose performance collapsed and had to be restarted. 'The concert must be called unsatisfactory in every respect,' wrote the Leipzig critic. Yet as observed by the writer and traveller J. F. Reichardt, the concerto was 'terribly difficult ... Beethoven played astonishingly well in the fastest possible tempi. The Adagio, a masterpiece of beautiful sustained melody, he actually sang on his instrument with a deep melancholy feeling which awakened its response in me.' So all was not lost; and the Fourth Concerto has survived to be one of the most valued and popular works in the repertory.

The final piano concerto, known as the 'Emperor', was not written by Beethoven for himself to play, as he was by then too deaf. Instead he writes out in great detail material that might have been improvised, including the bold opening flourishes for the soloist, and the unique transition from the magical slow movement to the bounding theme of the final Rondo Allegro. While the work certainly has aspects of the imperiousness of an emperor, the title was not Beethoven's. This huge and imposing work has stood the test of time at the heart of the piano concerto repertory, and marks the transition into the romantic vision of the virtuoso that would dominate the public concert world in the following decades.

Beethoven's life was continually tortured by two factors: his growing deafness, and his inability to form close personal relationships including marriage. Deafness caused him great depression and thoughts of suicide, expressed in the Heiligenstadt Testament of 1802 (a document he wrote that was never sent, but was intended to be read after his death): 'I must live alone like one who has been banished ... what a humiliation for me when someone next to me heard a flute in the distance and I heard nothing ... such incidents drove me to despair, a little more of that and I would have ended my life.' In fact, during the early 1800s he became increasingly successful, supported by a network of patrons who provided him with a stipend that ensured independence. Frustrated by his lack of a family, in 1815 on the death of his younger brother Caspar he became the guardian for his nephew Karl. This began a turbulent period of conflict with Karl's mother, Beethoven's sister-in-law Johanna, exacerbated after 1819 by total deafness and growing worry over Karl, concern about his own finances, and a general withdrawal from human contact. The political situation, with Napoleon finally defeated in 1815, did not help the performance of the large-scale works like the Ninth Symphony and the *Missa Solemnis* that Beethoven wanted to have played. His final years were depressive and isolated, and he caught an infection in 1826 from which he never recovered. But his death was marked by a large-scale funeral procession and public acclaim: the achievement of his music was recognised.

Beethoven's music in all genres developed through the periods of his composing life. His first set of piano sonatas appeared only after Haydn's last, when Mozart was already dead. In the developing world of the piano, instrument technology was moving on fast to create pianos of greater range and projection, to match the more public circumstances of performance. This produced a new world of the travelling virtuoso, among whom Johann Ladislaus Dussek (1760–1812) was outstanding. He originated the position of the soloist on stage playing side-on to the audience, so they could see his profile, and his impact was thus considerable: an account of a concert he gave in Prague in 1804 says that 'after the first few bars of his opening solo, the public uttered one general sigh. There was something magical in the way Dussek, with all his charming, graceful manner, and his wonderful touch, extracted from the instrument delightful and at the same time emphatic tones.' His music may not have lasted so well, but he clearly had an influence on Beethoven's style, as did the entrepreneurial Muzio Clementi (1752–1832), a publisher and promoter of pianos as well as a composer who did much to develop an idiomatic piano style. His understanding of emerging keyboard sonorities is very significant for Beethoven's work.

Beethoven was a very considerable pianist, as we learn from his pupil Carl Czerny: 'Nobody equalled him in the rapidity of his scales, double trills, skips, etc . . . his bearing when playing was masterfully quiet, noble and beautiful . . . his fingers were very powerful, not long, and broadened at the tips by much playing . . . he made frequent use of the pedals, much more frequent than is indicated in his work.' Beethoven learned from C. P. E. Bach and Haydn as well as Dussek and Clementi, and dedicated his first sonatas to Haydn. 'God knows why my piano music makes the worst impression on me, especially when it is badly played,' Beethoven scribbled in a notebook in 1804. Perhaps it was because he was being so original with the forms of the sonata. After the next sets of sonatas, Beethoven is increasingly inventive in structure. The single Sonata Op. 13, 'Pathétique', is a work of intense seriousness without remission. Beethoven unites the movements of the Sonata Op. 27 No. 1, calling it 'quasi una fantasia', where the impulsive form of the opening movements pushes the weight of the argument towards the finale. The same procedure returns in one of the most famous of all the sonatas, Op. 27 No. 2, later called the 'Moonlight' on account of its memorable and unusual opening movement, a melody over triplets marked Adagio sostenuto.

In his Sonata Op. 28 the 'Pastoral', Beethoven is breathing new life into old forms – here the drone bass which can be heard in eighteenth-century pastoral scenes and which features in the finale of Haydn's Symphony No. 104. The three sonatas of Op. 31 revert to an even more traditional plan, sometimes looking back to C. P. E. Bach in their spontaneity and fantasia-like improvisations. The Sonata Op. 53, the 'Waldstein' of 1804, is the culmination of the middle-period piano sonatas and also looks ahead to the writing of the late sonatas, exploiting the textures and range of the Érard piano that Beethoven had acquired from Paris the previous year. These innovations are intensified in the Sonata Op. 57 'Appassionata'. Only ten years separate this titanic work from his first piano sonatas, showing how rapid the development had been; the extremes of the keyboard, and wide dynamic and rhythmic contrasts, are constantly deployed.

In Beethoven's late piano sonatas and string quartets from the 1820s the personal nature of the communication takes us far beyond anything so far attempted. The sonatas still speak outwardly; the quartets speak inwardly. We struggle with their meaning and their logic; their rewards are deeply buried but intense. After the Sonata in A Op. 101, Beethoven concentrates on sculpting the forward movement of the whole piece in which the finale is a culmination. In the 'Hammerklavier' Sonata Op. 106, with its grand design involving a huge fugue, Beethoven proclaims the apotheosis of the 'display' sonata, here reformulated to express his life-and-death struggle, now visible on a public platform. It is a massive statement, drawing on every resource of the player; it should not sound easy to perform, as it is dauntingly difficult (and its finale, if taken at Beethoven's extremely fast metronome mark, is almost impossible).

The final sonatas turn inward: Ops. 109, 110 and 111 form a group all written around the time Beethoven was conceiving the *Missa Solemnis*. In Op. 109 in E the first movement presents two ideas, as a sonata is supposed to, but there seems to be no interaction between them. The final movement is a set of variations on a sublime theme that not only explore the theme but dissolve it. In Op. 110 in A flat the echoes of the baroque are very clear in the third movement which starts from a recitative and 'arioso dolente' that sounds like an echo of a Bach Passion, then moves into a fugue, the return of the arioso, and then an inversion of the fugue. Unlike the two other sonatas in this trilogy, this one ends with a hard-won triumph. In Op. 111 in C minor there are only two movements, as if the conflict of the sonata has been reduced to its barest essentials. It starts with a gruff call to action, a unison interval of the diminished seventh, but the Adagio movement that follows does not end in triumph. The variations do not behave in the usual way, varying the theme; they take it apart with rhapsodic trills and figurations of ever greater speed, which paradoxically attains complete stillness. At the final cadence, the whole of the music is both concentrated into one tiny moment and prolonged into timelessness.

The inward drama of the late string quartets, written between 1824 and 1826, is even more difficult to read, and equally rewarding to penetrate. Moving on from the mood he had explored in the 'Razumovsky' Quartets, with their extrovert drama and brilliant finales, Beethoven extrapolates that struggle on the largest scale in his daunting contrapuntal Grosse Fuge Op. 133, originally the finale to the Op. 130 quartet (it has also been arranged for string orchestra, where it seems marginally less awkward). In his Quartet in C sharp minor Op. 131, Beethoven takes us to an inner world with a dark but serene opening fugue, and then contradicts our expectations by offering seven linked movements, including a recitative, a set of variations, a scherzo, a little tragic Adagio in G sharp minor, and a final sonata-form Allegro – all linked into one transcendental sequence, with a clear sense of musical unity. These works took Beethoven far beyond the comprehension of his contemporaries, and some believed them to be simply the product of his deafness and despair. We wonder whether we understand them better than the audiences of Beethoven's time, given that they can now certainly be played well enough to allow us to try. They seem a key to an elusive personal, totally interior life in a way that is very rare in music.

With these concertos, his chamber music, and especially his nine symphonies, Beethoven stands at the heart of the canonic repertory that has come to dominate classical music performance. It is not difficult to see how this has come about, for Beethoven inspired the composers of the nineteenth century and continued to resonate through the twentieth century. Because of his relatively early death and often tragic life, Beethoven came to represent in vivid terms for the public the triumph of the creative artist against the circumstances of his life. That concept of the 'hero' is supported by the aspiration of so much of his music, from the 'Eroica' to the Ninth Symphony. And Beethoven's place at the tipping point from the classical spirit in music to the romantic imagination cannot be argued. But a great deal has changed since this first creation of the Western canon.

Beethoven still has a unique, central place in musical history, but for us the repertory has expanded vastly backwards as well as forwards. Composers today are much more likely to look back to a more distant past for inspiration, finding Beethoven's heroism foreign to their concerns. It is extremely noticeable how few contemporary composers cite Beethoven as a direct influence, and prefer instead to reach back to Bach, Purcell, Monteverdi or Machaut. It is a valid question as to whether Beethoven will continue to enjoy the central position for music-lovers that he has so far enjoyed. Partly this may relate to the freshness with which we approach the performance of his works, and the reinvigoration of interpretation brought about by the period-instrument movement has certainly aided that process. Whatever changing taste may swirl around his legacy, Beethoven's finest works will remain a cornerstone of what we believe to be, and agree to define as, great music.

12

Virtuosi

Musical eras are never clear cut: Beethoven's revolutionary art both brings to a close the classical period of the extended eighteenth century and also inaugurates the individualised personal expression of the nineteenth century. This sense of the obligation on the composer to be original, rather than to be a craftsman within an already established framework, is an essential part of the Romantic imagination. This brings with it a developed (some might say over-developed) sense of the self, of the contribution that only you can bring to artistic expression, and privileges individuality above all else. It leads to the concept of the 'great' composer and the 'great' work which has dominated so much of our thinking from then to now. It also begins to heighten the importance of the 'great' performer as a public individual through whom music speaks; and when composer and performer came together, as we shall see they did with Paganini the violinist and Liszt the pianist, the result had an electrifying attraction for audiences.

This is clearly another tipping point for the story of music: the moment at which the focus on the court and patronage becomes widened to include the whole public appeal of concert-giving and music-making, under the impact of radical social change in the first part of the nineteenth century. This had a profound impact on music-making. The decline of the aristocracy, and thus of the patronage that had supported so many composers, gave way to a market-led economy which threw the emphasis onto public events competing for the attention of paying audiences. The establishment of a strongly middle-class model of concert attendance and participation was a major factor in the life of great European cities, and lent a sense of ownership of the form to those newly minted members of the middle classes who wished to demonstrate their credentials. This is not to say that the tastes of the new middle class were always elevated, and popular light music featured in many concerts, but there was an aspirational element to their concert-going which supported the creation of a central repertory.

The balance between the importance of European cultural centres began to shift. The unquestioned leadership of Vienna at the end of the eighteenth century, with the succession of Haydn, Mozart and Beethoven, started to falter as its repertory became less adventurous. It passed instead to the rival cities of Paris and London, both expanding rapidly and consciously promoting concert life for a newly acquisitive and upwardly mobile public. Another key European centre was Leipzig, where Bach had worked. The Gewandhaus had been founded as a municipal organisation in 1781 and was well established; it was the home of Mendelssohn and Schumann; and many others came to perform or study there: Chopin, Berlioz and Brahms visited, Mahler worked there learning to conduct opera, from England the young Arthur Sullivan (p. 188) came to study, and one of the dominating figures of the nineteenth century, Richard Wagner, was born there.

Soloists and conductors began to travel internationally. The increasing ease of travel in the railway age, first around Europe, and then in America, enabled tours and concerts to spread reputations and create fame: the singer Jenny Lind gave a hundred concerts on her American tour of 1850–1. European musicians played in South America, and American conductors visited Europe to direct newly emerging ensembles. The standardisation of instruments, pitch and tuning became necessary, while publishers were in great demand to supply consistent performing parts and materials. A new professionalism, born of the marketplace, was emerging.

London's population more than doubled in size in the first half of the nineteenth century, and it has been estimated by the scholar Cyril Ehrlich that around 1840 there were some 7,000 active musicians in Britain. These were orchestral musicians as well as those who played in streets and taverns, and they were the backbone of an emerging profession. The Philharmonic Society in London brought together a professional orchestra in 1815 which was the first in Europe (among its innovations was support for the newest music: it paid Beethoven for the right to perform his Ninth Symphony, even though it had been dedicated and published in Vienna). There followed the Leipzig Gewandhaus under Mendelssohn from 1835 and the Vienna Philharmonic from 1842, while in Paris the Concerts du Conservatoire under violinist and composer François-Antoine Habeneck (1781–1849) developed an adventurous repertory and disciplined performances which were admired by Wagner among others. The public concert was now here to stay, and the growth of symphony orchestras as symbols of their cities was unstoppable: among the most famous, the Hallé in Manchester from 1858, and then in the 1880s the Boston Symphony, the Berlin Philharmonic, the Detroit Symphony and the Concertgebouw in Amsterdam all established themselves. A new performing tradition was being born.

One development to which this gave rise, which had immense influence from that day to this, was the gradual assembly of a 'canon' of musical works: a group of central pieces that were tacitly agreed to be at the core of the repertory. There had already been revivals of historic pieces by groups like the Academy of Ancient Music in London or François-Joseph Fétis's Concerts historiques in Paris in the 1830s, but this was on a different level. The importance of Beethoven was recognised early, and his work became regarded as central. Mendelssohn, Schumann and then Brahms followed, with some representation from Haydn and Mozart as the figures who prepared the way for Beethoven. It marked a new era in the emerging permanence of the world of music; it also inaugurated an era when the repertory became dangerously fixed in aspic. The oft-criticised 'museum culture' of orchestral concerts has its origins in this period.

On the other hand, the musician was still not treated with universal respect in the new world of social patronage. As reported by Wagner's biographer Ernest Newman, Carl Maria von Weber's son described the experience of a performer at a social gathering in London: 'his host greeted him condescendingly and pointed out to him his place which, in many salons, was separated by a cord from that of the guests ... He performed, was paid, and then had to leave without being regarded as one of the guests.' Clearly it was time for the performing musician to forge his own career, and establish his own relationship with his public.

The key aspect of the new world of public concert-giving was the growth of performers' virtuosity: that showy, demonstrative way of playing we have already encountered in the eighteenth-century concerto, one which draws attention to the performer's skill, sometimes at the expense of musical substance. This was one natural result of the building of larger concert halls, in which the performer had both to attract the public and to interact excitingly with them. Commentators were dubious: Claude Debussy, writing in his days as a critic, said, 'The attraction of the virtuoso for the public is very much like that of the circus for the crowd. There is always the hope that something dangerous may happen.' The first performer to successfully grasp the potential of extrovert virtuosity was undoubtedly the violinist Nicolò Paganini (1782–1840). In 1813 he gave his first concert in Milan which had the critics in raptures: 'genuinely incomprehensible. He performs certain runs, leaps, and double stops that have never been heard before from any violinist . . . in short, he is . . . one of the most artful violinists that the world has ever known.' He developed a specially dazzling style featuring the simultaneous use of the violin strings, darting arpeggios and the use of many hand positions which created a unique appeal. To the delight of supportive managers organising his travels, he mounted a great European tour in 1828–34 that created a furore. In London he gave fifteen concerts in the 3,300-capacity King's Theatre. Orchestras to accompany him had to be arranged, as well as other performers on the programme. Paganini was clever at choosing venues like opera houses that could accommodate bigger audiences than concert halls, even associating his performances with gambling in proposing a 'music casino' that combined them.

Paganini cultivated a special attraction with his audiences not only through his playing but through his devilish and haggard appearance; he cultivated the historic association of the violin with the devil across the ages. Some felt he even showed evidence of a Satanic origin, which only added to his allure. He single-handedly took on all the supposed traits of the dissolute artist: he gambled, he womanised, he self-advertised, but his technical prowess and his feats of dexterity were mind-boggling. When Heinrich Heine saw Paganini play in 1829, he described him as 'this vampyr with a violin, who would suck the money from our pockets', but was then completely won over by the force of his playing. The high prices that he and his promoters charged for his concerts created a sense of excitement and a sense of event: not only one of music's first public virtuosi, Paganini was also one of music's first great entrepreneurs, who knew his own value and exploited it to the utmost. His own music served his aims perfectly: several showy concertos for violin and orchestra, and the famous 24 Caprices which have challenged performers ever since and have stimulated variations by other composers (Plate 17).

The development of piano technology in the nineteenth century stimulated the growth of a virtuoso tradition among pianists. Already in Beethoven's output you can hear the impact of new pianos he acquired by the makers Érard and Broadwood on his musical style. Some pianos had extra pedals for special effects, such as percussion or the so-called 'Turkish stop' which activated a small bell. Large pianos with spans of seven octaves, strong metal frames and felt-covered hammers had a major impact; their sound was exponentially greater than the instruments of the late eighteenth century, and they created a style of piano playing which has remained fashionable to the present day. These pianos emerged from the concept of the 'English piano' developed by Broadwood and then by Pleyel, which favoured a big sound and deep tone, in contrast to the more precise small-scale Viennese pianos. This developed into a fusion of music and business with commercial results. Pianists would form alliances with manufacturers, and thus use their products exclusively (as survives today in advertisements for great pianists as 'a Steinway artist'); they would also publish their own material of piano tutorials and exercises. The growth of the piano as a domestic instrument provided a vital connection between public concert-giving and music-making in the home for the middle classes: you could hear a symphony in the concert hall and then attempt a piano-duet version in your salon. This was a new route to involvement in music-making.

The Romantic piano was also one of the factors which gave women composers and performers the opportunity to take the stage and escape from relative obscurity. Louise Farrenc (1804–75), teaching in Paris for most of her life, was encouraged by her husband to publish music and composed three substantial symphonies, a range of smaller studies, and variation sets for keyboard. Women composers active in the orchestral field are, regrettably, comparatively rare, but the German Luise Adolpha Le Beau (1850–1927) succeeded with the support of her parents in combating the opposition of the conservative musical establishment, and wrote a Symphony in F minor as well as an opera. Mendelssohn's sister Fanny Hensel (1805–47) and Schumann's wife Clara (1819–96) both made important contributions to this emancipation. Fanny can claim to have originated the concept of the 'song without words', some of which were published after her death, and she wrote in many of the genres her brother also cultivated. It was an unfortunate expectation, or perhaps it is just an expression of our subsequent prejudice, that women would compose music of less weight and substance than men, but Clara Schumann moved from writing light character pieces to more substantial chamber works influenced by Robert Schumann's engagement with Bach and the baroque. She became very well known as a performer (actually better known than her husband was as a composer), and her own Piano Concerto (*57), which she played in Leipzig conducted by Felix Mendelssohn, is now regularly performed.

On the cusp of the classical and Romantic eras, the piano and chamber music of Franz Schubert (1797–1828) explores new worlds, and yet is closely bound to the example of Beethoven whose legacy in Vienna was a dominating force. He is almost the polar opposite of a virtuoso in the generally small-scale nature of his works and their performance in domestic situations, far from the demands of the public concert hall (Plate 18). It is strange that at a time of great public demand, so few of Schubert's piano works were published in his lifetime, and some of his now most famous piano sonatas and impromptus appeared only in 1839. We now revere his last three piano sonatas of 1828 in C minor, A and B flat for their expansive lyricism and depth; his two sets of Impromptus from the previous year contain eight wonderfully contrasted movements. For domestic performance, he wrote superb piano duets, notably the turbulent Fantasia in F minor and the lyrical Rondo in A, and among his chamber works the String Quintet in C (*61) has a special place for its intensely lyrical themes and visionary slow movement.

THE LIFE OF MUSIC

The symphony as a genre in emerging Romantic music was heralded by Schubert's later symphonies, especially his 'Unfinished' Symphony No. 8 whose two completed movements explore new ideas of harmony and song-like melody; we do not know what it would have been like if ever finished, though some completions have been tried and Luciano Berio worked creatively with the sketches in his *Rendering* (p. 240). Schubert's 'Great' C major Symphony No. 9, a hugely ambitious structure which was praised by Schumann for its 'heavenly length', expanded classical models rather than replacing them. The musical language of Felix Mendelssohn (1809–47) moved into more Romantic territory through its relationship with the landscape; his 'Scottish' Symphony of 1842 reflects his love of the writings of Sir Walter Scott, the mythic literature surrounding the legend of Ossian, and the rising taste for tourism which led to his own early encounters with Edinburgh and the Scottish coast, which also inspired the gestation of the 'Hebrides' Overture. His 'Italian' Symphony of 1833 was written much faster, and captures the exhilaration the composer felt at the sights and sounds of Florence, Naples and Rome. There is a bustling opening movement in A major, a sober Pilgrims' March over an old-style walking bass line, a minuet and trio, and a whirling final tarantella which surprisingly begins and ends in the minor.

Mendelssohn's encounters with the concept of programme music resulted in these symphonies, and perhaps it was the fame of Beethoven's programmatic 'Pastoral' Symphony that encouraged this trend; it is a notable feature of art and literature as well as of music in this period, for countryside was one of the animating forces of the Romantic imagination. The rustle of leaves and the rising of the moon can be heard in the opening sequence of Mendelssohn's miraculous *Midsummer Night's Dream* Overture (*54) inspired by Shakespeare, written when the composer was just seventeen. He transports us into a fairy world that has its roots in the natural environment of the forest.

Even in Mendelssohn's abstract instrumental music, the scuttering harmonies of his precocious Octet for strings seem to breathe the spirit of the countryside. It is revealing that the young Mendelssohn, perhaps because of his understanding of himself as a Romantic artist inspired by nature, also became a skilled artist, a watercolourist who captured the scenes around him as he journeyed through

Italy and visited Britain. Coming from a highly cultured Jewish family, brought up to appreciate the world of German literature and the music of Bach, especially through his aunt Sarah Levy (who had been a pupil of Wilhelm Friedemann Bach) and his teacher Carl Friedrich Zelter, Mendelssohn became an advocate for the music of the past and staged an influential revival of J. S. Bach's St Matthew Passion in his own adaptation in 1829. This famous occasion was part of a gradual process of exploring Bach's music rather than a sudden discovery, but it was nevertheless a signal moment both in the Bach revival and in the renewal of interest in the music of the past.

To the song writers of the early nineteenth century, the natural world, the brooks, trees, sunlight, inns and journeys through the countryside, were central to their emotional state. Feelings, whether of love, despair or hate, took place within this natural environment and grew out of it. Franz Schubert wrote hundreds of songs in his tragically short life: there are story-telling ballads like *Erlkönig*, a powerful narrative of the death of a child, propelled by relentless triplets in the piano part and the terrible vision of the legendary Erlking. Schubert is sometimes taken as a typical example of a Romantic composer, but he is rather what we might call the classical Romantic: all his music is so perfectly shaped and contained, with even the most passionate and intense feeling occurring in strongly contained forms. In his song cycle *Die schöne Müllerin* he creates lyrical vocal lines that reflect the emotions of the poetry, with the piano adding perfectly sculpted, rocking, harmonious links that bind the whole together into a unity. At the end of his all-too-brief life, Schubert wrote his song cycle *Winterreise*, a winter journey in which a lover revisits the scenes of his now-vanished love; they lead him to some of his deepest and darkest thoughts, and end in bleak despair.

Robert Schumann (1810–56) constructed his supremely beautiful song cycles around the texts of Heinrich Heine and others, but it is their melodic impetus that carries the listener along. Here we are in a world where the formal bounds of Schubert's lyricism have been loosened, with visions which are rhapsodic and intense. Schumann's productivity was equally amazing: in the single year of 1840 Schumann wrote 140 songs. The wonderful cycle *Frauenliebe und -leben* Op. 42 tells a story of a young woman falling in love with an older man, marrying him, and having his child; then he dies. The cycles *Liederkreis* Op. 24 and *Dichterliebe* Op. 48 set Heine's poems without so much of a narrative thread, but with a natural grouping of themes and emotions: the propulsive movement of these songs is quite wonderful. Some of these songs have been criticised recently for their view of a woman's subservient place in society, but they represent the feelings of their era, and their emotions communicate vividly today. The *Liederkreis* Op. 39 to poems by Eichendorff, including the ethereally beautiful 'Mondnacht', makes for a perfect starting point (*55).

Schumann learned from both Schubert and Mendelssohn; he struggled with the symphony as an idea, but from 1841 he sprang into action, completing his 'Spring' Symphony No. 1 and working on what became his Fourth Symphony. Here with great foresight he looked forward to the emergence of the unified 'symphonic poem': he drew the four movements together into one without a pause between them, linking the themes and ensuring a dynamic, propulsive motion throughout the piece. (Mendelssohn also suggested that his 'Scottish' Symphony should be played this way.) Schumann's Symphony No. 2 in C, ebullient but troubled, and his Symphony No. 3 the 'Rhenish' are established in the repertory, with freshly minted performances with small forces such as those by Robin Ticciati bringing them to life, while the evergreen Piano Concerto of 1841 (opening with dramatic chords tumbling down the keyboard for the soloist) remains one of his most often performed works.

Schumann's chamber music includes rigorously argued string quartets and rather freer, imaginative piano sets of short movements, which gather rhapsodic pieces together into quasi-narratives, among which my favourite is the free-flowing *Kriesleriana* Op. 16; equally appealing are *Carnaval* Op. 9, the important *Fantasie* Op. 17, and the simple, practical pieces of the *Album for the Young* Op. 68. He had great success as a conductor, often appearing with his wife Clara, but his life ended tragically. Blighted by mental instability, he ended up in an asylum. It is revealing that neither Schubert nor Schumann had success in the field of opera: it was in smaller forms that their feelings flowed most naturally.

*

If we look for one blazingly creative figure who reinvented musical expression for the Romantic era, then it is surely the Frenchman Hector Berlioz (1803–69), a self-dramatist determined to make his impact on the largest possible scale. Notably, he did not come from the centres of music-making in central Europe, but from the newly expanded centre of Paris. From a cultured family, he went to the French capital to pursue a medical career but was far more attracted by the city's opera and theatre, where he conceived an obsession with the Anglo-Irish actress Harriet Smithson. Although he was not a performing virtuoso himself, he wrote about music, and he achieved Romantic expression through radical new forms and quirky examples of existing forms. *Harold in Italy* is a viola concerto called a symphony, while *Roméo et Juliette* is a cantata called a dramatic symphony. Berlioz's 'Romantic symphony', the *Symphonie fantastique* (*60), is a landmark in both orchestral technology and in expression, very adventurous for its date. In the 'dreams and passions' imagined by the fevered mind of the hero, nature is all around, in the setting sun, the sound of thunder; the country scene of the slow movement features shepherds with their pipes calling to one another, the witches' sabbath has its high dancing clarinets, and the fatal vision of the hero's march to the scaffold, making full use of the latest orchestral instruments of the time (including the ophicleide, a bass wind instrument only invented in the early nineteenth century), incorporates the ancient chant of the Requiem Mass, *Dies irae, dies illa* (*100).

Berlioz codified his thinking about orchestration in a very influential treatise of 1843, providing inspiration to generations of composers in imaginative scoring. One of my favourites among Berlioz's semi-dramatic works is the oratorio *L'enfance du Christ*, a gentle narrative of Christ's childhood which is exquisitely restrained and ethereal. It contains the famous 'Shepherds' Farewell', a chorus which has such an antique feeling that Berlioz published it under the name of an invented ancient composer, and then added two further movements 'in the manner of the old illuminated missals'. The three-part work telling the story of the Flight into Egypt is beautifully if occasionally sentimentally drawn, and ends with a visionary glimpse of the life beyond. Berlioz is one of music's true originals, not invariably successful but always pushing the boundaries of the forms within which he worked (Plate 19).

The Romantic imagination of Frédéric Chopin (1810–49) emerges in a quite different form, that of piano music. There are two concertos which are well written for the soloist but are less suited to the orchestra; Chopin sometimes performed them as solo piano pieces. He was born near Warsaw and always valued the Polish heritage which underlies much of his work. The perfection of his solo piano music, deriving so much of its power from his understanding of the keyboards of his time, is peerless. According to his lover George Sand, Chopin was a mixture of a spontaneous improviser and an obsessive reviser. He was not a demonstrative virtuoso performer himself, suffering for much of his life from tuberculosis; in his music his structural grip, methodical pacing and a clear sense of line go hand in hand with elaborate decoration and a vast emotional sweep. He often transformed the dance music of his Polish homeland in his mazurkas and polonaises, but in the more abstract forms of the sonata and his four Ballades he is creating new worlds of melancholic but rhapsodic expression.

As an outstanding example, Chopin's Ballade No. 1 in G minor (*56) is a touchstone of the Romantic piano style. It is assembled with consummate skill, from the striking opening unisons, moving from the flowing lyricism of its first subject to the melodic beauty of its second theme. The use of the extremes of the piano keyboard shapes the work, and the climax after the development of those two subjects is a thrilling link passage that leads into the final tumultuous coda with its pounding octaves in opposite motion. Here you feel a gripping story has been told with a perfect balance of compelling narrative, passionate feeling and ultimate resolution. As a skilled amateur pianist, the journalist Alan Rusbridger has given a vivid account of learning this piece in his book *Play It Again*. There are many other examples of this supreme skill in Chopin's piano pieces large and small, realised by virtuosi such as Arturo Benedetti Michelangeli, or poets such as Murray Perahia.

Chopin's piano writing seems all the more restrained beside that of Franz Liszt (1811–86), a composer who became the epitome of the nineteenth-century virtuoso performer. He was regarded by some as a charlatan: Mendelssohn, who had impeccable taste, said 'He performed works by Beethoven, Bach, Handel and Weber in such a pitiably imperfect style, so uncleanly, so ignorantly, that I could have listened to many a middling pianist with more pleasure.' But to others he was a superhuman genius who brought a new kind of music into the world. From a Hungarian background in the same Esterházy family that employed Haydn, Liszt had a relatively classic musical training, studying the piano with Carl Czerny and theory with Antonio Salieri. After the family's move to Paris from Hungary, he became famous as a travelling virtuoso, before breaking off in 1848 in order to pursue his career as a composer and teacher. He became the court music director in Weimar, conducting premieres including that of Wagner's *Lohengrin*, and fathering children with the Countess Marie d'Agoult, including Cosima, the future wife of Wagner. Bizarrely, he then abandoned his hedonistic life, moved to Rome in 1861, and became a member of the Catholic clergy as Abbé Liszt (Plate 17).

Liszt demonstrated the development in the relationship between the player and his audience; he had an almost erotic charge over those who listened to him, and you imagine his concerts as having the mood of religious revivalist meetings. Indeed, claiming to be inspired by a religious impulse, his aim was that 'all classes of society will finally merge in a common religious sentiment, grand and sublime'. He was a musical magician who held audiences in thrall. He created the typical idea of the Romantic artist, the ever-striving virtuoso, doing more and more to envelop his listeners in dazzling sound. As we have noted with many self-aware artists, he was conscious of his own reputation and responsible for organising his own success, making extensive use of the press in advancing his appeal, and exploiting his fame to the hilt. Images of his fevered performances with swooning audiences became famous, while reviews spoke of him as 'a magnetiser who conjures the electric fluid from every key . . . an amiable monster who now treats his beloved piano tenderly, then tyrannically'. Liszt was a pioneer of the instrumental recital as an art form in itself. His symphonic poems for orchestra, with their complex literary programmes, have never held a strong place in the repertory, though they are important for effectively developing the art of thematic transformation. I am never sure about Liszt's two piano concertos, especially the second with its ramshackle structure. But his solo piano music is another matter: here there is much of huge inventiveness and daring. Inspired by the virtuoso violin playing of Paganini, Liszt created transcriptions of his work for piano, and also made versions of Bach's organ works, Handel's operas, and a glorious fantasy around the music of Mozart's opera *Don Giovanni*. The composer Camille Saint-Saëns remarked that 'he not only illuminates the beauties of it but adds a commentary of his own that gives a new insight into them and helps us to appreciate more fully their supreme perfection and their immortal modernity'.

Liszt's last piano works seem to stretch towards the idioms of the twentieth century: spare, thin visions like *La lugubre gondola,* or *Nuages gris* with its weird harmonic language that has been analysed as a forerunner of atonality. The music always sounds as if it might resolve into a key, but never quite does. It is a telling illustration of the links across the nineteenth century that not only did Liszt know Beethoven, but he also lived long enough to encounter the young Debussy. On Wagner's death, he wrote *R.W. – Venezia* as a tribute, but though he admired Wagner's work, Wagner never returned the compliment, even after becoming Liszt's son-in-law through his marriage to Liszt's daughter Cosima.

The work that for me sums up the finest side of Liszt's achievement is his Piano Sonata in B minor (*53), a half-hour single movement which takes a glowering, gruff unison theme in the bottom of the piano and raises it through thematic transformations of all kinds, playing with three or four different musical ideas full of both falling melodies and fierce harmonic passages. It is as if the movements of a sonata have been rolled together and lapped over each other. Unlike in some of Liszt's more rhapsodically improvisational pieces, however, this sounds completely logical. This is persuasively argued music: just before the end, the music rises to a series of slow, high chords and in the hands of a great performer it is as if the whole structure of the piece is being lifted and concentrated into that one moment, before the music evaporates. In Liszt's lifetime the work was not widely taken up, and Hans von Bülow premiered it only in 1857. But now it has emerged as a key work in the world of nineteenth-century music, played by all the leading pianists of the day. 'If Liszt had written nothing else . . . it would still have sufficed to show what manner of man he was,' Richard Strauss said to the pianist Wilhelm Kempff. It has been interpreted by the leading pianists of our time, from Krystian Zimerman to Alfred Brendel.

1 Music, for or against?
St Cecilia has become the patron saint of music, but in Raphael's 1515 portrait, she rejects the sounds of instruments which lie crushed at her feet, the organ falling from her hands. Instead it is the purity of the heavenly choir above which commands her attention. Music as secular profanity or music as cosmic harmony: a constant tension across the ages (p. 30).

2 **The look of music**
How notation changes across the centuries:
above, Monteverdi's sparse scoring of his
opera *Orfeo* (1608, from the print of 1609),
with solo voice parts and *basso continuo*,
leaving much to be realised; below, Mahler's
dense autograph of his massive Symphony
No. 8 (1906), full of ultra-detailed
instructions for orchestra and chorus (p. 6).

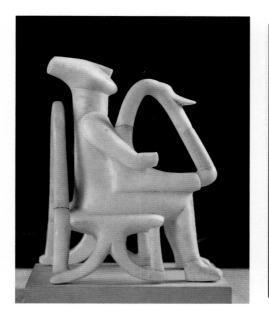

3 **Sounds from the Greek era**
An exquisite marble statue of a Greek lyre player, from the island of Keros in the Cycladic civilisation (above left); Hetaera playing a double aulós in a marble panel from the Greek Ludovisi Throne of *c.* 460–450 BC (above right); a Greek hydra by Phintias, *c.* 510 BC, portraying a young man being taught the lyre (p. 20).

4 The harmony of music

De institutione musica, a famous treatise by the sixth-century Greek philosopher Boethius, was not published until the Middle Ages, with this illustration of the three kinds of music in the right-hand panels: *musica mundana* (of the planets), *musica humana* (of the body and soul) and *musica instrumentalis* (audible music) (pp. 22–3).

5 A musical milestone

Sumer is icumen in, an isolated survival of medieval English music from the Benedictine abbey of Reading around 1280, has a jovial secular text and a Latin text underneath, and should be sung as a round, like 'Frère Jacques', with voices entering in succession with the same melody: its skipping score is still fun to sing today (p. 38).

6 Songs from Spain
The *Cantigas de Santa Maria* is a remarkable thirteenth-century collection of 400 songs, illustrated with intricate detail of both the instruments and their musicians, from the collection organised by King Alfonso X, 'El Sabio', who directs the proceedings. The mixed culture of Moorish and European influence is evident in the performers (p. 43).

7 **Composers become famous**
Portraits of named composers start to appear by the fifteenth century: at the top, colleagues Guillaume Dufay (with organ) and Gilles Binchois (with harp) depicted in Martin le Franc's *Champion des Dames*; below, the blind Italian Francesco Landini playing the organ in the magnificent Squarcialupi Codex from Florence (p. 55).

8 Even Ockeghem needed glasses
The composer Johannes Ockeghem was revered and admired by all: this is a miniature illustrating a poem written after the composer's death, praising a motet he had written for thirty-six voices. The monks gather round a single large score; no wonder Ockeghem needed spectacles to read from a distance! (p. 67)

9 Reformation and Counter-Reformation
Palestrina receives the blessing of Pope Julian III in 1554 for his new Mass which embodies the intelligibility desired by the Council of Trent. Meanwhile Martin Luther (or one of his followers) is vilified in this caricature by Erhard Schön, where he becomes the instrument of the Devil. Luther joked, 'Must the Devil have all the good tunes?' and wrote some of his own (p. 72).

10 Singing and dancing
Above, three women making music in 1520s Venice: the singer on our left looks nervously at the audience, the lutenist lifts her eyes to the heavens. Below, in this 1581 painting Queen Elizabeth I boldly dances the volta with the Earl of Leicester, to the admiration of her court: but how invented is her agility? (pp. 95–6)

11 **Music as power**

Celebrating the emperor: the magnificent series of woodcuts *The Triumph of Maximilian I* by Hans Burgkmair the Elder and others from 1526 shows a vast sequence of musicians as part of the emperor's imagined triumphal procession. Here, trumpets and drums on horseback above, crumhorns and wind instruments on a cart below. The project was never finished (p. 98).

12 A court portrait
Orlande de Lassus (also Orlando di Lasso) sits at the keyboard with his celebrated ensemble, the
Hofkapelle of Munich, for Hans Mielich's splendidly reverential and detailed picture of 1565–70. The
outstanding musicians are named in the panel below, showing their cosmopolitan origins. (As good a PR
portrait as any later orchestral photoshoot!) (p. 75)

13 Visual beauty
Two gorgeous images of design allied to
music. The architect, painter and sculptor
Bernardo Buontalenti designed the costumes
for the Florentine *intermedi* of 1589 (p. 102),
a spectacular display of scenic and musical
ingenuity. The teenage Louis XIV appears as
Apollo in the 1653 *Le ballet de la nuit*, giving rise
to his soubriquet 'Le Roi Soleil', the Sun King
(p. 107).

14 The baroque stage
Above, an amusing little-and-large parody attributed to Hogarth of the castrato Gaetano Berenstadt, the soprano Francesca Cuzzoni and the castrato Senesino, perhaps performing Handel's opera *Flavio* (p. 118). Below, an exquisitely detailed watercolour by Gabriel de Saint-Aubin of Lully's opera *Armide* being performed in 1761 at the Palais-Royal (p. 109).

15 **Serious and comic**
A pair of eighteenth-century Italian pictures which perfectly capture the contrast in genres
between the display of grand opera (top) and the emerging popular intermezzo (below).
Each is beautifully characterised with their different audiences: as with *Armide* opposite, the
listeners are an essential part of the spectacle (p. 122).

16 Family music-making
Above, around 1780 Johann Nepomuk della Croce depicts Wolfgang Mozart playing the piano with his sister Nannerl; their father Leopold listens, with the portrait of their mother Anna Maria, who died in 1778, looking on. Below, Johann Zoffany in 1775 shows George, 3rd Earl Cowper with the family of Charles Gore, who plays cello (with no spike) accompanied by a square piano.

17 Handing on the tradition
Above, Franz Liszt plays the piano in this
1840 painting by Josef Danhauser, with an
admiring audience including Alexandre
Dumas, Victor Hugo, George Sand,
Paganini, Rossini and Countess Marie
d'Agoult; the dominating bust of Beethoven
validates the new performer. Right, Nicolò
Paganini creates the image of a violin
virtuoso at the King's Theatre, June 1831
(p. 165).

18 **Concert-giving, private and public**

Two fine vignettes by Moritz von Schwind. Above, a sepia drawing of a musical soirée with Franz Schubert at the piano and the singer Johann Michael Vogl, with an attentively transported audience at the home of Joseph von Spaun. Below, an 1852 oil painting *The Symphony* – an interesting layout with orchestra and conductor at the back, piano in the centre, singers in front.

19 Big personalities

Right, Hector Berlioz causing
exuberant chaos in the audience
with his imperious direction of
his innovative and dramatic works
which expanded the sounds of the
orchestra (p. 171). Below, Johannes
Brahms, always tied to tradition, is
more restrained at the piano: we can
imagine him playing one of his late
piano pieces, unsurpassed for their
inward emotion (p. 194).

20 At Bayreuth
Behind the scenes at the unique opera house Wagner created: the mechanics by which the Rhinemaidens seemed immersed in water at the start of *Das Rheingold*; and the singers as they appeared in the opera's premiere in 1876: Minna Lammert, Lili Lehmann and Marie Lehmann (p. 183).

21 Balancing genius
Italian and French styles: above,
Italian Theatre by Delacroix
shows Rossini, the genius of
early nineteenth-century opera,
carrying leading characters from
his operas *Otello*, *Rosina* and *Il
barbiere di Siviglia* over his head;
below, an audience view into the
orchestra pit by Edgar Degas in
his *The Orchestra of the Opera*
of 1870, featuring his friend the
bassoonist Désiré Dihau.

22 Finding folk traditions
Béla Bartók was a pioneering collector of authentic folk music, seen here recording on a portable machine in Draž, Hungary, in 1907. Igor Stravinsky used the rich heritage of Russian folk music in his *Rite of Spring*, one of the century's most influential pieces: this is a photo of the Adolescents from the notorious premiere at the Théâtre des Champs-Élysées, Paris, in 1913 (p. 230).

23 Towering symphonists
Two musical geniuses whose symphonies expressed the twentieth century: Gustav Mahler, conductor as well as composer, captured in full flight in a caricature by Böhler, *c.* 1900; Dimitry Shostakovich photographed as a firefighter in Leningrad, part of the heroic narrative of his wartime 'Leningrad' Symphony No. 7 – he appeared on the cover of *Time* magazine (p. 203).

24 New media arrive
Above, Edward Elgar in a pioneering orchestral recording session in 1914 – but note, the musicians are crammed together for the photograph! Below, Vladimir Horowitz followed by cameras on stage after a recital at the Concertgebouw, Amsterdam. Like many later artists, his image was formed by the press as well as by performance.

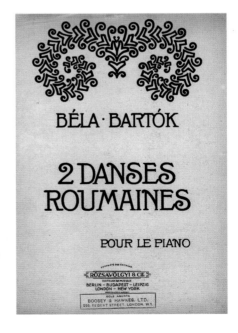

25 Nationalism in Europe
Varieties of national styles bringing distinctive colours
to early twentieth-century music: above, early prints of
Janáček's *Moravian Dances* capturing native folk-dance
traditions; above right, Debussy's *La mer* with its
iconic use of Hokusai's *The Wave*; and right, Bartók's
Two Romanian Dances, Budapest, 1910.

26 Operatic temples
The imposing exteriors of two great nineteenth-century opera houses in Vienna (above) and Paris (below), both built during the 1860s and photographed here around 1900. They were designed to impress and to create a feeling of privilege for those who entered; their sense of exclusivity contrasts strongly with the modern halls opposite.

27 **Bringing the audience closer**
Two recent European concert halls, both opened in 2017: the Pierre Boulez Saal in Berlin by Frank Gehry, an oval space totally surrounding the performers, seen here on its opening night; and the Elbphilharmonie in Hamburg by Herzog & de Meuron, with audience again surrounding the stage – a controversially expensive project but one which has become a symbol of the city.

28 Towards equality

The contribution of women to the classical music tradition has been hugely undervalued, but twentieth-century composers made their mark: top, sisters Nadia (left) and Lili (right) Boulanger in 1913; Imogen Holst, closely associated with the Aldeburgh Festival, conducting in Orford church *c.* 1950; and Sofiya Gubaydulina teaching in Lübeck, 2014 (pp. 234, 250).

29 Music on film
Popular genres transformed the public accessibility of classical music. Above, Walt Disney and Deems Taylor discuss with conductor Leopold Stokowski the innovative animated film *Fantasia* (p. 3). Below, George Gershwin at the piano with Fred Astaire and Ginger Rogers on the set of the 1936 film *Shall We Dance?* (p. 258).

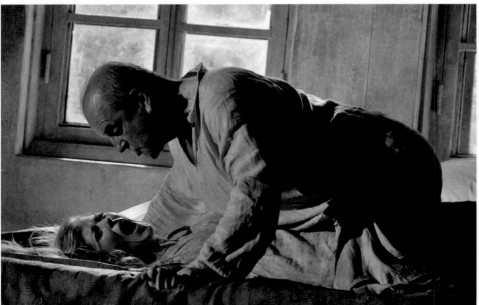

30 **Opera reborn**

Contemporary composers have relished the challenge of reinventing opera. John Adams broke through in 1986 with *Nixon in China*, here sung by James Maddalena, Russell Braun and Janis Kelly in 2011. Martin Crimp went back to a Provençal tale in his libretto for George Benjamin's *Written on Skin*, with Christopher Purves and Barbara Hannigan in Katie Mitchell's 2013 production (pp. 249, 255).

31 **Widening the range**

The diversity of classical music performers is broadening gradually but has so much further to go. Role models include the cellist Yo-Yo Ma, playing solo Bach to thousands – top, in Red Rocks, Denver, in 2018 – and leading the Silk Road Project; and the brilliant Kanneh-Mason family: cellist Sheku is seen here with young players from Liverpool's In Harmony project (p. 266).

Image: Hugo Glendinning

Image: Chris Christodoulou

32 **Inspiring the young**
Developing the music-making of a new generation is the most important task for musicians today: above, Sir Simon Rattle conducts the premiere of *The Hogboon* by Sir Peter Maxwell Davies with young people from LSO Discovery at the Barbican, London, 2016; below, the unique setting of the BBC Proms at the Royal Albert Hall, uniting people in inspiring musical experiences.

13

Music-drama

There is rarely one single stream of musical development. It is chastening to re-trace our steps and remember that Gioachino Rossini (1792–1868) was writing his hugely successful light-hearted operas at the same time as Beethoven was completing his utterly introverted late string quartets and serious symphonists were taking up Beethoven's daunting legacy. Opera had arrived at a moment when it was to achieve unparalleled success, a strand of music-making that originated in the warmth of populist Italy rather than in serious-minded Germany.

Rossini was born and bred in the Italian operatic tradition, growing up in Pesaro (where a festival devoted to his music flourishes) and studying in Bologna. His extrovert commercial success begins to emerge at the moment of the collapse of the Napoleonic era. His first successes in 1813 were both comic (*L'italiana in Algeri*) and serious (*Tancredi*). Rossini fever swept Europe, a fascinating example of early internationalism. It was reported that workmen in Venice sang Rossini arias in the street, and when the composer visited Vienna in 1822, the adulation was overwhelming: 'the entire performance was like an idolatrous orgy; everyone there acted as if they had been bitten by a tarantula', marvelled the normally re-served *Allgemeine musikalische Zeitung*. Rossini worked in Naples, then travelled to London and settled in Paris where his last success *William Tell* was premiered. Although there has been a revival of interest in his serious operas in recent years, it is the comic pieces that continue to hold the stage today: the wit and wisdom of

Il barbiere di Siviglia and *La Cenerentola* (*62) have kept those operas prominent in the repertory (Plate 21).

Rossini's music has an irresistible sparkle. When his mezzo-sopranos such as Cinderella are singing with emotion, they decorate with dazzling divisions. This is not unusual for the time, indeed empty copies of the style abounded, but Rossini's use of decoration was always purposeful: an elaboration resulting from an excess of feeling rather than from empty virtuosity; the brilliance of the singers' vocal lines is at the service of their emotions. Rossini developed one characteristic personal signature: the opera overture. His curtain-raisers are effervescent show-pieces which raise the audience's excitement to a fever pitch before the drama has even begun. With techniques going back a century to the 'Mannheim crescendo' of the early symphonists such as Stamitz (p. 138), extended with the orchestration of wind, piccolos and drums available to him, Rossini created a genre of his own. Rossini did not carry on producing great operas: his success gave him a comfortable life, his creative spirit declined, and he contented himself with somewhat self-parodying minor works like his 'sins of old age', *Péchés de vieillesse*. Among his later religious music, the quasi-operatic *Petite messe solennelle* is an entertaining mix of styles, while the *Stabat mater* is an extraordinary conflation which Rossini never wanted published. However, the scholar Julian Budden wrote entertainingly of the 'martial swing' of one movement and the 'jaunty syncopation' of another, which all adds up 'to form a perfectly balanced and consistent musical canvas'.

The spirit of Romanticism flourished in German opera where the confluence of art, literature and music produced a distinctively darker mix, although the form was slower to take root there until Carl Maria von Weber (1786–1826) wrote *Der Freischütz* for the Berlin court and then *Euryanthe* and *Oberon*, which created an extremely influential prototype of German opera. *Freischütz* is based around the powerful myth of the German forest, whether as a picture of rustic innocence or as a dark tangled landscape that hides secrets. Weber's orchestration is vivid, especially his atmospheric conjuring of the Wolf's Glen, and the opera was an immediate success at its Berlin premiere. Outside opera, Weber's brilliant writing for clarinet is a distinctive feature of his work and gave rise to two virtuosic concertos (*63).

Among his supporters was the influential writer, thinker and composer E. T. A. Hoffmann (1776–1822). He became a vital figure in articulating music's move into the Romantic era, and formulated the aspiration of music to be the greatest of the Romantic arts: 'one might almost say, the only genuinely romantic one – for its sole subject is the infinite'. His hero was Beethoven (p. 151) and he wrote of the Fifth Symphony in 1810 that 'Music reveals to man an unknown realm, a world quite apart from the outer sensual world surrounding him, a world in which he leaves behind all feelings circumscribed by intellect in order to embrace the inexpressible.' Hoffmann's important philosophy led inexorably to Wagner and his all-encompassing music-dramas (p. 182), and also to the notion that music could somehow float free of its social surroundings, supporting the concept of the isolation of the great creative figure, a powerful feature of later thinking around composers.

All this was in the context of a rapidly expanding network of opera houses and performers which stimulated public demand through the nineteenth century. It is said that by the beginning of the twentieth century there were some 3,000 theatres in Italy, most of them presenting opera, while Paris became the form's fashionable centre because of its large permanent company and extensive rehearsal time. In Paris, the era of 'grand opera' flourished, featuring historical melodramas laced with extravagant ballet and scenic effects. It was formulated by such composers as Daniel Auber (1782–1871) with his revolutionary drama *La Muette de Portici*, which features a dancer in the mute title role, and a scenic climax with the eruption of Vesuvius; and Giacomo Meyerbeer (1791–1864), who made an impact in the genre with *Les Huguenots*, a fiery depiction of the sixteenth-century conflicts between Catholics and Protestants during the St Bartholomew's Day massacre. These grand pieces were hugely popular in the nineteenth century but since then they seem to have fallen out of sympathy with our times, though they occasionally receive avant-garde stagings drawing out contemporary parallels in the stories. As with the countless symphonies and concertos of the late eighteenth century, only a tiny proportion of such operas survive in the repertory. Perhaps another day will come for Auber and Meyerbeer, or for Étienne Méhul (1763–1817), long regarded as the most important composer in France during the Revolution, and Simon Mayr (1763–1845), but at the moment their operas seem much further from today's concerns than those of Monteverdi and Handel from the previous centuries.

The one composer of the period who has acquired more appeal now than he had then is Hector Berlioz. *Les Troyens*, based on Virgil's *Aeneid*, a vast undertaking, was written between 1856 and 1858 but only partially premiered when the composer agreed to split the opera in two; Berlioz never heard it complete. Grand but also austere, inspired by classicism in art, Berlioz's style harks back to the ancients such as Gluck, while encompassing the full range of human emotions. Orchestral highlights such as 'The Royal Hunt and Storm', and the passionate love duet for Aeneas and Dido, show his typical flights of imagination. Perhaps as drama, especially at its full length, it will never rank among the most coherent of operas, but its music is compelling. The enthusiastic Berlioz revival in our time has also extended to the eccentric but thrilling opera *Benvenuto Cellini*, the story of the Renaissance sculptor, and even to stagings of his powerful oratorio *La Damnation de Faust*. Berlioz is a fascinating example of a totally individual composer who stands quite outside the German tradition that leads from Beethoven on to Brahms and Wagner. For that reason he has never been regarded as at the centre of the repertory by the mainstream German orchestras and opera houses. He establishes a different but equally characterful line of French colour, which shines from Lully and Rameau before him, to Debussy, Ravel and Boulez after him.

Rossini's true Italian successor was Vincenzo Bellini (1801–35), and the two men became good friends and colleagues, even though in his student days Bellini's teacher Nicola Zingarelli had tried to protect his pupil from being too directly influenced by Rossini's dominating success. Bellini was born in Catania in Sicily, where his body was returned after his death to be reinterred in the cathedral there, as a mark of the huge success of his career; I remember seeing his original coffin preserved in the Bellini museum, a rather grisly homage. His talent was spotted early: he was commissioned by Naples and then by La Scala, where he met the librettist Felice Romani, who became his closest collaborator. Their first success, and maybe the first thoroughly Romantic opera, was *Il pirata* for La Scala. The best place to start to understand Bellini's art is one of his most popular arias, 'Casta diva' from *Norma* (*59), which builds on the Rossinian belief that ornamentation genuinely means something. The heroine prays to the moon and the basic harmonic structure is simple, but the elaboration is wonderfully complex, with eloquent solo flute. This developed the singing style widely referred to as *bel canto*, unifying vocal technique into a long legato line capable of both sustaining melody and incorporating elaborate decoration. *La sonnambula*, with its title role of Amina, the sleepwalker, is a work of total maturity. Bellini was attracted to Paris, then moved there and wrote *I puritani*, taking Rossini's advice continually. It was a great success, but Bellini became ill and died later that year.

Then, also from the Rossinian tradition, came Gaetano Donizetti (1797–1848). His operas acquired originality through a very different approach to the vocal structure in *Anna Bolena*, which established him among the leading opera composers of the day. There followed *Lucrezia Borgia*, based on a play by Victor Hugo, *Maria Stuarda* and *Lucia di Lammermoor*, with its mad scene that Maria Callas made her own. These operas redefined Romanticism and it is these big serious works that have forged his reputation today. Astonishingly productive, Donizetti wrote some sixty-five operas which have been in and out of the repertory: his work suffered a declining reputation at the end of the nineteenth century but is increasingly accepted now. His more familiar comic achievements in *La fille du régiment* and *Don Pasquale* readily lend themselves to transposition to contemporary times in operatic production, so up to date is their humour; *L'elisir d'amore* with its winning melodies including the famous 'Una furtiva lagrima' is a continual delight (*58).

The phenomenon of opera was sweeping Europe, and what the opera houses needed were new works. It is an interesting sidelight that while orchestras were building a traditional repertory, in the opera houses of the day not many staple works were revived; the thirst was for adventure. A whole variety of contrasted genres grew up in response to audience demand: light opera, satirical opera and *opéra-comique*. That was the label under which Charles Gounod's (1818–93) *Faust* was first performed in 1859. Like *Carmen* by Georges Bizet (1838–75), these works originally featured a mixture of spoken text and musical numbers. But in accordance with the taste of the times they were later supplied with sung

179

recitatives, aligning them more to conventional operatic formats. For me, *Faust* is full of attractive melody and well-crafted scenes, demanding little of its audience. *Carmen* (*50) is a much more pungent proposition, based on Prosper Mérimée's novella, and was deeply suspect when premiered because of the dubious moral character of its heroine, a strong-willed gypsy who is determined to take control of her own life and in the end is murdered by her lover. With its gritty realism and the bullring as background and context, we can hear and see it now as anticipating some of the later mannerist, *verismo* Italian operas of the turn of the century, and we admire its hard-hitting modernity. It also contains some of the most memorable tunes in the entire operatic repertory, from the Toreador's swaggering song to Carmen's sensual seguidilla. Bizet never lived to see its success, although that emerged quickly after his death.

Alongside the exponential growth of the operatic repertory was the emergence of a new generation of star singers, whose technique helped to sell the *bel canto* style and ensure their popularity across nations. The outstanding Jenny Lind who toured widely across America has already been mentioned (p. 163). Among a host of others, the temperamental Maria Malibran brought brilliance to Rossini's heroines in London and New York; her younger sister Pauline Viardot García was equally distinguished in Verdi. Another pair of sisters, Giulia and Giuditta Grisi, were a famous couple singing Romeo and Juliet in the premiere of Bellini's *I Capuleti e i Montecchi*. Giulia became one of the famous singers of the age in repertory from Mozart to Meyerbeer. Giuditta Pasta had a voice of great range, beauty and power, creating the title roles in Bellini's *Norma* and *La sonnambula*, and travelling as far afield as St Petersburg. From a later generation, Teresa Stolz worked closely with Verdi and sang the role of Aida. Adelina Patti became famous in New York in Bellini's *La sonnambula* and in London for Verdi's *Aida*; she is among a group of singers whose style is preserved on early recordings and can be valuably studied for their restrained use of vibrato and considerable rhythmic freedom.

Male voices were arguably less feted than female soloists (at least until the arrival of Enrico Caruso in the early twentieth century – the first singer to become famous through recordings as well as performances, p. 3), but the Italian tenor Giovanni Battista Rubini was a close collaborator with Bellini and helped to develop his style. It is an endlessly fascinating exercise to see how vocal style has changed dramatically over the decades as opera houses expanded and composers wrote for the marketplace rather than for the court. Singers were dealing with bigger, louder orchestras and larger theatres, so projection became a necessity, and vocal style changed as a result. High notes were cultivated by composers and gave singers an opportunity to show off (Rubini reportedly sang an exceptionally high G through cultivating a powerful falsetto register). Various scores and singers' notebooks preserve elaborate ornamentation which was clearly thoroughly worked out rather than improvised; there are examples from Pauline Viardot written for a pupil, and several sources record how singers of the time ornamented an aria in Bellini's *Norma*, a role that was strongly associated with Giuditta Pasta – suggesting, writes Will Crutchfield, 'that her influence on the subsequent traditions of performing it were strong'. Thus individual performers came to have a significant impact on the way composers' music sounded in practice.

Later in the century, the first recordings by singers preserve their varied styles. Peter Schram recorded Leporello's arias from *Don Giovanni* in 1889, and many recordings testify to the rhythmic freedom and liberal use of *portamento* (sliding from note to note) that was then common, but which today's taste would find difficult to accept. Gemma Bellincioni, whom we know Verdi admired, recorded an aria from his *La traviata* in 1903 with flexible *rubato*, altered rhythms and added decoration, while Adelina Patti recorded Bellini's *La sonnambula* in 1906 with free elaboration; the practices continued until the Italian opera house reforms of Arturo Toscanini tried to take these liberties in hand in the 1920s. While there is thus evidence of their singing styles through these early recordings, we mostly have to guess at the acting styles that were used by these remarkable singers.

*

Few arguments in the arts are as conflicted and unresolved as that about the relationship between an artist's personal life and their work. Should we reject the creative output of an artist whose personal behaviour or views are abhorrent? Does the creation of extraordinary art exempt its creator from moral behaviour? Does the work exist independently of an artist's life and thus remain untouched by it?

There is no more troubling example in the world of music than that of Richard Wagner (1813–83), who is commonly acknowledged to be among the greatest original artistic geniuses of any age, but whose opinions, behaviour and relationships were deeply flawed. In his case there is the matter of his extreme and overt anti-Semitism, not just (as so often with others) implied by his actions, but made explicit in his tract 'Judaism in Music', first published anonymously in 1850 and then, greatly expanded, under his own name in 1869. This is an appalling vilification of Jews generally, and specifically pours scorn on the composers Giacomo Meyerbeer and Felix Mendelssohn, whom Wagner claimed to despise for holding back German music. This, alongside Wagner's single-minded egotism, which put the realisation of his grand artistic visions before everything else, and his philandering, indebtedness and destructive emotional behaviour, have left a difficult legacy, made all the more problematic by the Nazi regime's later appropriation of him as its patron composer. Yet he remains one of the most studied and written about of all musical figures, and the attraction of his mammoth operas to new generations shows no sign of abating.

Wagner's influence on composition and musical thought has been so overwhelming, so exhaustively discussed and debated, that it is difficult to recapture the freshness with which he burst onto the scene. While operatic fashion was dominated by the French and Italians, because of his German roots Wagner instead went back to Weber (p. 176) and delved into German folklore and Teutonic myth in order to overturn established operatic practice. Gone would be all the inessential trappings of recent grand operatic convention, especially the French traditions of inserted ballets, big processions and indeed the whole concept of clearly defined 'numbers', arias and ensembles. These would be supplanted by a continuous flow of 'endless melody', given logic and shape by the use of recurring musical phrases (*leitmotifs*) associated with people and ideas. This deep thinking, which took place during a period of compositional inactivity, came to be codified in his major 1849 treatises 'Art and Revolution' and 'The Artwork of the Future' and his 1851 book *Opera and Drama*, where first he formulated his idea of the *Gesamtkunstwerk* ('total art work'), a bringing together of all the arts, articulated in his praise of ancient Greek drama and then embraced as an ambition for his own new concept of music-drama. Interestingly, Wagner took his primary inspiration for music-drama from Beethoven and his symphonies, especially his Ninth – an odd choice, given that the symphony is primarily an instrumental work, albeit in this case one with text; nevertheless, it satisfied Wagner's belief that, as music was the greatest of the arts, it would lead this great synthesis of the art forms, yet be subsumed within it.

From his early work, which developed the existing German tradition – Weber was echoed in *Die Feen* – Wagner's first so-called Romantic opera, *Der fliegende Holländer*, produced in Dresden in the year he became conductor of the Dresden opera, began to explore these possibilities. *Tannhäuser* and *Lohengrin* drove his operatic revolution forward, while Wagner himself went into exile in 1849, leaving Dresden and seeking refuge with Liszt in Weimar. He then travelled to Switzerland, where his first marriage to Minna Planer was cooled by his infatuation with Mathilde Wesendonck, the wife of one of his Swiss patrons, and then with Liszt's daughter Cosima. She eventually persuaded her husband Hans von Bülow to grant her a divorce, and she married Wagner in 1870.

The real musical breakthrough came as he began work on the *Ring* cycle in the 1850s. *Der Ring des Nibelungen*, which was first performed in 1876, is a four-day opera of unequalled scope, length and power, an achievement still unsurpassed in Western music (though Karlheinz Stockhausen, in his week-long *Licht*, exceeded it at least in length: p. 238). The plots draw on German poems and Norse legends, retold in Wagner's own language, the reformulated texts perfectly suited to musical setting. The narrative may seem banal when reduced to a brief synopsis, but nothing can really prepare you for the sheer sound of these operas, which is their essence – shattering orchestral moments such as Siegfried's Funeral March from *Götterdämmerung* or 'The Ride of the Valkyries' which starts Act 3 of *Die Walküre*, whose sonic impact is unequalled. The passionate and exciting Act 1 of *Die Walküre* (*52), the most accessible of the operas that make up the *Ring*, is an unbeatable place to begin to understand the impact of the work.

The *Ring* was premiered in 1876, and the first performances celebrated the opening of the new theatre in Bayreuth. This had been specially built to Wagner's specifications and designed as a space in which total illusion can be assured: the orchestra is hidden in the pit, not visible, and there are no lights outside the pro-scenium arch so there is nothing to distract the audience from what is happening on stage. It fulfilled Wagner's oft-expressed conviction that 'there is only one thing that will enable my art to take root and not to vanish, totally misunderstood, into thin air. I need a theatre such as I alone can build.' And build it he did, thanks to the financially unlimited support of his patron Ludwig II of Bavaria (Plate 20).

Wagner's other works, written in the midst of the *Ring* and after it, demonstrate how he drew on Germanic myth in order to transmit it to a new generation, and in doing so took operatic form to its logical conclusion. *Die Meistersinger von Nürnberg* is intended as a paean of praise to 'our holy German art', a hymn to music, referencing the Middle Ages with its framework of a singing contest in a very typical German town and celebrated with an open, bold C major tonality in its famous Prelude. Although it contains much glorious music, the strain of nationalism it celebrates is difficult to identify with. Completely different is the mood of his last visionary opera *Parsifal*, which lifted Wagner's work out of a mythic framework and put it into an even more wide-ranging spiritual and religious one. The ideas behind *Parsifal* may be elusive, but the music is utterly compelling, the endless continuity of its argument so well drawn, that it is impossible not to get swept along by its inexorable logic and beauty.

It was in *Tristan und Isolde*, an opera composed after yet another personal crisis for Wagner following the ending of an affair, and dominated by the doomed love of its protagonists which can only be fully consummated in death, that Wagner's influence on the future of music was most keenly felt. When he wrote the opening passage of that score, he achieved something arguably even more seismic than an operatic revolution: he created a harmonic revolution. Instead of opening a work with a clear tonal chord or melody, he wrote a few bars of extreme uncertainty, using a chord made up of the notes F, B, D♯ and G♯ which has become known as the 'Tristan chord'. Nothing here is firm or fixed; the notes do not belong to any of the usual harmonic combinations. Scholars and analysts have argued for decades as to how to describe it. The nineteenth-century Czech scholar Carl Mayrberger's analysis, which is claimed to have been approved by Wagner, describes it as a *Zwitterakkord*, 'an ambiguous, hybrid or possibly bisexual or androgynous chord'.

Yet it sounds completely convincing, utterly memorable, and is repeated through-out the opera. It had an enormous influence on those who tried to trace its origins back to Machaut, Gesualdo and Beethoven, and on those who quoted it humor-ously, such as Debussy and Britten. Whatever its source, it moved music towards dissolving the traditional boundaries of tonality and ushered in the increasing chromaticism of the decades to come. With that single chord sequence Wagner issued a harmonic and musical challenge to the whole of the twentieth century.

*

The apogee of music-drama as popular engagement was undoubtedly the oper-atic art of Giuseppe Verdi (1813–1901), which stretches across the second half of the nineteenth century. He was a revolutionary, genuinely in touch with the people who worked extremely hard with him from what he called his 'galley years' onwards, and (thanks to the growing system of copyright protection) earned enough from his music to retire comfortably. He withdrew from operatic life to take up a role as a successful landowner, which has led to criticism from some commentators, but in comparison with Wagner he is a model of humanity with an underlying integrity, leading his biographer John Rosselli to 'admire him, warts and all . . . even when he is being unreasonable or wrong'. The period of his cre-ativity moves from his first successful opera *Nabucco* to the triumphs of *Rigoletto* and *La traviata*, the latter two based on French literary models by Victor Hugo and Alexandre Dumas respectively. Here it is real people who compel our atten-tion. The pathos of the comic entertainer Rigoletto as he discovers his daughter's murder; the gradual descent of the anti-heroine of *La traviata* towards her death by tuberculosis: these are masterpieces of characterisation. Verdi's melodic clar-ity and shapeliness is one part of his remarkably constant appeal. His orchestra-tion is detailed and his concentration on real human drama is outstanding. It was also his political commitment, which associated his work with the Risorgimento movement, that endeared Verdi to a wide public who heard him championing freedom, moreover a freedom which could be theirs, in vigorous choruses. He did not always conform to expectations in the form of his operas, but as he wrote when asked to provide an aria for a singer in *Rigoletto*, 'I have conceived *Rigoletto* without arias, without final tableaux, just as an endless succession of duets because this form alone satisfied me. If others say, "He should have done thus and thus," I answer, "That may well be so, but what I have done is the best I can do."'

After outdoing French grand opera at its own game in *Les vêpres siciliennes*, Verdi's middle period develops fresh ways of bringing the narrative together with new combinations of forms. His political engagement caused problems with *Un ballo in maschera*, originally alluding to the assassination of Gustav III of Sweden in 1792, which was thought so direct by the Italian censors that the plot had to be changed and reset in seventeenth-century Boston with its Governor as the protagonist; triumphing over the tribulations of its creation, the opera contains gripping music and has been a great success. *La forza del destino*, written for St Petersburg, is a bleak religious parable with some passionate music, which in the original ended with the suicide of the protagonist; this was later changed to a rather weaker spiritual ending, but that does not invalidate the music in the rest of the score. The full maturity of Verdi's imagination can be heard in the magnificent score of *Don Carlos* in French and the powerful drama of *Simon Boccanegra*. His orchestration becomes ever more adventurous and subtle, illuminating his characters and expressing their unspoken conflicts; the climax of this period is *Aida*, which has always been popular because of its vast spectacles, harking back to the traditions of grand opera with processions and the famous triumphal march; the paradox, however, is that at its heart it is a compellingly intimate piece.

Verdi's final triumph was in the two operas that he was persuaded out of comfortable retirement to write: *Otello* in 1887 and *Falstaff* in 1893, both based on Shakespeare in skilfully adapted libretti by Arrigo Boito. That such groundbreaking works could be composed at the end of the nineteenth century seems extraordinary, and it is an achievement that such maturity and adventure can be found so late in the life of the genre. From its stunning opening storm scene to the pathos of Desdemona's prayer 'Ave Maria', with shrewdly drawn characters and dramatic set pieces, *Otello* is a masterpiece which spans the whole range of emotion. If this is the apotheosis of grand opera, *Falstaff* (*42) achieves the same function in comic opera, one in which comedy is raised to the highest level with a warmth surely never surpassed, full of genuine hilarity and humane understanding, culminating in a final backward-glancing fugue as its uplifting finale.

Verdi enabled a traditionally based musical language to continue to be used in opera, albeit with great imagination. By the end of the nineteenth century in Italy there were other trends, notably the emergence of *verismo*, which paralleled the growth of literalism in literature. The aim of *verismo*, not unlike the operatic reforms of the mid-eighteenth century, was to bring opera down to earth, to show ordinary people's struggles and emotions based in the everyday, rather than creating far-off historically based scenarios. The two most famous results of this short-lived movement were one-act operas that are frequently performed together, *Cavalleria rusticana* by Pietro Mascagni (1863–1945) and *Pagliacci* by Ruggero Leoncavallo (1857–1919). These are vivid portraits of local Italian life. Set in Sicily, *Cav*, as it is nicknamed, is a grim tale of love betrayed, most famous for its instrumental Intermezzo which has often been used out of its operatic context. *Pag*, meanwhile, is a similarly violent story, but is more striking and horrific in its outcome, with one of the great tenor roles in opera in Canio, which has attracted the greatest singers of our age. It deserves a place in any history of performance, as it was the first opera to be recorded complete, in 1907, and the first to be filmed complete in 1931. There was a further film directed by Franco Zeffirelli in 1982 with Plácido Domingo as Canio, and countless subsequent recordings.

The route of musical continuity with a generally traditional language was vigorously pursued by Giacomo Puccini (1858–1924), whose deeply conservative approach produced some of the most appealing operas of the period. He came from a family of church musicians in Lucca, and was expected to follow in their footsteps, but a performance of Verdi's *Aida* in Pisa turned his creativity towards opera, and he became a hugely successful composer in the form for which he felt destined. As he put it, 'the Almighty touched me with his little finger and said: "Write for the theatre, mind, only for the theatre!" And I have obeyed the supreme command.' His tragic heroines give their names to many of his operas, and while their emotional scope is arguably limited, their musical and theatrical command of situations and atmosphere is superb. Start with *La Bohème*, whose unforgettable melodies frame a simple, touching story of impecunious students and lovers. *Tosca*, with its brutal scenario ending in the deaths of both protagonists, is more crudely dramatic, but is far from being the 'shabby little shocker' as it was puritanically castigated by a later critic. If there is a Puccini opera that is emotionally manipulative, it is surely the heart-rending but sentimentalised situation of *Madama Butterfly*. *Turandot* was unfinished at the time of the composer's death but has been completed by others. At his best Puccini is unmatched for wit and sheer natural musical exuberance. *Il Trittico*, first seen in New York, is a set of three one-act masterpieces on very different themes, each perfectly realised: *Il tabarro* is a grisly *verismo* tale of passion and betrayal; *Suor Angelica* a weird vision of relationships in a nunnery; and finally the immortal *Gianni Schicchi* (*30), a hilarious comedy centred around the dictation of a false will, in which not a note is wasted. Puccini's work has always been sniffily regarded by critics and academics, but it is among the most popular operatic legacies of all time. Sometimes we just need to accept what the public is telling us, and the triumph of Puccini is such a case.

Alongside grand opera and *opéra-comique*, another strand of lighter music flourished in the second half of the century: operetta, led by the cleverness of Jacques Offenbach (1819–80). For pure fun in the French operatic field, it is difficult to beat his *Orphée aux enfers*, a clever send-up of Gluck's *Orfeo*, full of parody of the gods and mortals alike, set to racy and attractive music. He followed it with a rapid series of satirical and witty operettas including *La belle Hélène* and *La Vie parisienne*. Light-hearted operetta soon spread fast, and in Vienna Johann Strauss 'the Younger' (1825–99), already an established composer, hit the jackpot with *Die Fledermaus*, full of great melodies and using the idiom of the Viennese waltz (of which he had himself written the best-known examples), and then *Der Zigeunerbaron* (The Gypsy Baron). The tradition was continued in slightly more saccharine mode with *The Merry Widow* by the Hungarian Franz Lehár (1870–1948), whose sweeping tunes proved popular everywhere, including London, and encapsulated an increasingly decadent *fin de siècle* culture.

For those of us brought up in an English tradition, the real inheritors of the comic opera genre in the late nineteenth century are the operettas of W. S. Gilbert (1836–1911) as librettist and Arthur Sullivan (1842–1900) as composer: a true partnership which has ensured that (most unusually) the librettist's name has equal billing. Sullivan, with his training in Leipzig helping to form an acute ear for continental operatic style, managed to place whimsical parody alongside genuinely touching melody; there is a Donizetti-inspired ensemble in their early one-act opera *Trial by Jury*. Whether responding to the skilful patter of 'I am the very model of a modern major general' in *The Pirates of Penzance* or creating an artless melody for 'A wand'ring minstrel I' in *The Mikado*, Sullivan captures the moods of Gilbert's ingenious lyrics perfectly. Some of the finest music is in the through-composed finales, and especially the opening sequence of *The Gondoliers* (*45). The vein of gentle satire that so appealed to early audiences has remained remarkably fresh, for instance in the political advancement without evident talent of the First Sea Lord in *HMS Pinafore* or the aspirations of the feminist college in *Princess Ida*. When I first came to know *The Yeomen of the Guard*, *Patience* and *Iolanthe* – all of which marked the peak of my performing career when I sang their leading ladies as a boy! – I had no idea of the operatic models of which they made fun, nor many of their satirical barbs; I took them on their own terms. I can still remember so many of their perfectly crafted words and so much of their entirely memorable music. As examples of the ability of the British to laugh cheerfully at themselves, they sum up a national character in a totally appealing way.

14
Reinvention

In a period of turbulent social change, led by industrialisation and the growth of the well-off middle class, composers from the most conservative to the most adventurous found themselves operating in a world where the old structures of patronage and performance had disappeared. Their task was musical reinvention, reflecting the movements in society and the framework in which their music would be heard. At the start of this shift in the second half of the nineteenth century we have to go back to Johannes Brahms (1833–97), to find a great master of the symphonic form when the tradition itself was being questioned: he is a composer who seems to speak directly to the preoccupations of the time, increasingly aware of the burden of European history, absorbed by the tradition he had inherited from music's past, reluctant to reject it but rather working to renew it.

Brahms was a puzzling character, continually active but curiously unfulfilled. He had played the piano as a boy in the waterside bars of Hamburg, and later said that what he saw there had made a deep and dark impression on him; he certainly acquired some difficulties in the area of personal relationships, remaining a bachelor for the whole of his life in spite of one engagement and his continually warm and close relationship with Clara Schumann. Brahms was obsessed, almost overwhelmed, by the music of the past. He studied with the pianist and composer Eduard Marxsen who had a strong appreciation for the music of previous eras from Bach onwards, and had personally known both Schubert and Beethoven.

This was the period when the historical impetus towards the music of the past took root, and the collected works of the great masters began to be gathered, edited and published. Brahms played a leading role in this process: he venerated Mozart and owned the autograph score of his Symphony No. 40, editing the Requiem for the Mozart Edition. He revived the choral works of previous generations, including music by Schütz, Gabrieli, Bach and Beethoven's *Missa Solemnis*, performing them with his Gesellschaft der Musikfreunde in Vienna.

It is easy to see that this extensive absorption in the past might have caused some problems for Brahms in the creation of his own music. He laboured long and hard over his First Symphony, feeling that the ghost of Beethoven was bearing down on his shoulders. When it was finished in 1876 (having been begun some twenty years earlier), it was hailed as 'Beethoven's Tenth', so close was the resemblance of the hymn-like melody of the finale to that of Beethoven's Ninth Symphony; but as Brahms himself quipped when this was pointed out to him, 'any fool can see that'. The best answer was given by the great scholar and critic Friedrich Chrysander when he reviewed the symphony: 'the reference to Beethoven's last or Ninth Symphony is so obvious here that we cannot postulate a weak, unproductive imitative intent. What we have here is a conscious intent, an artistic will that gives the work its historical significance.' This placed Brahms at the heart of the developing symphonic tradition, combining an acknowledgement of the past with a new form of expression. Beethoven was not the only composer echoed in the First Symphony: others have heard in the relentless triplet tread of its opening the influence of the start of Bach's St Matthew Passion.

Like so many of his predecessors, Brahms was drawn to Vienna where he performed as a pianist and conductor, becoming part of the city's musical life. Alongside his chamber music and symphonies, he wrote striking choral works, of which the most famous became the German Requiem, setting biblical texts in German rather than the words of the Latin Requiem Mass, with antique fugues and stirring melodies. He met the great composers of the day, and had an ambivalent relationship with Wagner, who regarded him as too unadventurous and derivative in his music. Yet Brahms's Second Symphony, composed in 1877, was stirring and successful, exploring the open, major key of D in comparison to the First's

C minor, with a gently swinging first movement in triple time. After two beautifully orchestrated central movements, its exhilarating finale, crowned by brass fanfares, creates one of the most triumphant conclusions in the orchestral repertory.

His Third Symphony in F followed in 1883 and his Fourth in E minor in 1885. By now Brahms's fame was well established and both works were immediate successes. Melodies from the Third Symphony, which is the least assertive of the set, with a quiet ending, have become often quoted in popular culture and film; it is a concise and consoling work with a strong strain of melancholy and owes something to the influence of Schubert and Schumann (whose 'Rhenish' symphony is echoed in its opening), allowing exuberance to break through occasionally but never to triumph. The Fourth Symphony is a magnificent, much more outgoing symphony, though being in the key of E minor it retains a stern monumentality. Its first movement, with its sweeping first theme, is powerfully argued, the second movement breathes the spirit of nature with its opening horn call, while the third movement is a real scherzo that accumulates amazing power in the final pages. For his finale, Brahms activates a plan he had been considering for some years: it is built on a ground bass which he took from an early Bach cantata, *Nach dir, Herr, verlanget mich* (No. 150), adding a chromatic note to propel it into the nineteenth century, and making it a passacaglia theme over which he constructs a sequence of variations embodying what has been called a spirit of 'wintry resolve', before ending in triumph.

It is difficult to overestimate the extent to which Brahms's four symphonies established a central place in the orchestral repertory in the succeeding years, providing a fulcrum around which some European orchestras orientated their work, featured in repeat performances by great orchestras such as the Berlin Philharmonic and the Vienna Philharmonic under conductors from Wilhelm Furtwängler and Herbert von Karajan to Claudio Abbado and Christian Thielemann. Smaller-scale accounts with chamber orchestras by Charles Mackerras and Robin Ticciati have reflected more closely the forces with which the symphonies would originally have been performed, while other conductors like Roger Norrington have gone further, using the instruments of the time to counter the argument that

Brahms's orchestral textures are too dense and clogged. Whatever the forces used, Brahms's symphonies remain a cornerstone of the repertory, and their freshness of appeal has only been increased by new performing styles.

Before his later hard-won symphonies, Brahms provided four gifts to Romantic virtuosi: the two massive piano concertos, one violin concerto, and an unusual double concerto. These are among his greatest musical achievements, and it is surely part of their appeal that they in no way feel like mere showcases for virtuosity. The First Piano Concerto, completed in 1858, was the result of considerable struggle, reflecting Brahms's involvement with Schumann, who had tried to take his own life in 1854 after which he was confined to a mental institution. It had begun life as a work for two pianos, which was then altered and adapted as a partnership with orchestra. There is a sense of titanic struggle expressed by the fiendishly difficult octave trills in the first movement piano part. By contrast the slow movement seems to echo Brahms's involvement with the religious music of the past, made explicit by the inscription 'Benedictus qui venit in nomine Domini', a direct quotation from the text of the Mass – but also an inscription at the abbey where E. T. A. Hoffmann's literary character Kapellmeister Johannes Kreisler finds rest, giving the allusion a Romantic twist. Brahms's Second Piano Concerto, which is a later work from 1881, is another masterpiece, but in a more restrained vein, the mood set by its quietly lyrical opening with horn and rippling piano figuration. There is a paradoxical chamber-music quality to this big work, especially in the slow movement where a solo cello partners the piano. The outgoing finale with its Hungarian mood and gypsy rhythm represents another essential side of Brahms's nature – but is no less difficult for the pianist.

The third of Brahms's great contributions to the concerto repertory is the Violin Concerto of 1878, where a Hungarian flavour also colours its last movement, while the central movement also features a solo instrument, here the oboe with a memorable melody elaborated by the violin. The first movement bears the weightiest structure, but also achieves the widest emotional range, especially in the final pages after the soloist's cadenza, where the music floats wonderfully around the themes until it gathers for the conclusion. The concerto was written for the famous violinist Joseph Joachim, whose advice Brahms sought (but did not always take) on the technical issues of violin writing. Also written for Joachim and a colleague, the late Double Concerto for violin and cello is a more mellow and lyrical piece using a tricky combination of instruments skilfully; it was Brahms's last orchestral work.

There is another aspect of the idea of reinvention in the solo piano pieces that Brahms created towards the end of his life. Here he is reimagining every facet of keyboard writing that he inherited from Beethoven and Schubert. They require virtuosity but of an inner kind, a mastery of the keyboard that allows every subtlety to tell. From the final decade of the nineteenth century, the Intermezzi Op. 117 and the Klavierstücke Op. 119 are among the most eloquent of all piano pieces. The lullaby inspired by a Scottish folk song that opens the Op. 117 in easeful E flat major is a simple and moving melody, yet subtly turned with accents in both twos and threes; the second intermezzo is tinged with sadness and regret; while the more assertive Op. 117 No. 3 also relates to a Scottish folk song. These pieces certainly link back to the final pianistic thoughts of Beethoven and Schubert, but there is also a sparseness and a restraint which echo Liszt's attempts to dissolve tonality in his late music. Brahms does not challenge tonality, and remains anchored to a key, but in the ethereal chord sequences of Op. 119 No. 1 in B minor (*43) he seems to question the future, and reach beyond the music to another world (Plate 19).

The symphonist who became most popular with audiences alongside Brahms was the Russian Piotr Ilyich Tchaikovsky (1840–93). This is striking, because Tchaikovsky did not come from the European classical tradition like Brahms, but from the Russian nationalist school (p. 207). His reputation has continually been divided between those who felt his music was not Russian enough, because it incorporated so many elements of the Western symphonic tradition, and those who felt it was not symphonic enough because of its roots in a nationalist idiom. We might now regard his final sequence of dramatic, heartfelt symphonies as too self-obsessed, but they cut to the heart of the Romantic dilemma. Tchaikovsky was expressing his personal traumas – of which there were many – through music in an extrovert way, and they gained wide acceptance at least partly because they are so skilfully written for the orchestra, and partly because they were psychologically penetrating in a way with which audiences could identify. It is intriguing that Tchaikovsky, whom we now consider a prime exponent of a heart-on-sleeve musical emotionalist, revered Mozart the classicist above all previous composers.

Tchaikovsky was trained as a civil servant before entering the St Petersburg Conservatory and studying with Anton Rubinstein, and then teaching in Moscow. He became successful as both a conductor and composer, but the nature of Tchaikovsky's personal relationships caused him much unhappiness. Although he was certainly homosexual, he first became engaged to the Belgian soprano Désirée Artôt and then, more disastrously, married Antonina Milyukova, a former student, for a short time in 1877. The relationship that seemed to give him stability was with the wealthy widow Nadezhda von Meck, who became his patron, but bizarrely, despite their long and regular correspondence, they agreed never to meet. Instead she wrote to him passionate commentaries on his work: 'your march, Peter Ilyich, is so beautiful that it lifts me, as I had hoped, into that mood of blissful madness in which one can forget all that is bitter and offensive in the world. It is impossible to describe the chaos which reigns in my head and heart when I hear it . . .' Torn between his desire to remain out of the limelight and his need for success as a musician, Tchaikovsky gradually acquired the acclaim he deserved at home and abroad, culminating in the first performance of his Sixth Symphony which he conducted in 1893 in St Petersburg.

While his earlier symphonies, including the attractive Second, the 'Little Russian', have not been regularly performed, the final three are among the most often played of all symphonies. His Fourth Symphony is dark and powerful, in a traditional format with a strong first movement, but moving towards an innovative use of blocks of undeveloped material in close juxtaposition. The Scherzo with its pizzicato strings and burbling winds conjures up what the composer calls 'fugitive images that pass through one's mind when one has had a little wine to drink and is feeling the first effects of intoxication'. The Fifth Symphony is the most traditional in form, but uses a motto theme to link together the powerful movements, all with the aim of depicting fate and 'the inscrutable design of Providence'. The final Sixth Symphony in B minor, with its later nickname the 'Pathétique', became his trademark. Here he moves from a slow introduction to a sombre first movement, then translates a waltz into five-in-a-bar, and creates a terrific, assertive but despairing march. Audiences are ready to applaud as if it is the end of the symphony, but a final slow movement follows, capturing utter despair – fading away with a dying fall that pre-echoes the close of Mahler's Ninth Symphony (p. 199).

The reception of Tchaikovsky's last symphony has been all the greater (rather like that of Mozart's Requiem: p. 150) because just a few days later the composer died, whether through illness or suicide we will probably never be quite sure. But his legacy lives on at least as much in his operas *Eugene Onegin* and *Queen of Spades*, his flamboyant First Piano Concerto, his beautiful songs, and especially his ballets. For an introduction to Tchaikovsky's music at its most ingratiating and winningly scored, do try his three dance works – *The Nutcracker* with its precisely characterised sequences like the 'Dance of the Sugar Plum Fairy', and *The Sleeping Beauty* and *Swan Lake* (*49) with their endless waltzes. When Tchaikovsky could escape his personal torment, he wrote music of subtle charm, perfect craftsmanship and great beauty.

While Tchaikovsky was composing and Brahms was still struggling with the challenge of the symphony, Anton Bruckner (1824–96) was already active in expanding the form and hugely extending its range and length. A church organist from Linz, he created massively sonorous symphonies that specifically evoke the organ in long, sustained passages for wind and brass and soaring melodies for strings. He vastly expanded the scope of the symphony without radically changing its form; the content of his music is unusual because of its almost hypnotic repetitiveness, some of its effects anticipating the minimalism of composers a century later. His symphonies are monumental, and they aspire to a new type of musical architecture, built across large spans of material that do not always develop. Bruckner, untypically among composers, was extremely insecure in his judgements of his own music: he often revised his scores at the suggestion of conductors and others, giving rise to several different versions of his greatest works.

The first of his great symphonies after the uneven earlier works (No. 2 is 'Bruckner Too Long', a conductor once said to me) is the Fourth, called the 'Romantic', which originally came with a naïve programme describing its antique scenes: dawn in a medieval town, hunting and processing knights. The Fifth Symphony is a good starting point for its sheerly magnificent sound, but contains many surprises in its unpredictable use of tonality. It was only with the Seventh Symphony (*47), with its glorious opening theme for the cellos, that Bruckner began to be widely noticed as a composer, after the great conductor Arthur Nikisch premiered the work in Leipzig on 30 December 1884. Hermann Levi and then Hans Richter took it up, as have most of today's leading conductors, notably Bernard Haitink who made it his own.

Bruckner paid tribute to Wagner in his magnificent Eighth Symphony with its slow movement using the special instruments from Wagner's *Ring* cycle, known as Wagner tubas, to create a sonorous and unutterably beautiful sense of calm. Then, in his unfinished Ninth Symphony he strove to create a final testament (which has been completed from the surviving sketches by various hands) and described it as a farewell to life. Bruckner's legacy is equally felt in his smaller religious works, gem-like motets (*Os justi, Ave Maria, Ecce sacerdos magnus*) and a splendid *Te Deum*, but very little chamber music.

Bruckner's younger contemporary Gustav Mahler (1860–1911) took the symphony into the twentieth century and dissolved its formats in a series of often disturbing visions. Mahler's works have been felt to portray the potential end of the symphony as a form, though in the succeeding decades the symphony as an idea has proved surprisingly resilient. Born in Bohemia, and always bringing echoes of its folk tradition and poetry into his music, Mahler was a demanding conductor as well as a composer, an intensely practical indicator of every detail in his scores so that performers could be in no doubt as to his intentions (p. 6). First at the Vienna State Opera and in his last years at the New York Metropolitan Opera, Mahler raised standards ('tradition', he famously said, 'is laziness') until his life was cut short by heart disease. He worked obsessively through many tragedies, the death of his daughter, and the faithlessness of his wife Alma with the architect Walter Gropius, provoked by Mahler's relentless refusal to allow her own creative career as a composer to develop alongside his. He concentrated his composition into his summer breaks from conducting, when he would retire from the city to the lakes and mountains that stimulated his creativity (Plate 23).

Only Mahler's stirring First Symphony retains the outlines of a form he had inherited from Beethoven and Brahms; he conceived it with a programme in five movements, and originally called it 'Titan', but resolved it into four movements: it is perfectly paced to end in a raucously affirmative climax. Adding vocal and choral forces to his Second Symphony, the 'Resurrection', Mahler creates a life-to-death sequence of movements which end in overwhelming glory: this has now become one of his regularly performed, probably over-performed, masterpieces. Already by the nature-inspired Third Symphony, Mahler is eschewing the grandiose climax for something much warmer and broader, ending the symphony with an elegiac, hymn-like movement marked 'slow, peaceful, with feeling', and including children's playground voices in the fifth movement; the Fourth Symphony ends with a vocal movement, an innocent solo song of a child's view of heaven, 'Das himmlische Leben', that lifts the work into the harmony of the angels. In his conducting work in Vienna, Mahler was preparing the music of Wagner and Mozart (reviving the then neglected *Così fan tutte*) and perhaps that work is reflected in the development of his own musical language. In an earlier age of confidence, the end of a symphony was the resolution of the musical arguments it had presented, as in Beethoven's Fifth. The problem of how to resolve Mahler's intensely personal conflicts within the format of the symphonic musical argument preoccupied him: he succeeded in bringing the three-part, five-movement Fifth Symphony (*40) to a close with a final triumph after the bittersweet Adagietto, a movement made famous by its inclusion in Luchino Visconti's film *Death in Venice*.

Some have criticised as banal the almost cheerful resolution of the five-movement Seventh Symphony with its two eerie *Nachtmusik* ('night music') movements, though in a really good performance the triumph is organic. Mahler avoids resolution altogether in the apocalyptic and magnificent Sixth Symphony, which reverts to a four-movement model, but fills it with the most turbulent vision of a new century, the individual struggling against implacable fate, symbolised by the three hammer blows in the finale, ending in what sounds like despair. Then Mahler reaches still further in the massive but flawed vision of the Eighth Symphony, with its thousand performers (in an ideally large-scale performance) and text from the old Latin hymn *Veni, creator spiritus* (Part 1) juxtaposed with Goethe's *Faust* (Part 2), imagining, as he put it, the universe ringing and resounding. It is an ambitious concept that has magnificent moments but arguably does not quite

manage to unify the old-style choral approach to the Latin text in the first part
with a soloistic approach to the Goethe setting in the second.

Mahler's last completed symphony, his Ninth, expires with one of the longest,
most drawn-out deaths in all music, the hymn-like melody of its final movement
torn apart and dislocated into tiny shreds, spread through an orchestra which
seems frozen by despair. It is an unearthly and moving end to an odyssey which
had taken the composer from the nineteenth into the twentieth century, developing the symphonic form beyond anything that had been thought possible by
his predecessors. He was to attempt to go further in beginning his Tenth Symphony: its opening Adagio survives complete, while the composer's sketches for
the other movements have been completed by Deryck Cooke, with Colin and
David Matthews.

Mahler did complete the song cycle *Das Lied von der Erde* for two soloists and
large orchestra. Mahler had heard recorded cylinders of Chinese music, and they
certainly influenced the musical language in this piece. He set the words of Tang
dynasty poets, notably Li Po, which he found adapted in a volume of poetry called
The Chinese Flute by Hans Bethge. As these texts were already changed from the
originals, Mahler felt free to adapt them further to reflect his universal concerns
about the relation between humanity and nature. 'I seek peace for my lonely heart.
I wander to my homeland . . . everywhere the good earth blossoms into spring',
reads the final poem in Mahler's own text. The underlying message derived from
the Chinese philosophy of the poetry is ever present, and so *Das Lied von der Erde*
takes far more from the East than the superficial sound of its music: it takes us to
the heart of its message, especially in the final painful *Abschied*. Some of Mahler's
song cycles were scored for orchestra from their piano versions, and are among
his most successful works: the *Lieder eines fahrenden Gesellen* and the series of
settings of poems *Des Knaben Wunderhorn*, with the tragic *Kindertotenlieder* set to
texts by Friedrich Rückert.

Mahler's symphonies were not always successful in the composer's lifetime,
and were accounted failures when given in under-prepared performances. But
they have come into their own as central works of the renewed classical tradition
in the twentieth century, a clear example of the fact that great art can take time

to communicate to audiences. It was the continued devotion of conductors like Bruno Walter (Mahler's choice as his assistant at the Vienna Court Opera), then the advocacy of a new generation led by Leonard Bernstein, who brought them into the mainstream. Now they represent a peak of symphonic performance to which many conductors aspire, and which audiences crowd to hear. They need, perhaps, to be taken in moderation.

The days of the big affirmatory symphony were numbered, but not before two symphonies by Edward Elgar (1857–1934) touched a nerve with the public in Britain and Europe and, like so much English music, achieved new things late in the life of the form. Following the early success of his orchestral *Enigma Variations*, these early twentieth-century symphonies deserve to be counted alongside the greatest. The First Symphony, with its initial noble motto theme, touches the heights of eloquence in its lamenting slow movement, and then brings back its motto theme in unsullied triumph at the close. The Second Symphony, which starts with a burst of optimism, ends not in triumph but in nostalgic yearning, longing for a world that was rapidly evaporating. From being regarded as quintessentially English and so unexportable, Elgar's two symphonies were taken up by conductors such as Georg Solti, André Previn and Daniel Barenboim, and often heard in Europe, and it is fascinating to hear the First Symphony played with European skill and non-vibrato eloquence by the Southwest German Radio Symphony Orchestra under Roger Norrington. Elgar was to struggle with the challenge of a post-war Third Symphony that had been commissioned by the BBC at the insistence of George Bernard Shaw, and though he wrote many sketches, he was never to complete it. It took Anthony Payne (1936–), a contemporary composer with a deep understanding of Elgar's idiom, working with the support of conductor Andrew Davis, to memorably bring the Third to fruition in 1995.

Elgar's other signal contribution was the revival of the oratorio, so long moribund in nineteenth-century England, with the drama of *The Dream of Gerontius* to a text by Cardinal Newman that Dvořák once considered setting. Although it was a failure at its ill-prepared premiere in Birmingham (Vaughan Williams reported memorably that the Gerontius sang 'in the correct tenor attitude, with one foot slightly withdrawn'), it soon became recognised as an inspiring example of what could be achieved in the form, influencing Britten, Walton and others. Following his large-scale, big-boned Violin Concerto, in his more concentrated Cello Concerto (*28), written after both the First World War and the death of his wife Alice, Elgar creates an unforgettable farewell to an era, shot through with tender regret. It acquired a particular poignancy as the signature performance of the cellist Jacqueline du Pré in the years before her illness.

The twentieth-century symphony flourished in the hands of the leading Finnish composer Jean Sibelius (1865–1957), whose seven symphonies provided a much-needed boost to the core orchestral repertory, with a strong nationalistic tinge that ensured wide acceptance. Indeed Sibelius's First Symphony looks back to Tchaikovsky's models, with a sweeping melodic drive. But the contrast between Sibelius and Mahler as contemporary symphonic composers could not be more marked. They once met and discussed their approaches. While Sibelius talked about severity of style and a profound logic that linked motifs, Mahler disagreed, saying that the symphony 'must embrace the whole world'. Sibelius's symphonies are regarded by many as outstanding twentieth-century examples of the form, skilfully balancing exactly the structural and emotional elements that the composer debated with Mahler. Sibelius's Second Symphony with its broad themes and bold orchestral textures is an immediately approachable work, rising to a noble climax (perhaps with nationalist allusions) in its finale. The Third Symphony moves away from this extrovert mood to a more inward style which still manages to end in triumph, while his Fourth takes the move to severity still further, and has been called his most austere symphony, dark and brooding. The Fifth marks a return to a more outward-facing style, edgy and energetic, evidently inspired by Sibelius's glimpses of the natural world, struggling towards its glorious climax with sudden silent pauses just before the end of the piece which never cease to astonish (*25). The Sixth is once again enigmatic in tone: the composer described it as 'very tranquil in character and outline'; it maintains the four-movement symphonic form, but the Seventh, conceived around the same time, condenses the whole argument into a single movement, restless, turbulent, but in the end full of positive affirmation. After his Seventh Symphony, Sibelius drastically slowed his productivity and completed no more symphonies. Their popularity has waxed and waned during the twentieth century, as they lay outside the modernist mainstream, but their strong appeal to conductors and listeners ensured a revival later in the century. Continuously popular have been his colourful tone poems, especially *The Oceanides*, the subtle *Tapiola* and *The Swan of Tuonela*, and most of all his Violin Concerto, which is superbly written for the soloist, balances lyricism with virtuosity, and is among the greatest twentieth-century concertos.

The Danish Carl Nielsen (1865–1931), whose six symphonies are at once more eccentric and wilder than Sibelius's, took longer to establish himself. His Third Symphony 'Sinfonia espansiva' emerged from a period before the First World War when Nielsen described his vision: 'Our work is a continual protest against the thought of death, and an appeal to and cry for life.' Under the influence of the war, Nielsen became ever more desperate to affirm the message of music, and called his Fourth Symphony the 'Inextinguishable' (*31), meaning for him 'in one word what only music has the power to express in full: The Elemental Will of Life. Music is Life, and like it inextinguishable.' Its finale pits two sets of timpanists on opposite sides of the orchestra against each other. He was much less sure of his position by the 1920s when he wrote his more pessimistic and tortured Fifth Symphony, where a single side drum attempts to interrupt the progress of the entire ensemble, but the piece wrenches itself into an upbeat conclusion.

Dmitry Shostakovich (1906–75) is now emerging with audiences as one of the most important composers of the twentieth century. His music will never be endorsed by advanced modernists, for whom it is insufficiently complex and challenging. (Pierre Boulez, for instance, never conducted his symphonies, though most other leading conductors from Bernard Haitink to Mariss Jansons and Andris Nelsons have responded to their power.) For audiences his music communicates directly, especially when aligned to narratives about his persecution by the Soviet authorities. Such stories came to light with the 1979 publication of *Testimony*, described as Shostakovich's memoirs dictated to Solomon Volkov, though argument still rages about the authenticity of that material. His successful opera *Lady Macbeth of Mtsensk*, premiered in 1934, was withdrawn after *Pravda* denounced it as 'muddle instead of music'. Subsequently Shostakovich always kept his true opinions and feelings carefully under wraps in his verbal pronouncements, even though the weight of his musical meaning could be heard by anyone with ears to hear. It must have been agonising for him to create within the restrictions and criticism that he faced, and on his public appearances he always seemed a tortured personality; but his music has survived to triumph over the Soviet regimes that censored it.

Shostakovich's precocious First Symphony had been a big success for a prodigy, and it was taken up by leading conductors such as Otto Klemperer and Leopold Stokowski. It led on to the titanic Fourth Symphony which Shostakovich had to withdraw in the wake of the denunciation of his opera. Hidden for years until it could be performed in 1961, eight years after the death of Stalin, the Fourth Symphony made an overwhelming impression and Shostakovich confided that he felt it 'stands much higher than my recent ones'. Instead, as a follow-up to the fated opera, he wrote the emotionally simpler and more strident Fifth Symphony which he labelled, surely ironically, as 'a Soviet artist's reply to just criticism'. It was perceived as the sort of music the regime wanted, yet its spirit of repression in the painfully powerful last movement is audible: it had a triumphant reception from an audience who surely grasped what was being said. The Seventh Symphony, called the 'Leningrad', was written during the Nazi siege of the city (1941–4) where the composer was serving as a firefighter, which lent the work a certain glamour in the West (Plate 23). *Time* magazine featured Shostakovich resplendent in fire helmet on its cover in July 1942, and the score was smuggled out so that Toscanini could give its premiere. Its occasionally crude music was briefly parodied by Béla Bartók in his *Concerto for Orchestra* (p. 211). Deeper and more affecting is the extended Eighth Symphony, still a wartime work but one that feels more abstract in its concerns, though no less urgent; it was written in an extraordinary heat of intensity across some forty days. It conveys both hope and desolation in equal measure, and its winding evolution of themes is compelling, though the final evaporation at the end of the last movement leaves the strongest memory.

In his intense series of post-war string quartets, Shostakovich found his favourite medium: as critic Alex Ross puts it, the intimate quartet form 'gave him the freedom to write labyrinthine narratives full of blankly winding fugues, near-motionless funeral marches, wry displays of folkish jollity, off-kilter genre exercises, and stretches of deliberate blandness'. Although not part of the most advanced post-war music, Shostakovich's symphonies continued with the concentrated and hard-hitting Tenth Symphony (*14), with its galvanising Scherzo, right up to the intense vocal settings of the Fourteenth Symphony which are preoccupied with death. The enigmatic final Fifteenth Symphony, like his late Viola Sonata, both from the 1970s, is shot through with quotations from earlier music as the composer strips down his musical language to the very barest essentials. In these pieces Rossini's *William Tell* Overture and Beethoven's 'Moonlight' Sonata appear as ghostly echoes of a long-dead musical past.

15

Homelands

Nationalism – a creative flourishing of those strands of music inspired by the vision of a single country, and expressive of a particular cultural identity – was one of the most fruitful movements in nineteenth- and early twentieth-century music. Yet, taken to extremes, nationalism as a movement divided nations in conflict rather than uniting them, and eventually lay behind some of the worst wars mankind has seen. Historians have seen the origin of the nation state as the inevitable result of a movement from an agricultural society based on the land to an industrial revolution which created the need for state control and organisation based on the city. Among the many artistic changes that resulted were the creation of cultural centres in the heart of the major cities, and in the musical sphere the establishment of concert societies and the provision of music for the educated middle classes. Conflicts such as the Franco-Prussian War of 1870–1 hastened the establishment of strongly national cultural organisations. Great exhibitions, such as that of 1851 at the Crystal Palace and the Exposition Universelle in Paris in 1889, expressed the formulation of a national identity and purpose. Twentieth-century composers with the memory of world conflict spoke of their desire to rid their music of specifically national traits and to conceive universal idioms. Yet the identity of a country – America's wide-open prairie spaces, or England's green countryside – has proved a resilient source for the imagination of composers. And for a flourishing period, national identity produced great music whose very success, paradoxically, was its ability to transcend national barriers and to be widely appreciated (Plate 25).

Nationalism rooted in the traditions of the past was especially powerful in eastern Europe, where the pace of industrial change had been more gradual, and the old folk repertory was still prominent. How far these traditional songs and dances could be said to represent a newly emergent national identity is arguable, but they provided an appropriate source for composers expressing a new cultural idiom. The Czech composer Bedřich Smetana (1824–84) was one of the first to successfully colonise this repertory and to create an idiom out of Bohemia's woods and fields, which became the title of one movement in his hugely popular nationalist portrait *Má vlast* (My Homeland). His compatriot Antonín Dvořák (1841–1904) drew on local traditions in his expressive and exuberant *Slavonic Dances* in Prague, and kept a balance between traditional symphonic argument in his Seventh Symphony and nationalist exuberance in his Eighth Symphony (*44), deftly conjuring a rhapsodic portrayal of the countryside and village life.

When he was invited to New York in 1892 to teach at Jeannette Thurber's National Conservatory of Music of America, which even in a time of segregation admitted Black students, it was through an African-American student, Henry Thacker Burleigh, that Dvořák was introduced to spirituals, and these made their way into his music. Far from his national roots, it was in America that he composed his famous Ninth Symphony subtitled 'from the New World', using both pentatonic scales and a spiritual-like melody in a highly polished and sophisticated context. Dvořák was a cosmopolitan figure who travelled widely, and in his music, nationalism acquires a broad humanity: his glorious Cello Concerto is one of the very few successful concertos for that instrument with a full symphony orchestra, which is so difficult to balance with the solo, low-pitched cello.

Leoš Janáček (1854–1928) was born into a generation of Czech nationalists, and his music was a very late flowering of great originality. He remained opposed to the Austro-German tradition on his doorstep, and in a series of late operas created a musical world entirely of his own. Janáček's music sounds like no one else's, and that is because of his dependence on the speech rhythms and natural inflections of his native Moravia, which he transcribed and transformed into a unique musical language. *Jenůfa*, premiered in 1904, brought him wide attention only after being performed in Prague in 1916; then followed in rapid succession the naturalistic tragedy of *Katya Kabanova*, the anthropomorphic fantasy of *The Cunning Little Vixen*, the gripping parable *The Makropoulos Affair*, and the bleak prison tale *From the House of the Dead*. These operas only took root elsewhere after the Second World War, but they have now become part of the international reper- tory thanks to the advocacy of certain conductors, especially Charles Mackerras. Janáček's piano and ensemble music, the dazzling fanfares of his Sinfonietta (*24) for large orchestra and the 'outdoor' pagan splendour of the *Glagolitic Mass* have ensured that his special take on nationalism flourishes in the present.

In Russia, Mily Balakirev (1837–1910) was a noted teacher of an important generation of Russian composers, and one of a group famously characterised as the Mighty Handful who together created a distinctly nationalist sound. These composers formed a group of iconoclasts who opposed conventional authority and went their own way through shared experiences and intense dis- cussions of music they liked or disliked. The Russian composer and music critic César Cui records how disrespectful they were of Mozart and Mendelssohn; they preferred Liszt and Berlioz, and 'worshipped Chopin and Glinka'. Although Balakirev wrote symphonies (one of which I recall playing as an amateur bassoon- ist that included a note that was too low for the instrument, a problem solved by inserting a cardboard toilet roll into the top of the bassoon), he is more com- monly heard in piano recitals with his exotic fantasy *Islamey*, a work which has also been orchestrated.

His pupil Modest Petrovich Mussorgsky (1839–81), like several of this group a professional in his own right as an army officer, was determined to express a strong Russian nationalism in music, and his great opera *Boris Godunov* tells the story of Russian history through the lens of a national struggle. (Dvořák interest- ingly wrote a much less well-known opera, *Dimitrij*, whose plot begins exactly at the point where *Boris* ends.) *Night on the Bare Mountain* and *Pictures at an Exhibi- tion* (*51) are both powerful depictions of Russia, the former based on national legends, the latter on the paintings of Viktor Hartmann. Originally conceived for piano, *Pictures* was orchestrated by Maurice Ravel to sumptuous effect.

The scoring of *Night on the Bare Mountain* was colourfully revised by Nikolay Rimsky-Korsakov (1844–1908), another member of the Mighty Handful. He also completed Mussorgsky's opera *Khovanshchina* after the death of the composer, whose work had been interrupted by financial crises and alcoholism; and Rimsky-Korsakov worked on *Prince Igor* by Aleksandr Borodin (1833–87), yet another member of the Handful, who was well known in his day as a chemist as well as a composer. Rimsky-Korsakov was most successful as reviser and teacher, passing the nationalists' heritage on to Stravinsky and Prokofiev. His own fifteen operas have never securely held the stage outside Russia, though some, including *The Golden Cockerel*, *The Invisible City of Kitezh* and *The Snow Maiden*, all based on Russian legends, are revived and are popular with his supporters. Like his compatriot Glinka, Rimsky-Korsakov's nationalist leanings not only had a Russian outcome, but also led him to Spanish music in the skilfully scored *Capriccio espagnol* and the equally exotic *Scheherazade*, where tales of the *Arabian Nights* are retold in lavish orchestration.

Spanish music was among the strongest national schools to attract international attention: its distinctive idioms drew all manner of composers and provided material for their work. Rimsky-Korsakov's homage in the *Capriccio espagnol* followed Bizet's *Carmen*, Édouard Lalo's *Symphonie espagnole* and Emmanuel Chabrier's *España*. The Spanish composer Manuel de Falla (1876–1946) was in Paris for seven years from 1907 when both Debussy (in his *Ibéria*) and Ravel (in his opera *L'heure espagnole*) were absorbed in Spanish music. Falla went on to write hard, gem-like pieces owing much to their folkloric background. His first opera, *La vida breve*, which premiered in Nice in 1913, mixed folk inspiration with a tinge of modernism; it was gradually accepted and revised, then performed in Spanish in Madrid in 1914 to huge acclaim. He wrote successful, sharply scored ballets, notably *El amor brujo* and *The Three-Cornered Hat*. Among all these Spanish-influenced composers, Falla is a real original, and not one of his works is conventional: for Wanda Landowska he wrote a fierce Harpsichord Concerto; he created a puppet play within a puppet play, *Master Peter's Puppet Show*, based on an episode from Cervantes's *Don Quixote*; and he laboured long and hard on his unfinished dramatic oratorio *Atlántida*, which survives only as a fragment.

The small extent of Falla's output is made up for by the scrupulous quality of every piece.

Isaac Albéniz (1860–1909) developed the Spanish tradition, especially in his characteristic piano music: he followed in the footsteps of Liszt as a travelling piano virtuoso and improviser, creating the extravagant and difficult suite *Iberia*, which was said with some sarcasm to contain nothing that a good three-handed pianist could not master. Enrique Granados (1867–1916) wrote *Goyescas*, first as a piano suite and later as a one-act opera. Highly typical of the time was the Spanish native operetta called the *zarzuela*, which originated in the seventeenth century as a local genre of music-theatre, and then flourished in the second half of the nineteenth century and the first half of the twentieth century as a genuinely popular genre of light operatic music, with an emphasis on melody and homespun culture, on a par with Johann Strauss in Vienna or Gilbert and Sullivan in England. Like the latter, *zarzuela* has remained something of an acquired taste outside its native land.

Reflecting other national identities was Edvard Grieg (1843–1907) and a group of Scandinavian colleagues. Grieg's incidental music for Ibsen's *Peer Gynt* captures the essence of Norway with an impressionistic gift for sound-painting. Grieg absorbed German culture through his time at the Leipzig Conservatory, and wrote in traditional forms too. It would be hard to hear any primarily nationalistic tinge in his famous Piano Concerto, which became so popular that he grew to dislike it because of the number of times he was asked to play or conduct it. Grieg's chamber music includes three violin sonatas and a cello sonata of considerable subtlety.

In France, nationalism received a boost from the formation of the Société Nationale de Musique in 1871, whose motto was 'Ars gallica'. César Franck (1822–90) was a late developer whose first major success was his Piano Quintet written when he was fifty-seven. Even later, in 1888 his Symphony in D minor, which uses a unified thematic approach across its three movements, became the leading example of French symphonic art; the fine Violin Sonata in A with its canonic treatment of its main theme in the finale is a masterpiece. His lively and attractive *Symphonic Variations* for piano and orchestra is all too little heard today. French music itself was on the cusp of a revolution (p. 227) but its native traditions were still being developed in the music of Gabriel Fauré (1845–1924), who wrote *mélodies* setting the symbolist poetry of Paul Verlaine in his song cycle *La bonne chanson*.

Fauré's greatest achievement, and for me one of the most serenely beautiful works in existence, is his choral Requiem (*48), on which he worked over many years, expanding the orchestration from the small-scale original which had no violins, with the collaboration of Roger-Ducasse. Far from the terrors of death conjured up in the Requiems of Verdi or Berlioz, this gentle piece points to a transcendental calm in the afterlife, hinted at in the horn calls of the Sanctus, summed up by the calm melodic flow of the solo Libera me and choral Agnus Dei, and sealed by the untypical choice of the text 'In paradisum deducant angeli' (May the angels lead you into paradise) as the eloquent final movement. Nadia Boulanger, who conducted its first performances in England in the 1930s, said of the Requiem, 'no doubt tarnishes its unassailable faith, its quiet confidence, its tender and peaceful expectation'.

Camille Saint-Saëns (1835–1921), who led the Société Nationale, was active as a composer of operas which have not lasted (with the exception of *Samson et Dalila*), piano concertos of which the lively No. 2 is the most played, and fine chamber music. His Third 'Organ' Symphony unusually features the grand organ as the central solo instrument; modern technology has enabled it to be played in halls not containing an organ by beaming in the sounds from a local church or cathedral. His *Carnival of the Animals* (*46) was so popular that he banned its publication until after his death, and it remains hugely enjoyable. At the end of his life Saint-Saëns wrote a series of fine, neglected sonatas for wind instruments: oboe, clarinet and bassoon. He was deeply committed to the music of his country's past and edited the complete keyboard works of Rameau.

The most compelling evidence of the depth of nationalist feeling in these years is the work of researchers to collect the folk traditions of their native lands. Béla Bartók (1881–1945) in Hungary was tireless in his efforts to ensure that the music was captured before it disappeared (Plate 22). Bartók travelled far and wide in this quest, and used the discoveries in his own music – not as some English composers did, in literal quotation, but as a way of analysing a new way forward for music that was not dependent on the classical tradition. Bartók's 'deep folk' style produced his chilling one-act opera *Duke Bluebeard's Castle* and his piano concertos, and later embraced a wider palette in his orchestral masterpiece, the *Music for Strings, Percussion and Celesta* (*19), making use of antiphonal exchanges between two groups of players and creating an eerie, winding fugue to start, an atmospheric night music movement, as well as an exuberant folk-inspired finale. After the war took him to America, he forged a more inclusive style in the *Concerto for Orchestra* (poking some fun at Shostakovich). Bartók is one of the most successful composers of the twentieth century to have created a new language from old traditions. His constant collaborator in collecting and publishing folk material was Zoltán Kodály (1882–1967); his fine compositions were equalled in importance by the constant commitment he showed to music for young people through the development of the 'Kodály method' in choral singing. He was a true pioneer of popular, excellent education for all, creating both musical material and methods of delivery that had a major influence.

Equally individual within a very different sound-world, using folk influence with lush and sonorous effects, is Karol Szymanowski (1882–1937), who skilfully mixed the influence of his Polish roots with a wide knowledge of advanced European music. His one opera *King Roger* is a ritualistic and deliberately static work set in Sicily, full of magnificent music, which after a long period of neglect is now entering the repertory; his wonderful *Stabat mater* carries on a long tradition of setting this Marian text by reworking it as a sumptuous choral fresco. Immediately appealing are his two violin concertos from 1916 and 1933 (*22), superbly written for the instrument; the first uses a large orchestra with great colouristic subtlety.

American composers played a major part in bringing nationalism onto a wider world stage. Charles Ives (1874–1954) was one of the major innovators of his time, drawing on the half-heard sounds around him to create collage-like tapestries of everyday life based on the music of New England: hymns, marching songs, landscape and ambitious philosophical thoughts in his 'Concord' Sonata for piano. His Symphony No. 2 is a good introduction to his music; his Symphony No. 4 is a massive, bewildering assembly of great effects. Most atmospheric to start with is the triptych *Three Places in New England* (*39), with its noisy evocation of 'Putnam's Camp', and then the deep impressions made by nature in its final movement 'The Housatonic at Stockbridge'.

Ives's predecessor Edward MacDowell (1860–1908) incorporated Native American melodies into his works, notably in his Second (Indian) suite for orchestra, as did George Chadwick (1854–1931), using Protestant hymn melodies. Chadwick was an adviser to Amy Beach (1867–1944), the most successful woman composer at a time when composers were still generally assumed to be men. (It was only in 1893 that a piece composed by a woman was played by a major American symphony orchestra: Margaret Ruthven Lang's *Dramatic Overture*, by the Boston Symphony Orchestra.) Beach was already a talented pianist when she married and determined to pursue a largely self-taught composition career. The use of folk melodies and indigenous music in her work marks her out as a nationalist composer, and her *Gaelic Symphony* is an example of the fine integration of native themes. This work, written partly as a reaction to Dvořák suggestion that American composers should use spirituals – which she countered by saying that the melodies of European immigrants could be equally suitable material – was widely performed both in the United States and Europe.

William Grant Still (1895–1978) achieved a breakthrough for African-American composers, and had success in traditional Western forms of opera, symphony and chamber works in the wake of the success of his *Afro-American Symphony*. The best-known name among the Black composers of the era is Scott Joplin (?1868–1917). His ambitious ragtime opera *Treemonisha* did not succeed at its premiere, which hastened Joplin's early death in 1917, but it has been revived since. However, his ragtime piano music (*37) has enjoyed a popular revival thanks to its advocacy by pianist Joshua Rifkin and its inclusion in the film *The Sting*. Successful Black composers of the period included the Canadian Robert Nathaniel Dett (1882–1943), who was active for many years in New York and incorporated a wide range of African-American melodies into his work. More recently George Walker (1922–2018) has emerged as an important figure whose music is beginning to be revived: he was the first African-American to receive the Pulitzer Prize for music in America in 1996. But it is chastening to recall that Duke Ellington (1899–1974) was turned down for a Pulitzer in 1965, and received one only posthumously in 1999. It has taken a long time for the impact of jazz and all Black music to be fully acknowledged by the broader music community.

Aaron Copland (1900–90) was the leading composer in giving American music an identity and an unmistakably nationalist sound. He captured the spirit of the wide open spaces in his Third Symphony and *Appalachian Spring*, while his ballet scores *Rodeo* and *Billy the Kid* sum up a distinctively American exuberance in their pungent sound-worlds. Perhaps the burden of being thought of as the first truly American composer weighed heavily on him, and a brush with the notorious House Un-American Activities Committee (which was not pursued) caused a reorientation of his idiom. Not all his later music flirting with twelve-note idioms, like the acerbic *Connotations* for the opening of the Philharmonic Hall in Lincoln Center, is so successful. Before retiring into silence, Copland became a leading educator, and his little book *What to Listen for in Music* remained a classic for generations.

Perhaps the best American symphony of the period remains the muscular Third Symphony of Roy Harris (1898–1979). But the full range of idioms from late Romanticism to adventurous modernism was cultivated by American composers. On the conservative side is Samuel Barber (1910–81) in *Dover Beach*, the Violin Concerto and most memorably the evocative narrative *Knoxville: Summer of 1915* for soprano and orchestra, nostalgically looking back across the era between the wars. By far his most famous work is the *Adagio for Strings*, arranged for string orchestra from the second movement of his String Quartet Op. 11, which has become used as a frequent memorial piece and arranged as a choral Agnus Dei. The cutting edge of experiment was advanced by Henry Cowell (1897–1965) with his use of piano clusters, playing the inside of the piano, and non-Western musical sources from India, Japan, Bali and all around the Pacific Rim. Ruth Crawford Seeger (1901–53), whom Cowell encouraged and published, wrote some fascinating music but then turned to collecting and preserving folk music. Together they wrote the book *New Musical Resources*, anticipating some of the approaches of the post-war avant-garde to musical organisation.

Scarcely nationalist in outlook, but most extreme of all in his originality, and one of the defining composers of the interwar era, was the French-born Edgard Varèse (1883–1965). He moved to New York in 1915 and created a knockout homage to his new country in *Amériques*, a strident and noisy essay for huge orchestra. Obliterating

213

the support structures of both tonality and its replacements, Varèse created pictures of pure sonic effect: *Offrandes*, the smaller but fierce *Hyperprism*, *Arcana* for large orchestra and *Ecuatorial*. He was a constant supporter of living composers, and in New York founded both the International Composers' Guild which gave many premieres, and the Pan-American Association of Composers. His thorough-going, uncompromising radicalism has attracted the interest of avant-garde composers in both the classical and non-classical arenas: one of his biggest admirers and promoters was the rock musician Frank Zappa.

*

The turmoil across Europe in the first decades of the twentieth century caused some composers to lose their way and struggle to find their voice: the shock was just too great to assimilate, and the demands created a block in their creativity. To others, however, war and social change were a powerful stimulus, either towards expressing conflict or seeking escape. Political engagement was never far from the surface, and the pressures of working within repressive regimes would become a major force in the careers of those composers who chose not to escape them, or felt unable to do so.

The nationalist impetus is tellingly demonstrated by the choices of composers who were based in Russia. After the Revolution of 1917, music in the Soviet Union increasingly came under centralised control, with taste determined by such groups as the Union of Soviet Composers from 1933. Sergey Rachmaninov (1873–1943) left Russia immediately and became a cosmopolitan populist, making a career as a piano virtuoso in the United States. His totally memorable Piano Concerto No. 2 became his most successful work, reinforced by its use in the 1945 film *Brief Encounter*. That concerto had been a recovery from the earlier abject failure of his First Symphony, and after it he felt able to return to the symphony as a form: his Second Symphony is a big-boned, ambitious work, as critic David Fanning has described it, 'drawing on the full arsenal of his technique, synthesising Russian symphonic trends with the glamour of the Lisztian symphonic poem'. It has proved continuously popular with conductors and orchestras as it can display their prowess to the full. A later hugely successful work, written for

214

himself to play, is the *Rhapsody on a Theme of Paganini* inspired by the violin virtuoso of the previous century and including a quote from the plainsong *Dies irae* (p. 30). Rachmaninov's career was an object-lesson in how a performer can create his own personality and aura, expanding his reputation from Russia to Europe to America, writing the pieces that would project his pianistic skills to perfection. The support of conductors such as Mahler at the New York Philharmonic, with whom he played his Third Piano Concerto (*34) in 1910, helped to enhance his reputation; the Russian-born virtuoso Vladimir Horowitz took up that concerto and made a famous recording.

Sergey Prokofiev (1891–1953) also left Russia after the Revolution, and wrote his surrealist opera *The Love for Three Oranges*. He had already conceived the brittle brilliance of his early Classical Symphony, which directly inspired Benjamin Britten (I hear its last movement in the fugue theme of Britten's *Young Person's Guide to the Orchestra*). Prokofiev created a strong showpiece in his earlier Third Piano Concerto (*26), which he premiered successfully in Chicago. It became one of his most popular pieces, full of virtuosity but also of memorable melodies. But for reasons that remain unclear, less connected with nationalism than with the promise of commissions, Prokofiev returned to Russia in the mid-1930s and wrote some of his most successful works there: the dramatic ballet *Romeo and Juliet* and the children's story *Peter and the Wolf*. This remains an all-too-isolated example of a musical tale for narrator that works for a young audience, perfectly illustrated by the character of the instruments used: innocent strings for Peter, a flute for the bird, an oboe for the duck, a clarinet for the cat, a bassoon for the grandfather, and a group of horns for the wolf itself. It has been narrated by a succession of starry actors, not all of whom have managed to keep to the score: at a performance I attended Peter Ustinov became so lost that he had to insert the line 'the hunters came out of the woods – *again*'.

As a result of his dependence on the approval of the Soviet authorities, Prokofiev wrote a large amount of forgettable music in this period, as well as some that is regrettable. But his cantata *Alexander Nevsky*, drawn from his film music, is a taut and impressive bow to Russian history, while his most successful symphony, the Fifth, found favour and has remained prominent in the repertory since. The composer described it as 'a symphony of the greatness of the human spirit' and in it he managed to reconcile the demands of nationalism with the rigours of symphonic form in a way that gained wide appeal – though personally I have never found its busy optimism very convincing. Ironically, one of his finest works, the 1948 opera *War and Peace*, based on Tolstoy's epic novel, coincided with Prokofiev being denounced for 'formalism' by the authorities: a major setback for one who had been so loyal to them. Prokofiev composed little else after this before his death – which occurred on the same day as Joseph Stalin's.

The years after the First World War saw political turbulence force the movement of many composers across Europe and to America. In Weimar Germany, Kurt Weill (1900–50) absorbed the adventurous idioms of the time and created a sharply innovative style in his radical collaborations with Bertolt Brecht, *The Threepenny Opera* (*23) and *The Rise and Fall of the City of Mahagonny*. These fierce parables of challenges to civilisation matched the temper of the times, and Weill's music, with its jazz-influenced orchestration, is some of the most pungent of the interwar period. Its cutting edge is still powerful today, especially in the idiomatic early recordings whose sound captures the sultry atmosphere of cabaret and nightclubs. Weill's work in Germany was cut short after the premiere of his opera *Der Silbersee* in 1933, a socially engaged parable about extreme riches and poverty which deserves wide revival as it mirrors so much in our own times. He fled the country for Paris and then America, bringing his brand of strong engagement to the American musical in 1940s works such as *Street Scene* and *Lady in the Dark*, with their deftly crafted scenes and melodies. Weill's music has never quite broken through to the mainstream, though all his works are well-made and emotionally powerful; his time will come.

The moral dilemmas of those who remained in Germany after 1933 were acute in the face of the blanket suppression of music by Jewish composers. A German composer who suffered from the changing political situation was Paul Hindemith (1895–1963), who taught in Berlin but whose advanced music was denounced by the Nazis for its atonality. His rapid move into a late-Romantic idiom enabled the authorities to stop short of total denunciation; instead they tacitly encouraged his involvement in music education abroad. But then his opera *Mathis der Maler*, which explores issues of the relationship between art and society based around the life of the painter Matthias Grünewald, was forbidden to be performed in Berlin; it had to be premiered in Zurich. Hindemith moved to the United States and taught at Yale, becoming very involved in the revival of old music. Among his orchestral works worth exploring are the *Symphonic Metamorphoses on Themes of Carl Maria von Weber* and the *Symphonia serena*, while his earlier series of *Kammermusik* pieces includes practical works for a huge range of instruments.

While Hindemith was alert to the political conflicts of the time, no such scruples seemed to affect Carl Orff (1895–1982), who remained in Nazi Germany and also worked extensively to provide educational materials for children to learn music. He also produced one of the most popular choral works of the era in the *Carmina Burana*, based on the old drinking songs of the Middle Ages (p. 48). In its exuberant, pounding rhythms and insistent melodies this work seems to prefigure some aspects of minimalism; the use of secular Latin texts proved so successful that Orff repeated the device in two more oratorios, *Catulli Carmina* and *Trionfo di Afrodite*, which have never quite had the same success. Like Hindemith, he was deeply involved in early music: Hindemith explored the music of Bach, while Orff made new performing versions of Monteverdi, Schütz and Bach.

The equivocal position of musicians and composers in interwar Germany proved challenging to many, though not visibly to Richard Strauss (1864–1949). He is an ambivalent figure in twentieth-century music, whose personal and political stance, avoiding conflict with the Nazis at a time when so many other musicians suffered, was at best dubious. Yet in the first decade of the twentieth century he had created some of the most overwhelming new music of the century: the operas *Salome* and *Elektra* alone would ensure him a place in the pantheon. The modernist expressiveness and extreme emotions of those two operas, full of brutal, oppressive sounds, seem to have reached a limit for Strauss; his next opera, *Der Rosenkavalier*, is a heady brew of languorous sensuality, a peerless evocation of a fading era. But it begins a strain of nostalgia for the certainties of the old world that Strauss explored repeatedly in his later works. The huge and richly orchestrated philosophical vision *Die Frau ohne Schatten*, *Intermezzo* and *Arabella* take us further away from the world of the present. Oddly, the last works, which are

without any relevance to their time, are perhaps the most affecting with their Mozartian echoes: the one-act operas *Daphne*, based on ancient myth, and *Capriccio*,
on words and music.

Among his concert works, Strauss's extrovert early orchestral showpieces are
easy to engage with, especially the lively storytelling of *Till Eulenspiegels lustige
Streiche* (*41) and the hero's life of *Ein Heldenleben*, though perhaps worth avoiding
is the banal *Sinfonia domestica*. Strauss's engagement with the music of the past was
centred around Mozart, whose opera *Idomeneo* he arranged for a then rare revival,
and Gluck, whose *Iphigénie en Tauride* he also arranged. At the very end of his life,
after the war was over, Strauss wrote the gloomy and impressive *Metamorphosen* for
twenty-three solo strings which quotes the funeral march of Beethoven's 'Eroica'
Symphony, and the beautiful *Four Last Songs* (posthumously premiered in London
by Kirsten Flagstad): they signal the end of an era that had actually long passed.

*

In Britain, the nationalist revival that had focused on the folk-song research by
Cecil Sharp, and the re-creation of the church hymn tradition, had been galva-
nised by the arrival of Elgar and his path-breaking oratorio *The Dream of Gerontius*
whose overtones were Wagnerian rather than English pastoral. The interwar years
were a period of cultural renaissance and widespread engagement with music of
many genres, fuelled by the arrival of broadcasting in the 1920s. Light music and
classical music were available to all through the newly formed BBC, which also
took over the promotion of the Proms from 1927. Visits from leading European
orchestras, including the Berlin Philharmonic under Wilhelm Furtwängler, demonstrated how slipshod were the standards of British orchestral playing, and this
led to the foundation of two outstanding new orchestras, the BBC Symphony
in 1930 and the London Philharmonic in 1932. Led by the strongly contrasting
figures of the reserved Adrian Boult and the effervescent Thomas Beecham, these
orchestras raised the standards of ensemble playing and attracted international
conductors, notably Bruno Walter and Arturo Toscanini; the latter gave an in-
cisive Beethoven symphony cycle with the BBC Symphony which made a great
impression, just before the outbreak of the Second World War.

British new music of this period reflected both the impact of the First World War and a newly vigorous emancipation from the inheritance of the Edwardian era. Ralph Vaughan Williams (1872–1958) is remembered for his work exploring the folk-song tradition and the revival of English hymnody; he was also a major symphonist. His First Symphony of 1910 had been a big choral setting of Walt Whitman's poetic vision of the sea; his Second, completed in 1913, a vivid and often nostalgic orchestral soundscape of the bustling capital city of London; while after the First World War he wrote his Third in a quieter pastoral tradition featuring wordless solo voice. The echoes of his experiences in the First World War, and perhaps a foreboding feeling of the Second that was to come, can be heard in the excruciating dissonances of the Fourth Symphony. Written before and during the Second World War, the Fifth Symphony is surprising for the time: a picture of peace and harmony, warm and consoling, based on material Vaughan Williams had assembled for his opera *The Pilgrim's Progress*, reflecting John Bunyan's humane vision. The nationalist impulse which led Vaughan Williams and his colleagues towards collecting folk song and reworking old music inspired him to write the *Fantasia on a Theme by Thomas Tallis* (*33) based on a modal hymn tune, for string orchestra with a solo quartet.

Vaughan Williams was equally devoted to Bach, conducting annual performances of the St Matthew Passion at his music festival in Leith Hill in Surrey, though he preferred large forces, insisted on singing the texts in English, and scorned the revival of older instruments, dismissing 'those gross bagpipes which in Bach's day stood for an oboe'. The rhapsodic *The Lark Ascending* in its version for violin and orchestra has become one of the quintessential works of the English tradition, as the violin soars and floats above the orchestral textures, conjuring up the countryside which inspired the composer. Vaughan Williams remarkably went on writing symphonies up until his death at the age of eighty-five. Notable are the Sixth, with its use of solo saxophone, representing a formidable new development in his post-war style, and the Seventh, *Sinfonia antartica*, based on music for a film project, *Scott of the Antarctic* – film was a medium which was becoming increasingly important for British composers of the period, both creatively and financially. Vaughan Williams's music has been labelled as an example of the English pastoral style, but with his symphonic skill and continental influences he pushes it forward, and his contribution to British music is central to the century.

For other English composers it was not necessarily the symphony that enabled them to flourish musically in this period: Vaughan Williams's close colleague Gustav Holst (1874–1934) came to prominence through his classic orchestral suite *The Planets* (*29). Its form had been suggested by hearing Schoenberg's Five Orchestral Pieces at the Proms in 1914, but its idiom is very different. Inspired by Holst's interest in astrology, this is a brilliant place to start for anyone interested in the sonorities of twentieth-century music, including as it does insistent war music in the first movement 'Mars', stirring melodies (Holst later adapted 'I vow to thee my country' from the big tune in 'Jupiter'), and a long-distance evaporating chorus at the end of the final 'Neptune'. (Following the discovery of the planet Pluto in 1930, the composer Colin Matthews (p. 256) later added a movement to the suite which is sometimes performed with it.)

Holst was always interested in Hindu literature and studied Sanskrit, writing his chamber opera *Sāvitri* to his own libretto. A strong vein of exoticism helped to create Holst's choral masterpiece *The Hymn of Jesus* and his sets of songs from the *Rig Veda*. One of his most characterful orchestral works, *Egdon Heath*, drew the attention of no less a modernist than Pierre Boulez, who rarely performed British music. Always a generous and inspiring teacher at St Paul's Girls' School and elsewhere, Holst had a major influence on the succeeding generation of British composers. For him, nationalism operated with a wide, diverse cultural base.

William Walton (1902–83) came from Oldham in the north of England and was a young choirboy at Christ Church Cathedral, Oxford. His stylish social connections with the fashionable Sitwell family led to the writing of crisply original music over which Edith Sitwell's poems were spoken: *Façade*, a sort of upper-class English *Pierrot Lunaire* (p. 223), proved a long-lasting hit. Some of his early chamber music had a more modernist edge and his First String Quartet was heard at the festival of the International Society for Contemporary Music in the 1920s, but Walton disowned it as 'full of undigested Bartók and Schoenberg'. His First Symphony, in particular its finale, was a long time coming to completion, but especially in its propulsive first movement it proclaimed a strong individual voice. Somehow his promise was unfulfilled: he is remembered for his effective concertos of the interwar period, for viola and violin, and for the tremendous impact of his choral masterpiece *Belshazzar's Feast*, a regular favourite with choral societies; but little written after the Second World War matched that.

Meanwhile a growing strand of women composers was becoming prominent. In the wake of the women's suffrage movement there were growing calls for the achievement of women composers to be recognised. The pioneering figure was Ethel Smyth (1858–1944), who had been a suffragette herself; she had studied in Germany and was encouraged by Thomas Beecham and Henry Wood, and frequently conducted her own music at the Proms. Her operas are beginning to be revived, and *The Wreckers*, premiered in Leipzig and brought to London by Beecham, has been recorded. In a later generation, Elisabeth Lutyens (1906–83) was both prolific in 'advanced' chamber music and a successful composer for film, while her friend Elizabeth Maconchy (1907–94) had her cantata *The Land* performed at the Proms and wrote a very fine series of string quartets. The conductor Iris Lemare and the violinist Anne Macnaghten created the Macnaghten-Lemare concerts, an important initiative which in the 1930s supported the performance of new British music and gave opportunities to many young female musicians. This is a development which has continued to gather pace as more opportunities for women conductors and programmers open up – and the Master of the Queen's Music is now a woman, Judith Weir (p. 257). But there is still a long way to go before women play a truly equal role in the creation of our musical culture.

16

Revolutions

Retracing our steps to the beginning of the twentieth century, the transition from the nineteenth century is always seen as a major fissure in the development of music. Composers recognised it themselves: speaking with the benefit of hindsight, Béla Bartók said, 'The excesses of the romanticists began to be unbearable for many. There were composers who felt: "this road does not lead us anywhere; there is no other solution but a complete break with the nineteenth century."' There was a feeling that the increasingly complex world of chromatic harmony could go no further; even an essentially Romantic composer like Franz Liszt recognised this in his late piano pieces, where he began to pare down his material to shreds of themes and elusive harmonies. Thus, new sounds and new harmonic languages began to transform the sound of music around 1900. We have already seen one unusually sudden change, a tipping point from the equal-voiced music of the Renaissance to the soloistic world of the baroque (p. 85). This is another tipping point in the story of musical evolution, though it resulted not in a singular line of development, but in two contrasting ways forward to the revolutions in music of the twentieth century: changing sonorities, and radical reinvention.

'I feel the air from another planet': few musical texts have carried so great a resonance beyond their literal meaning than the words of the soprano singing in the last movement of the Second String Quartet of 1908 by Arnold Schoenberg (1874–1951). The addition of a voice was unusual in itself, but as she sings you can feel the bonds of tonality being loosened, and with it the grip of a whole musical tradition. Here is one strand of twentieth-century music laid bare: Schoenberg sets off into uncharted waters. It is possible to feel that music was transformed by him and his contemporaries in the early years of the twentieth century to a greater extent than had occurred any time in the three previous centuries. The question remains as to how permanent a transformation that has turned out to be, but it is unarguable that their new approach to the creation of a melodic line, to harmony and to texture had a deep influence on a generation and more of musicians – even on those who rejected the theory and wished to move beyond it.

It was not until later that Schoenberg fully codified his method of working with all twelve notes of the chromatic scale on an equal basis. Other composers made similar moves: I have been fascinated by the similar theories of Josef Matthias Hauer (1883–1959) whom Schoenberg knew; but Schoenberg's resulting music is much finer. It is as usual dangerous to attempt to simplify the process, but essentially the decision was to move beyond the organisation of themes and harmony through the use of major and minor scales (which determined the sequence of notes around which both melody and harmony were conceived), and instead to treat the twelve notes of the chromatic scale as equally important. What became known as atonality implied both the abandonment of traditional tonal schemes, and the construction of new harmonic and melodic methods of organising sounds. Not all twelve-note composers, as they became known, were as thoroughgoing in their methods as Schoenberg, and even he moved gradually towards his chosen goal.

He had written late-Romantic essays in small and large forms, from the expressionist *Verklärte Nacht* (Transfigured Night) for string sextet to the massive vocal and choral *Gurrelieder* (first performed in 1913) with its strong Wagnerian overtones: this oratorio-like fresco is always worth catching if you spot a rare live performance. Then he struck out in a newly rigorous direction with his twelve-note Three Piano Pieces of 1909, written in the same year as the Five Orchestral Pieces, which Henry Wood famously premiered at the Proms with a baffled orchestra and a resistant audience in 1912. With *Pierrot Lunaire* in that same year Schoenberg created a radical new idea for a half-speaking, half-singing voice described as

Sprechstimme with small ensemble, and cast off into the harmonic unknown with a surreal setting, working towards the formulation of the twelve-note method which he then strove to perfect. This music can still seem awkward, yielding its secrets only slowly. But it has its own beauty, and a logic which compels attention.

In moving from a language based on the familiar tonal scales of major and minor, which had in any case become increasingly modified by Romantic composers' use of chromatic material, Schoenberg was both reacting against established tradition and making a conscious attempt to create a new tradition. That was what he hoped the twelve-note style was to become, and he was fully aware of the difficulty of this new language for performers. It is revealing that as his compositional work progressed, Schoenberg felt the need to create performances that were properly rehearsed by players who understood the music. Hence the formation in 1918 of the Society for Private Musical Performances in Vienna, a pioneering venture that supported the promotion of works by a wide range of composers from Bartók, Berg and Busoni to Mahler, Schoenberg himself and Webern. Small-scale reductions of large works were made, including, in an attempt to make some money, miniature arrangements of Johann Strauss waltzes, but the Society eventually closed after some 117 concerts for lack of financial support. Schoenberg's other major achievement of this period is the gripping monodrama *Erwartung* (*36) from 1909, which was not performed until 1924. This is a huge tableau for solo soprano and orchestra, in which he explores with great penetration the desolation of a woman abandoned by her lover and searching the forest for him, where the density of the orchestral writing mirrors the thickness of the vegetation that surrounds her to oppressive effect. Although there is little dramatic development, as an evocation of atmosphere this is powerful. Schoenberg's work was never successful in financial terms. When the Nazis came to power in 1933, he immigrated to America, and took up academic posts in southern California; he went on write a Piano Concerto there, and progressed his major opera *Moses und Aron* which remained unfinished at his death but has been effectively staged in its truncated form. Its strong choral writing and wild orchestral 'Dance of the Golden Calf' make an impact, but even the composer's supporters complain of what has been called his 'determined unapproachability'.

Schoenberg's pupils and followers included two major composers of great but contrasted strengths. Anton Webern (1883–1945) concentrated the twelve-note method into fragmentary sounds, reducing it to movements of a few notes which however speak with complete authority. He wrote a few early orchestral works with a late-Romantic aura that are performed, such as *Im Sommerwind* and the *Passacaglia*, yet the most characterful works are his chamber and piano pieces such as the Variations Op. 27, in which the spareness is audible. I find there is a wonderful sense of angular beauty in these pieces, with their seemingly random notes and thin chords plucked out of the air and acquiring their own inexorable logic. Webern was inspired by the complex work of medieval composers (p. 34) and made an analytical orchestral arrangement of the six-part Ricercare from Bach's *Musical Offering*. For a hugely impressive introduction to his idiom, listen to the large-scale original version of his Six Pieces for Large Orchestra Op. 6 (*35), especially as conducted by Pierre Boulez; there is such a powerful logic that you sense these could not be any other notes.

Alban Berg (1885–1935) took Schoenberg's method and linked it back into a collusion with the past that ensured sensuality and colour in his music. His Violin Concerto (*21) has established its firm place in the repertory partly because of the subtle way in which its lyricism is created. Berg uses a twelve-note pattern of pitches that is not random, but is constructed from overlapping rising major and minor tonal triads in different keys. So from the start his atonal melody has a strong tonal background in the listener's mind, whether consciously or not. A further link is provided by the final movement, which is a set of variations on a chorale 'Es ist genug' from Bach's Cantata No. 60. The listener feels grounded in the music of the past, while the sounds are distinctively those of the present. The concerto is dedicated 'to the memory of an angel', a reference to the early death of Manon Gropius, the eighteen-year-old daughter of Walter Gropius and Mahler's widow Alma, who were close friends of the Bergs.

Berg's two operas, *Wozzeck* premiered in 1922 and *Lulu* (which was left unfinished at his death but has been completed by others from Berg's sketches), have profoundly human qualities that made an immediate impact. *Wozzeck* is one of the greatest creations of the century, based on a drama of 1836 by Georg Büchner yet resolutely contemporary in its understanding of human passion and revolutionary fervour. The opera perfectly aligns emotion with structure: there are five scenes in each act, all linked by themes and motifs, and the characters are drawn with great precision, especially the two central characters Wozzeck and Marie, who seem redeemed from the tragic fate that engulfs them by the music they sing. The sequence of orchestral interludes in *Wozzeck* is truly shattering, and while both it and *Lulu* dwell on the dark side of human character, lyricism is not absent; it acquires an awful irony when surrounded by bleakness. Berg's Three Orchestral Pieces Op. 6 and his chamber Lyric Suite express this drama on both larger and smaller canvases: of the twelve-note composers, he is the most expressive and surely the most approachable.

Other composers loosened their ties with tonality in different ways. The Russian Aleksandr Scriabin (1871/2–1915) will always remain an esoteric figure, since his complex post-chromatic language makes his music difficult to absorb. But he should be credited for his extremely original approach to the problems of twentieth-century musical language, and for his links with mysticism and synaesthesia, associating different keys with a colour spectrum. His orchestral tone poems include the very intense *The Poem of Ecstasy*, and *Prometheus*, for which he stipulated that coloured light should flood the hall. His piano music, inspired by Chopin, is where his individual language is most clearly developed, and where it has found most acceptance among such outstanding performers as Horowitz and Richter; although Rachmaninov played his music, Scriabin felt his understanding of it was limited.

*

The contrasting new direction from the tipping point of early twentieth-century music was born of a radical approach to sonority, new sensibilities and changing influences; it was not a theoretical language like the twelve-note idiom of Schoenberg, but it was equally revolutionary in its results.

The music of the East had opened up to composers such as Mahler (*Das Lied von der Erde*), and made a major impression on Claude Debussy (1862–1918). He heard a gamelan orchestra from Bali at the Paris Exhibition of 1889 and declared that it made Palestrina sound primitive by comparison. The rhythmic and melodic sophistication of that music awoke a response in Debussy and his music in the following years explored something of that freedom, experimenting with oriental scales and rhythms in his pieces for the piano. Pierre Boulez suggested that modern music was born with the single flute line that opens Debussy's orchestral *Prélude à l'après-midi d'un faune*. Certainly it abandons the usual idea of a key centre, the fluid opening line resisting any notion of symphonic development, and the piece's ideas fleetingly come and go with sensual effect. It is also remarkable, for such adventurous music, in having been an instant success with audiences unused to its idiom.

There are many continuities that can be demonstrated as music crosses the boundaries of the nineteenth and twentieth centuries, but we feel a fundamental change when we hear the music of Debussy. He did not so much reject the language of tonality as dissolve it, making his understated and emotionally restrained music intelligible within a new framework. He draws on the inheritance of French music with its liking for colour and decoration, derived from Rameau in the eighteenth century and Berlioz in the nineteenth (who were themselves both theorists of harmony and orchestration), but in place of big symphonic structures Debussy presents small tantalising fragments with programmatic clues. In his *Préludes* for piano, these titles are placed at the end of each piece; at the beginning of each there is only a tempo marking. But what contrasting worlds he conjures up in these tiny essays, each born from a single idea! We are reminded of the inventiveness of François Couperin's character pieces for harpsichord from an earlier age (p. 113). Debussy focuses on a rhetorical device to unify each piece – the parallel chords of 'La cathédrale engloutie', the halting syncopations of 'Des pas sur la neige'. A challenge to amateur pianists, there is so much pleasure to be gained from the perfect characterisation of 'La fille aux cheveux de lin' or the gentle jazz parody of 'Minstrels'.

Beauty of sonority lies at the heart of Debussy's music. Both his piano music and his orchestral scores conjure up a world that has had the easy label 'impressionist' rather too often attached to it. There are certainly fully descriptive pieces in his output: the orchestral trilogy *La mer* (*38), which he called 'Three

Symphonic Sketches', is a direct tribute to the sea, with a first movement called 'from dawn to midday on the sea' (of which the sardonic composer Erik Satie commented that he liked the bit about quarter to twelve). Yet the impact of this tremendous piece is not so much its description of the sea, but the emotions it conjures up, the assault it makes on the senses. This is achieved with a wonderful ear for orchestral colour, using a muted trumpet and cor anglais that set the waves going; the rhapsodic but perfectly controlled final movement creates an increasingly powerful picture, musically transparent and pulsing with power. We feel we have been thrust into the eye of the storm.

Debussy's greatest contribution to defining the sound of the twentieth century was his single completed opera, *Pelléas et Mélisande*. With a profoundly original approach to declamation and structure, he created a continuous ebb and flow of sound with the most beautiful orchestral textures supporting the vocal lines. This 'endless melody' he certainly derived from Wagner and his *Tristan und Isolde* (p. 182), but the sound is completely different. The elevated emotional temperature of the symbolist story is combined with a continual sonic coolness which creates what is to my mind a completely unique operatic atmosphere. It stands in opposition to the *verismo* tendencies then current in Italy, though Puccini greatly admired *Pelléas*, as did Olivier Messiaen for whom it became an essential part of his composition teaching.

Maurice Ravel (1875–1937) is always linked with Debussy under the banner of impressionism, but his musical influences were even more diverse than Debussy's. Both were fascinated by the music of the French past, and Ravel reworked it more consciously, from the early piano piece *Menuet antique* to the late *Le Tombeau de Couperin* which anticipates the emergence of neo-classicism in the 1920s as a major musical trend. Ravel was a fastidious composer, who did not compose a note more than was needed; he claimed that he spent much time 'eliminating all that could be regarded as superfluous in order to realise as completely as possible the definitive clarity so much desired'. (You could wish some other less disciplined composers had taken this path.) As a result, there is nothing out of place in his perfectly finished scores; they echo the classical tradition in his String Quartet, frequently played and recorded as an ideal companion to

Debussy's String Quartet and later Violin Sonata. Taking Debussy's colouristic virtuosity to new levels, the exquisite precision of Ravel in his large-scale piano music *Gaspard de la nuit* and *Miroirs* are exhilarating for their sheer display of technique, but they leave amateur pianists behind: the simplicity of the *Pavane pour une infante défunte* is more practical.

Ravel's orchestral scores are masterly in technique and atmospheric in effect: the biggest of them, *Daphnis et Chloé*, is an hour-long ballet written for the impresario Sergey Diaghilev from which two orchestral suites are usually played, the second an uplifting picture of dawn, the evocation of Pan, and a lavishly scored final eruption of colour. Its positive exuberance is matched by the much more ambivalent sound of *La valse* (*27). This masterpiece surely marks the final disintegration of nineteenth-century opulence and excess: it is a portrait of the destruction of the old world. Here, waltzes swirl around the textures, ostensibly celebrating the Viennese waltz tradition but actually deconstructing it. Ravel creates, in his words, 'a fantastic and fateful whirlpool' which sucks up the triple-time rhythms, collides them with each other, and at the end throws them to the wind. For all its supposed elegance, this is a viciously turbulent picture of a civilisation on the edge.

Although they stand at the head of one twentieth-century musical revolution, these French composers had strong links to the past which they did not reject. The same is true of the towering figure of twentieth-century music, Igor Stravinsky (1882–1971). He was hailed as a revolutionary, and liked to portray himself as a radical original, but it is now becoming clear how much Stravinsky owed to his Russian ancestors and to the folk music of the time. Just as Stravinsky was premiering his precocious *Scherzo fantastique* in 1908, Diaghilev, who had commissioned Ravel's *Daphnis*, was seeking a composer of ballets who would not be too expensive. Having been turned down by some leading composers for the Russian fairytale ballet he needed, Diaghilev took a risk on the young Stravinsky. The result, *The Firebird*, with its superb understanding of the orchestra, vivid colours, sharp characterisation and rhythmic flair, was a triumph; it was repeatedly performed, even though in later life Stravinsky was critical of the score and made several different versions before settling on a substantial Suite. It was quickly followed by *Petrushka*,

Stravinsky's own concept of a folk story from pagan Russia which enabled him to weave into the score the folk melodies that were part of his upbringing, but with radical twists as he combines and alters their melodies. The puppet-like, mechanistic sound of the score perfectly reflects the mythology of the story, while the depictions of the traditional dances, with all the energy of the local Shrovetide Fair, come together in an orchestral showpiece.

It is the third of these great ballets, *The Rite of Spring* (*32), that stands uncontested at the head of a century of invention. As a landmark of innovation whose impact continues to the present day, it is unequalled and has been subject to deep analysis. Yet this ballet too is shot through with the traditional music of Stravinsky's homeland. Here he reworked everything that he had learned of Russian folk music and the orchestral practices of his predecessors Glazunov and Rimsky-Korsakov, the latter his teacher, but thrillingly recreated them for a new century. The harmonic and rhythmic intricacies of the *Rite* have been studied by countless teachers and composers, but it is the earthy immediacy of the score that makes an immediate impact on the first-time listener who is confronted by its evocative directness. The opening solo, high on the bassoon, is a challenge to players then as now and sets the tone for a succession of blocks of sound: traditional symphonic development is largely absent here as one slab of hard-hitting orchestral colour follows another, climaxing in a Sacrificial Dance of rhythmic complexity and elemental brutality.

The first performance of *The Rite of Spring* at the Théâtre des Champs-Élysées in Paris on 29 May 1913 has become a famous landmark in twentieth-century music because it provoked a riot among an audience outraged both by its unfamiliar music and by the choreography of Nijinsky. But very quickly this became mythologised. The reports of the rebellion were adopted by a fashionable audience, especially in Paris, who were keen to be shocked by the music of the moment: the narrative of the *Rite*'s reception became part of a significant move away from a traditional concert-going audience absorbed in the weighty canonic symphonic repertory to a new crowd thirsty for innovation and excitement. *The Rite of Spring* also marks another development: the growing importance of recordings in shaping our musical world. The new technology of the phonograph invented and refined by Thomas Edison was crucial to Stravinsky in accessing Russian folk music, as he asked his mother to send him 'folk songs of the Caucasian peoples that have been phonographically transcribed'. This gives the lie to the idea that the sounds Stravinsky imagined for his ballet were wholly new: like so many others he was reinventing the past. However, he was doing so with a radical imagination that left an indelible mark on twentieth-century music (Plate 22).

It was a big challenge for Stravinsky to develop after the triumphs of those three ballet scores, which remain among the cornerstones of the twentieth-century orchestral repertory. Still working for Diaghilev, he turned to a smaller scale and became more neo-classical in *Pulcinella*, with a reworking of eighteenth-century music that he believed was by Pergolesi but was mostly by other more minor figures. In line with Stravinsky's uncanny ability to rationalise his own story, he claimed that *Pulcinella* was 'my discovery of the past, the epiphany through which the whole of my later work became possible'. In *Pulcinella* music's past was literally evoked, but with its witty dislocations, quirky scoring and rhythmic surprises, the composer's input was supremely imaginative. In his brilliant reimagining of an old world for new purposes, Stravinsky was taking the fragile vessel of twentieth-century music into uncharted waters, steering it between the dogma of serialism and the reaction of post-Romanticism. He then achieved the same refreshment of tradition with his post-Second World War opera *The Rake's Progress*, set to an excellent libretto by W. H. Auden and Chester Kallman. Full of copious echoes of Mozart and others, it used an eighteenth-century story of decline and fall based on the story of Tom Rakewell in the engravings of Hogarth, creating a neo-classic sharpness which has held the stage. While some have criticised its reliance on the past, Stravinsky's wistful irony is here entirely appropriate to the subject and creates set-piece arias and ensembles of poise and power. The reference to the past language of music is not only well matched to the story but entirely typical of the changing taste of the day.

*

Alongside the revolutions of serialism and impressionism, the radical anti-Romantic feeling at the start of the twentieth century was reflected in further attempts to disrupt and reconstruct the conventional languages of music. Schoenberg's twelve-note method in the attempt to reinvent tradition was one; Debussy's loosening of tonality in the search for expression was another. Béla Bartók's recourse to the language of folk traditions provided another route. The absorption of idioms from popular music and jazz became a fourth fork in the road. Erik Satie (1866–1925) took a different path. He was a radical outside the mainstream, a complete individual who created such eccentric pieces as *Embryons desséchés* and the *Sonatine bureaucratique*; as early as 1888 he wrote the famous *Trois gymnopédies*, an advanced but simple work, inventing new scales and harmonies around the whole-tone scale. Part of the fashionable world of Paris in Montmartre, but always slightly remote from it, Satie was then commissioned to provide ballet music by the impresario Diaghilev. He created in 1917 the ballet *Parade* to a scenario by Jean Cocteau, sets by Picasso (more recently they were memorably redesigned by David Hockney) and choreography by Léonide Massine.

From being regarded as a slightly mad outsider, Satie was suddenly lauded as having captured the spirit of the times. *Parade* reflected the sharp, simpler, pared-down style of the moment, as opposed to the intellectual pretensions of the twelve-note composers. He integrated everyday sounds like typewriters, pistol shots, sirens and a lottery wheel into his score, along with echoes of the music of cafés and the streets. It was a big success; though it is striking that, like Stravinsky's *Rite of Spring* four years earlier, it took a scandal around the controversial first performance to propel it to fashionable attention. Satie went on to write the cantata *Socrate* and then *Relâche*, a bizarre ballet to a scenario by the leading Dada artist Francis Picabia (for which the two of them starred in an absurdist film shown in the interval, called *Entr'acte*). Satie's genius declined soon afterwards and he became inactive, leaving behind many piles of manuscript sketches and unworn suits. His greatest influence was yet to be seen: his philosophical belief in simplicity of utterance and avoidance of any decoration laid the groundwork for the musical minimalists of later in the twentieth century, from John Cage onwards to Philip Glass and Steve Reich (p. 245).

Satie, especially as idolised by Jean Cocteau in his publication *A Call to Order*, was the inspiration for a group of younger composers working in Paris called Les Six. Although they were individually very different, they espoused for a while a common aesthetic: lightness of tone and clarity of utterance were prized; heaviness of scoring was avoided. Germaine Tailleferre (1892–1983) drew on the French baroque for her Piano Concerto; Georges Auric (1899–1983) followed Satie closely, though any lover of classic British film is most likely to have heard his music in the scores for *Passport to Pimlico* and *The Lavender Hill Mob*. Darius Milhaud (1892–1974), incredibly fluent and productive, found the greatest success. He collaborated with Satie on so-called furniture music, *musique d'ameublement* (intended as unobtrusive background); he was heavily influenced by jazz in the very effective small-scale ballets *Le boeuf sur le toit* and *La création du monde*. These created the most successful syntheses of classical and jazz idioms before Gershwin, making as Milhaud put it 'wholesale use of the jazz style to convey a purely classical feeling'. This was a vital development in the broadening of classical music's language, but as the composer implied, it was one that used the style to refresh the classical tradition, rather than respecting the roots of the style it adopted, which could lead it to be criticised today.

Arthur Honegger (1892–1955), Swiss by birth, also struck out on a successful career of his own, with some highly individual works that have stood the test of time. Two dramas draw on well-known stories, one biblical (*Le roi David*), with big choral effects, and one historical (*Jeanne d'Arc au bûcher*), both using spoken narration. He greatly influenced the early years of cinema, for which Honegger created many scores, beginning with Abel Gance's *Napoléon*. Honegger developed traditional forms in his five symphonies (No. 3, the 'Liturgique', based on plainsong themes, is the strongest), but his best-known orchestral work has always been the clever portrait of an accelerating train, *Pacific 231*.

Most successfully among the Les Six composers, Francis Poulenc (1899–1963) caught and expressed the culture of France between the wars and after. He is supremely witty in the short opera *Les mamelles de Tirésias* and deeply disturbing in the full-length opera *Dialogues des Carmélites* which tells the story of a group of nuns persecuted and executed during the French Revolution. His final dramatic piece is totally original for its time: *La voix humaine* for solo voice and orchestra sets a monologue sung by an abandoned lover on the telephone. His finest music, notably the choral *Stabat mater* (*15), adds a religious fervour to a rich sound-world. Poulenc also cultivated a warm, extrovert version of neo-classicism in his instrumental pieces such as the Concerto for Two Pianos, which owes much to Mozart, the lyrical Flute Sonata and the cheerful Sextet for piano and wind. Forming a duo with the baritone Pierre Bernac, Poulenc as pianist and composer recreated the age of the French *chanson* with new repertory, setting texts by Apollinaire and others. He did not worry about not being totally original, saying 'I think there's room for new music which doesn't mind using other people's chords.'

It is a rebuke to the male-centred musical world of our time that it took so long for the remarkable talent of Lili Boulanger (1893–1918) to be recognised. Regrettably, her brief life did not enable her to fully develop her talent, but she had an early success, winning the Prix de Rome in 1913 with her cantata *Faust et Hélène* – the first woman to do so – and her settings of Psalms 24 and 130, which have now been recorded, are anguished music of deep feeling. Her *Clairières dans le ciel* was among the first works to be premiered in Paris after the First World War and represented a widespread search for a new French idiom. She suffered throughout her short life and died of tuberculosis at twenty-four. Her elder sister Nadia Boulanger (1887–1979) devoted much of her time to preserving and performing Lili's work, wrote some music herself, which is beginning to be revived and recorded, and became an outstanding teacher in her own right. Indeed, if we search for the influential figures who have formed the sound of mid- to late twentieth-century music, Nadia Boulanger emerges as a key force. Her famous classes at Fontainebleau from 1921 and elsewhere, including America during the Second World War, taught analysis and composition, reflecting and encouraging a melting pot of trends. She welcomed a host of young composers, such as Aaron Copland, Elliott Carter, Leonard Bernstein, Lennox Berkeley, Walter Piston, Virgil Thomson, Darius Milhaud and Heitor Villa-Lobos, as well as performers and scholars such as Daniel Barenboim and John Eliot Gardiner; she taught Philip Glass and even encouraged the Argentinian Astor Piazzolla (p. 267) to write tangos. Her methods were rigorous but supportive, and she was a leading light in the revival of Monteverdi and other early music; her pioneering recordings of his works, with herself playing piano continuo, are historical documents of the first importance.

17

New Worlds

The end of the Second World War brought peace to Europe, but it did not stem the turmoil of the musical world. Radical new music which pushed forward the adventurous inheritance of the pre-war period became ever more abstruse, some would say dangerously remote from audiences. Ironically this occurred at a time when more and more people were hearing and enjoying music, thanks to the availability of radio, and the many wartime activities stimulated by organisations such as the Council for the Encouragement of Music and the Arts (CEMA, ancestor of today's Arts Council England), which brought music to new audiences. Radio had become a central part of people's musical experiences during the 1930s, and this only increased during and after the war: as Simon Frith has written, radio 'transformed the use of domestic space idealising the family hearth as the site of ease and entertainment'.

New orchestras were formed, the Philharmonia and the Royal Philharmonic, and new festivals in Edinburgh and elsewhere advanced the cause of music for all, culminating in the Festival of Britain in 1951. Benjamin Britten was active in creating the festival in Aldeburgh where he lived with the singer Peter Pears. The Proms, which moved after the bombing of the Queen's Hall in London to the Royal Albert Hall, became ever more populist under the conductorship of Sir Malcolm Sargent and drew large audiences. He introduced large-scale choral works such as Verdi's Requiem and Elgar's *The Dream of Gerontius* to the repertory; they had not featured in Henry Wood's Proms, which were almost entirely orchestral, but unlike Wood, Sargent did not support adventurous new music.

An emphasis on the well-known works of the repertory was also encouraged by the burgeoning record industry, which began to issue the central pieces in collectable form on long-playing records. This focus on popular works reflected the fact that, as distinct from the public service of the BBC, which could afford to be adventurous in its repertory, the record industry was a commercial undertaking that had to turn a profit. Success in the 1950s and 1960s enabled the recording and re-recording of vast swathes of the classical music repertory bringing fame and fortune to those artists whom the companies decided to record and promote. A new emphasis on musical appreciation and learning, both in Britain and America, helped to advance this process with speed, enabling self-improvement through the supply of subscription mail-order recordings by organisations like Reader's Digest.

The selections made by the record industry and the media proved highly influential on the listening habits of the public. Arturo Toscanini became a national figure in the USA after the war through his work with the specially created NBC Symphony Orchestra, his concerts broadcast on television. The conductor Herbert von Karajan, supported by the influential producer Walter Legge, became a top-selling classical recording artist. Live music and recording fed off each other, promoting each other, and this propelled conductors with a shrewd business sense like Karajan into positions of considerable power, able to choose their projects and their repertory.

While all this popularisation was moving on apace, the strand of advanced contemporary music was becoming ever more experimental, perhaps precisely in reaction to the growing populism around it. When the French composer Olivier Messiaen (1908–92) created his experimental *Mode de valeurs et d'intensités* at the end of the 1940s, he took to an extreme the organisational elements of musical language that had been preoccupying those composers who believed tonality was dead. Every element of the piece was determined by a calculation: not only were the pitches ordered with all twelve notes of the scale in equal prominence and regular order (as Schoenberg had formulated), but so too were the dynamics and the rhythms. By this method both the lengths of the notes and their loudness were each organised in rigorous series. Messiaen took the organisation of musical sound to a new level, creating a whole system of 'modes of limited transposition' which formalised all the different modes and symmetrical groups possible within the twelve-note chromatic scale. This created an extremely dry idiom, difficult for the ear to appreciate, and began to define a strand of modernism in music that privileged construction above all else. To some, expressiveness as an aim in itself was suspect, while the demonstration of a robust constructionist approach to the notes on the page was what counted (and in the extreme cases, a great deal of counting *was* involved). Pierre Boulez later claimed that this kind of 'total organisation' only lasted for a very short period of time. Yet, as we can recognise, the balance between constructivist and expressive approaches to composition has been a theme since the Middle Ages.

Messiaen was no dry dogmatist: at other times his music is some of the most gloriously sensual of the twentieth century. His *Turangalîla-Symphonie*, for huge orchestra, and featuring the swooping sounds of the unusual instrument the Ondes Martenot, is a rhapsodic hymn to love, as is the virtuoso song cycle *Harawi*. No one can listen to these works and find them over-organised or under-expressive. Messiaen always insisted that his greatest inspiration came from nature and the sounds of birdsong, which he collected in the countryside and reworked into piano music with great imagination: his *Catalogue d'oiseaux* has seven books of material reimagined from his precise notations. Messiaen wrote his *Quatuor pour la fin du temps* during the war when confined to a concentration camp, and it speaks of eternal truths with great humanity in its eight movements for clarinet, violin, cello and piano. A sequence of religious works, from the sublime *Visions de l'Amen* for two pianos to *Et exspecto resurrectionem mortuorum* for massed wind ensemble, all bear witness to the composer's transcendental aspiration, and they lead up to the huge opera *Saint François d'Assise*, which brings together many of Messiaen's preoccupations in a spiritual vision that has continued to draw many performers into its unique world. Perhaps his most personal and characteristic religious works are his long series of organ cycles, based on the improvisations he would play when organist of the church of La Trinité in Paris. From *La nativité du Seigneur* (*20) onwards, they respond to the centuries-old Catholic liturgy in great detail and intensity, and often use plainsong as their source.

Messiaen's technical innovations inspired a generation of the new avant-garde, including two great dominating figures of the post-war scene who studied with him, Karlheinz Stockhausen (1928–2007) and Pierre Boulez (1925–2016). Their names have become synonymous with the remoteness of 'modern music' from its audience, yet their music has an expressive intent and sonorous appeal. Stockhausen moved away from the strict regime of twelve-note music to different modes of serial organisation, and even managed to incorporate jazz influences in his super-organised *Kreuzspiel*. He created a masterpiece, *Gruppen*, for three orchestras all following different rhythmic patterns in an enthralling mix; this was followed by *Carré* for four orchestras and choirs. Stockhausen experimented extensively with live electronics, and created the evocative *Gesang der Jünglinge* for boy treble and electronic sounds. One other immediately approachable work is the meditative *Stimmung*, for six voices alone with microphones, based entirely on the vocal overtones of a single bass note. He became increasingly interested in philosophy and embarked on a massive week-long opera *Licht* with instalments for each day, many sections scored for his musical family and collaborators. This seemed to aim to rival Wagner's *Ring* cycle (p. 183) in its ambition and to exceed it in its pretentiousness. *Licht* requires massive resources to bring it off – in some sections beyond anything previously required, notably the 'helicopter quartet', for four airborne helicopters, each one carrying a member of the performing string quartet.

Pierre Boulez established a rebarbative reputation as the composer who rejoiced in Schoenberg's death as the end of a false tradition, and proclaimed Webern as the only true model for composers of the future. Active like Stockhausen in the contemporary music courses of Darmstadt, writing works of 'total serialism', he also embarked on a parallel career and became an outstanding international conductor. The chamber score *Le marteau sans maître* was his first piece to make a big impact. His music always has a French colourist's instinct, the same quality recognised in Berlioz and Debussy, which is why the surface allure of *Pli selon pli*, the rapturously sensual early cantata *Le visage nuptial*, and the much later *Sur incises* (*3), dazzlingly scored for trios of pianos, harps and percussion, are so totally engaging. His own late orchestrations of several early piano pieces from the 1940s, *Notations*, create some of the most coruscating sounds to be heard from a modern orchestra. Boulez's razor-sharp recorded interpretations of other composers' music have ensured him a major legacy in our age of re-creation: in his transparent, translucent performances of Debussy, Mahler, Stravinsky and many others he reflected the taste of the times quite as directly as did the pioneers of the early music revival (which is ironic, given that Boulez detested the appeal to historical information as a basis for performance). He made all the music he conducted seem completely freshly imagined, and through his choice of repertory he illuminated the evolution of twentieth-century music. Boulez is a prime example of the influence of a gifted interpreter in the world of today's music-making.

Far less visible than Boulez, but thoughtfully concerned with the essential materials of music, Henri Dutilleux (1916–2013) produced beautiful work in the French colouristic tradition. Start with his string quartet *Ainsi la nuit*, his Cello Concerto for Mstislav Rostropovich, *Tout un monde lointain*, and his late, lyrical song cycle for soprano and orchestra, *Correspondances*. Less well-known among Messiaen's pupils is Iannis Xenakis (1922–2001). Born in Greece, he moved to France and worked with the architect Le Corbusier; he used the calculations of his score for *Metastaseis* to inform the design for the Philips Pavilion for the World's Fair of 1958, which housed Edgard Varèse's electronic piece *Poème électronique*. Here the individual string glissandos formed a visual shape on the page of the score as well as an architectural shape, a fascinating link between music and design. Xenakis used computer programs to generate chamber pieces, while conceiving orchestral works of stark power, a ballet for orchestra *Antikhthon*, and chamber works which may look more conventional, such as the hard-hitting string quartet *Tetras*, but sound fiercely original.

The international avant-garde, especially those with political alignments, had a strong base in Italy. There had already been the individual voice of Luigi Dallapiccola (1904–75), who had suffered under Mussolini and made an impact with his one-act radio opera *Il prigioniero*; all his music is scrupulously conceived and realised. Luigi Nono (1924–90) was a colleague of Stockhausen and Boulez who married Schoenberg's daughter Nuria. He created strongly engaged concert pieces which espoused directly political causes: the greatest are the elaborate music-theatre work

Prometeo and the cantata *Il canto sospeso* setting texts condemning fascism. Nono's severe, political idiom was initially matched by the German composer Hans Werner Henze (1926–2012), who settled near Rome and became a committed communist. His oratorio *The Raft of the Medusa*, a requiem for Che Guevara, was the scene of student rioting in 1968 which caused the cancellation of the first performance in Hamburg, but it was later premiered in Vienna. Henze's long line of finely written operas, including *Elegy for Young Lovers*, *The Bassarids*, *We Come to the River* and *Venus and Adonis*, have music of voluptuous beauty in their vocal and orchestral scoring. Neither these often rhapsodic operas nor his ten symphonies and vast smaller output really place him with the avant-garde. Henze strove for a positive compromise between his political views and his musical language, which was fertilised by a combination of his German roots and his long residency in Italy. Henze's music is so well conceived and technically realised as to compel attention, and in works such as the Symphony No. 7 (*8) he explored both his national heritage and the legacy of German guilt in music of great orchestral beauty.

Less politically aligned than Henze but also growing from the world of the avant-garde was Luciano Berio (1925–2003). What distinguishes his music, as it did his personality, is a thorough-going humanity laced with a strong sense of wit. He creatively interacted with several pieces of incomplete past music including Bach's *Art of Fugue*, Mozart's *Zaïde* and Schubert's 'Unfinished' Symphony (in *Rendering*). He relished his involvement with history: one of his most involving works is *Sinfonia* of 1968 (*12) for orchestra with the voices of the Swingle Singers, which draws on Mahler's Second Symphony, Debussy, Ravel, and a host of other existing music to create his own music of the future. Both *Coro* and *Folk Songs* employ the native music of many different regions, and Berio created a series of pieces called *Sequenza* using advanced techniques for solo instruments and voice. I found his opera *Un re in ascolto* with its surreal libretto by Italo Calvino, playing with ideas of perception and reality, one of the most absorbing and stimulating premieres of recent decades.

A composer who took elements of the advanced avant-garde and used them in a wholly individual and humane way was Witold Lutosławski (1913–94). From the early extrovert *Concerto for Orchestra* through to his rich late works, he does not avoid melody: his Symphony No. 4 opens with a beautiful clarinet solo. Lutosławski's most distinctive contribution is his use of free, random passages within otherwise fully notated works; these aleatoric effects, calling on individual members of the orchestra to improvise around given material, are always carefully controlled. His Polish compatriot Krzysztof Penderecki (1933–2020) made a big impact with his St Luke Passion, writing concertos for leading soloists including the cellist Rostropovich and the violinist Anne-Sophie Mutter. His style became increasingly conservative and saccharine in later years, but a range of his work, including the famously gritty *Threnody to the Victims of Hiroshima*, was used to great effect in the films *The Exorcist*, *The Shining* and *Children of Men*. In a mirror of John Cage's 4'33" which started with a title and then became a timing (p. 13), Penderecki's *Threnody* started as a timing, 8'37", and only later acquired its programmatic title.

A British school influenced by the continental avant-garde grew with the new generation. Studying together in Manchester, Peter Maxwell Davies (1934–2016), Harrison Birtwistle (1934–) and Alexander Goehr (1932–) went on to produce work that has transformed British music and travelled far. Maxwell Davies's inspiration from medieval music and plainsong was evident in his major opera *Taverner*, with its use of chant and old instruments, and peaked with the densely worked and thrilling *Worldes Blis*. He was then stimulated by a move to Orkney in the north of Scotland, where he produced symphonic work inspired by the landscape, and practical music for young performers in the St Magnus Festival that he founded. Birtwistle has continued to evolve through massive orchestral tableaux such as the magnificent *The Triumph of Time*, *Earth Dances* and *The Shadow of Night*, as well as intensely original smaller works like *Pulse Shadows* juxtaposing soprano and string quartet. Goehr worked in both small-scale music-theatre and full-length opera; he wrote the powerful music-theatre piece *Triptych* and set the libretto of Monteverdi's lost opera *Arianna* (p. 105). All three composers have deep links to the music of the distant past, deriving stimulus and inspiration from the medieval, Renaissance and baroque repertory rather than from their immediate predecessors. Since then, the English tradition has been carried forward by such individual figures as Nicholas Maw (1935–2009), whose impressive *Odyssey* is one of the longest single spans of orchestral music, and Hugh Wood (1932–), whose *Scenes from Comus* was a successful Proms commission. Richard Rodney Bennett (1936–2012) straddled the worlds of serious and popular music with ease, learning from Boulez but writing eclectic and successful film scores for such hits as *Murder on the Orient Express*.

Reflecting quite different aspects of the modernist tradition are two Hungarians. György Ligeti (1923–2006) wrote fantastically inventive concertos for violin and piano, and orchestral essays such as *Apparitions*, *Atmosphères* and *Lontano*, which along with the multi-layered choral Requiem, with its links back to the medieval past, could not be mistaken for the music of anybody else, such is their originality of gesture and individual harmonic language. He developed a long series of *Études* for piano from 1985 (*7) which are masterpieces of modern virtuosity. His surreal opera *Le grand macabre* is a bizarre and hilarious apocalyptic vision which has had great success in different productions. Ligeti seems to me less the inheritor of a modernist, constructionist aesthetic and more the successor to Stravinsky in his darting magpie-like ability to make anything sound distinctively his own. His compatriot György Kurtág (1926–) has a sharp wit and deep wisdom, especially inventive in the long and often aphoristic series of piano miniatures called *Játékok* (Games) which are by turns quirky, amusing, expressive and pungent; he played them with his late wife Márta alongside touching Bach transcriptions. His first music-theatre piece has now been premiered: *Fin de partie* is based on Samuel Beckett and draws on operatic tradition going right back to Monteverdi, a moving and eloquent piece from a master who never compromises.

*

It has never been easy to predict which streams of musical development will become established, and which will wither over time. The arrival of twelve-note music produced some masterpieces, and was followed by Boulez's proclamation that Webern was the way forward rather than Schoenberg. But it did not turn out to be the single path its adherents hoped for. Similarly, for a time, it seemed possible that 'pure' electronic music, long generated in universities like the Massachusetts Institute of Technology and continental radio studios, which offered limitless textural possibilities and could be reliably performed without performers, was a way forward for post-war music. There have indeed been successful electronic pieces, but the best of them, such as *Mortuos plango, vivos voco* by Jonathan Harvey (1939–2012), have a human element; it includes the recorded voice of his son alongside a bell of Winchester Cathedral. Sophisticated technology allied to live performers has been a positive development of recent years, especially since Boulez founded his research institute IRCAM at the Pompidou Centre in Paris. The combination has been notably successful in Boulez's *Répons*, which uses the real-time electronic modifications of the sounds of an ensemble of live musicians, and in the electronic enhancements of his *Anthèmes* for solo violin.

Especially in America, universities with their resources have provided a haven for advanced composers, enabling their work as research but arguably cutting them off from the wider public. Some composers seemed to revel in remoteness: Milton Babbitt (1916–2011) wrote one of the most famous polemics of the post-war era, arguing that 'the composer would do himself and his music an immediate and eventual service by total, resolute, and voluntary withdrawal from this public world to one of private performance and electronic media', so that he was not distracted by questions of public reception, acclaim or the reverse. It was not a theory that matched the spirit of the times, though Babbitt's large output of inward-looking music includes some beautiful works including *Philomel* for soprano, recorded soprano and tape. An American maverick who created pieces purely for machine, though not an electronic one, was Conlon Nancarrow (1912–97) whose *Studies for Player Piano* took the potential of the mechanical piano to such limits of virtuosity that live musicians were inspired to try and match it.

Has there been a moment when modernist complexity triumphed? The finest American examples in post-war music have surely turned out to be the increasingly valued and frequently performed works from the protean imagination of Elliott Carter (1908–2012). Beginning from a closeness to Charles Ives rather than to the avant-garde mainstream, Carter took a nationalistic neo-classical stance in his Symphony No. 1, but moved towards writing an intricate and many-layered polyphony. He found highly original ways of combining different time schemes within the same piece, and giving each note a purpose and weight without resorting to over-determined structures. This was a technique developed especially through his remarkable series of string quartets and notably in his String Quartet No. 3, which at its British premiere I found one of the most challenging yet one of the most rewarding scores of the early 1970s. The experience of hearing a Carter piece for the first time can be disorientating, yet as with all great music, however unfamiliar, there is a perception that this makes sense and is worth exploring.

Carter's orchestral works grew from the approachable *Variations for Orchestra* up to the marvellous, graphic *Symphony of Three Orchestras* (referring back to Mozart's use of three separate orchestral groups in the Act 1 finale of *Don Giovanni*), whose literary inspiration from Hart Crane's poem 'To Brooklyn Bridge' elucidated its multi-layered structure. Towards the end of his long life, Carter's idiom gave way to a more open, simpler style in his last pieces, *Interventions, Instances* and *Epigrams*. After a long period when his works were felt to be daunting to perform and would not appeal to audiences, he roused enthusiasm among leading conductors, ensuring continuing commissions and performances which lasted after his centenary. Reflecting on the influence of great performers on the course of musical history, it is worth noting how the reputation of Carter's music was advanced by key interpreters: the pianist and writer Charles Rosen, the conductors Pierre Boulez, Oliver Knussen and Daniel Barenboim. Even Igor Stravinsky acclaimed Carter's work. With powerful advocates like these, there was a sense that we had to take notice.

Yet in terms of popular recognition, these composers are surely overshadowed by creators of American music in a very different tradition, which takes us beyond the scope of this book. Duke Ellington, Charlie Parker (1920–55), Miles Davis (1926–91) and John Coltrane (1926–67), among many others, have brought jazz into the mainstream of modern music. Composer–performers such as Dave Brubeck (1920–2012), Herbie Hancock (1940–) and more recently Wynton Marsalis (1961–) as the energetic director of Jazz at Lincoln Center, have built bridges across the genres.

18

Diversity

One story of this book has been that music has rarely progressed in a straight line: advances create a reaction, and an aim to imagine something new meets opposition from those who want to preserve the past. That has been true across musical history, but it was especially so after the Second World War, when there was a parting of the ways. Some composers perceived the modernists who dominated advanced music as going down a blind alley, and reacted productively against them by a myriad of varied routes, taking music's development in unexpected new directions. This was not quite a tipping point, because the future towards which it led is so diverse, but it was certainly a crisis.

One way forward was silence. Not total silence: we have already suggested that 4'33" by John Cage (1912–92) is a profound and witty statement about the nature of sound (p. 13). But in the context of the post-war era, as complexity proliferated, Cage's piece had a symbolic importance. It challenged the conventions of the day, harking back to the radical stance of Satie rather than the inheritance of Schoenberg, and gave an unspoken challenge to music to reinvent its roots. That approach was perhaps what Schoenberg referred to when he said that Cage was a great inventor rather than a great composer. Cage's ear for sound was very acute: the *Sonatas and Interludes* (1946–8) are sonically beautiful. I remember being entranced in a downtown New York loft in the presence of the always gentle, always appreciative composer, by the noises emerging from the instrument with its added percussive devices which gave a new edge to the piano sound.

Cage moved philosophically from a position where his early works had beginnings, middles and endings, as he wrote in *Changes*: 'The later ones do not. They begin anywhere, last any length of time, and involve more or fewer instruments and players.' You will come across pieces like his *Fontana Mix* or *Cartridge Music* in many different versions. Concepts like his *Musicircus*, where you wander round random groups of performers playing and singing varied repertory, can be experienced in any number of different combinations and settings, with material provided by the musicians. This was building on echoes of the music of Charles Ives, who captured the clash of sounds that he encountered in real life; Cage's radical thinking led the way for a whole post-war generation of composers who rebelled against ever-increasing complexity.

Attempting to strip away all unnecessary elements, composers tried for a new simplicity. A close colleague of Cage was the craggy figure of Morton Feldman (1926–87); they were said to have met after a performance in New York of Webern's Symphony Op. 21, escaping before the music of Rachmaninov that was to follow. While using notated techniques, Feldman created lengthy, slow-moving music of ethereal beauty for those with the stamina to encounter it: *String Quartet II* lasts an uninterrupted six hours. There are more approachable pieces for orchestra, notably *Coptic Light*, a late work which has been revived and recorded, and I found it a spiritual experience to sing in his intensely atmospheric choral piece *Rothko Chapel*, its slowly moving textures evoking the powerful dark-hued paintings of Mark Rothko as hung in the famous chapel in Houston, Texas. Feldman wanted his material to communicate directly: asked by Stockhausen what his secret was, Feldman said, 'I don't push the sounds around', to which Stockhausen replied: 'Not even a little bit?'

La Monte Young (1935–) was the first of what have been called minimalists, though this is far too limiting in terms of what the music has now become. You have to abandon yourself to the language of this music, and be taken over by its timescale – which is more or less the same approach you have to apply to a Handel or Wagner opera. La Monte Young's amazing *Well-Tuned Piano* matched

Feldman in its length (more than six hours) and hypnotic sound. He became associated with the innovative and inventive downtown New York scene associated with the artistic Fluxus group and the multi-talented Yoko Ono. He wrote pieces of solely verbal instructions, for instance one based on releasing butterflies into the concert hall in the series *Compositions 1960* (p. 12). One member of La Monte Young's ensemble was Terry Riley (1935–) who created *In C* with its tiny repeated phrases and loops and continual repeats of the note C on the piano, using techniques derived from electronic manipulation but with live musicians; it is a piece which has become a classic of the genre, as has his 1969 album *A Rainbow in Curved Air*.

Minimalists like Riley incorporated elements from non-Western music, especially Indian and African traditions; initially this was for a limited, connoisseur audience that shared the same tastes, but it quickly appealed to a far wider audience. The first composer to break through to this larger public was Steve Reich (1936–), who was gripped by his early encounters with Ghanaian music. His rigorously organised early pieces, like his earliest *It's Gonna Rain*, presented musical or spoken fragments which gradually fell out of synchronisation with each other; this 'phasing' made the listener concentrate on the very slow changes in the material. The fullest articulation of this technique is the still-fresh, intensely involving subtlety of *Drumming*, a work which brings together the influence of African drumming and phasing techniques and (like so much great music) can be heard either purely instinctively or with careful attention; each approach is rewarding. Reich presented *Music for 18 Musicians* (*11) with his ensemble, a superb tapestry of subtly shifting harmony in glittering sounds, which gained instant acceptance and has become one of the classics of the genre. He went on to devise interactions of voice and music in *Different Trains* and film and music in *The Cave* but has never ventured into conventional opera.

Philip Glass (1937–) came from a traditional musical background and was classically trained at the Juilliard School, studying with Nadia Boulanger and then Ravi Shankar in Paris. After encountering Reich's *Piano Phase* in New York, he began to move towards a more minimalist approach; he developed his own phasing technique while working in film and theatre, and then formed his own ensemble which played his *Music in Twelve Parts*. This multi-section minimalist essay, full of repetitive consonance and melody, became a cult work, its use of extensive amplification enabling it to cut through to a pop and rock audience; I experienced it in New York with a crowd of devotees who turned it into a celebration of its era, pounding and insistent. The climax of this period of Glass's work was the stand-out achievement of *Einstein on the Beach* (*10), written in conjunction with avant-garde director Robert Wilson; in a highly unusual arrangement, it was put on for sold-out evenings at the Metropolitan Opera in New York, but as an independent promotion, not as part of their opera season. This practically plotless music-theatre piece thrives on symmetry and pattern-making, with vivid visual pictures punctuated by five 'Knee Play' sections, which draw the audience through nearly five hours of its compelling repetitive material. You have to be willing to be drawn into the codes and structure of *Einstein*, but it has an extraordinarily compelling power; when it was revived in London in the 2000s, although audiences were encouraged to come and go during the five hours, there was very little movement as they sat hypnotised. Glass went on to write more conventionally plotted operas with equally original minimalist music, *Satyagraha* based on the story of Gandhi, and *Akhnaten* on the story of the Egyptian pharaoh, both of which have been regularly revived and imaginatively staged in recent years in New York (during the Met's main season) and London. But his move into the symphonic mainstream with concertos and symphonies has felt less natural, more forced.

Inevitably over time minimalism became more sophisticated, and indeed less minimal. John Adams (1947–) was never a hardcore minimalist, and he gave the genre a human face with his beautifully scored orchestral sounds and eloquent vocal writing. His choral and orchestral *Harmonium*, setting texts by Emily Dickinson, is among his most purely expressive works, while *Harmonielehre* jumbles both modern and classical styles to exhilarating, post-modern effect. Among all those who started as minimalists, Adams has been the most successful at moving into the mainstream concert repertory, recently using his links with brilliant soloists to write a violin concerto for Leila Josefowicz, *Scheherazade 2*, and a stunning piano concerto for Yuja Wang, *Must the Devil Have All the Good Tunes?* (*1) His operas have become the most consistently successful of the 2000s. His 'fanfare for orchestra', *Short Ride* *in a Fast Machine*, has an irresistible energy and forward movement and seems to reach back across time (p. 13). Because of its descriptive title, it had to be twice dropped from the Proms concerts in London, once in 1997 after the death of Diana, Princess of Wales, and once in 2001 after the 9/11 attacks in America. Adams probably now wishes he had named it after the time it takes to perform it.

Adams's operas have made a major impact in the repertory. *Nixon in China* was based on the 1972 visit of President Richard Nixon to Mao Zedong in China. The librettist was Alice Goodman, and the director (and conceiver of the whole show) was Peter Sellars. If any modern opera can be said to have already become a classic, *Nixon in China* is it: a human drama set to enthralling music, full of wit, humanity, satirical divertissements for dancers, with jokey moments but also moments of deep interior emotion – all the ingredients of great opera through the ages. It set contemporary opera on a new course, and John Adams's music has gone from strength to strength in the years that followed (Plate 30).

He hit a political minefield with *The Death of Klinghoffer*, a dramatisation of the hijacking of the cruise ship *Achille Lauro* in 1985, which was accused of pro-Palestinian bias for its depiction of terrorists amid Arab–Israeli tensions; it nevertheless triumphed in sold-out performances at the Metropolitan Opera in New York. Adams has gone on to flourish in both orchestral and operatic work such as *Doctor Atomic*, telling the story of the first atomic bomb and the personal struggles of J. Robert Oppenheimer; the oratorio-style drama *El Niño*, around the narrative of the birth of Christ; and *The Gospel According to the Other Mary*, in which Adams (and Sellars, who semi-staged them both) drew on powerful religious and humanitarian themes to tell their story with acute contemporary relevance.

Another opera linked to familiar material is *Marnie* by the American Nico Muhly (1981–), cleverly based on Hitchcock's film and stylishly staged in London and New York. Its crossover idiom of minimalism-plus owes much to Glass and Adams but develops its own voice. Muhly has traversed many boundaries between classical and contemporary music, and has been a skilled rearranger of old music for new forces.

The important Russian strain of minimalism, never wholly simplistic, finds a voice in the music of Alfred Schnittke (1934–98), a unique and influential figure whose combined assault of parody and self-criticism produced some of the toughest yet most engaging music of our time. Continually referring to other music and subjecting it to fierce dislocation (even the innocent carol *Stille Nacht* receives this treatment in his version for violin and piano), Schnittke uses a wide set of references. Sometimes his music is filled with hilarious jokiness, as in his collage-like First Symphony (1969–72), which deconstructs the symphonic form with manic entrances and exits to and from the stage by the performers, creating a surreal drama. Sometimes he sends up an entire idiom, as in his Concerto Grosso No. 1, satirically playing with the baroque and classical style. The great work to start with in listening to Schnittke is the Viola Concerto that he wrote for Yuri Bashmet, austerely beautiful, weaving his name into the score and hinting at Bach. His later symphonies, the Sixth, Seventh and Eighth written during his periods of ill-health, become ever barer and more attenuated, while still retaining a weary integrity; he left an outline of a Ninth Symphony.

That fierce integrity also shines through the music of his compatriot Sofiya Gubaydulina (1931–), whose music brings together a range of influences from her Tartar origins, her love of Bach, evident in the big violin concerto *Offertorium* based on the theme of Bach's *Musical Offering*, and her Eastern philosophy. The result is an extraordinary originality of voice. Often criticised through official channels in Russia, she left for Hamburg in 1992 and was one of a group of major composers commissioned to write a new Passion for the millennium year which produced her bold, ritualistic *Johannes-Passion*, later followed by the equally large-scale *Johannes-Ostern*, two biblical narratives with big choruses and massive organ parts. Gubaydulina is not a minimalist in the sense of relying on repetition and gradual harmonic change, but her works have a spareness in which not a note is wasted.

The religious tradition underpinning many of her works is also evident in a rather different line of minimalist beauty. Arvo Pärt (1935–) came from an Estonian background, worked in a Communist country, adopted some modernist principles, and his earlier music (influenced by what he was able to hear of the Western avant-garde on the radio) is acerbic and uncompromising. His *Nekrolog* was denounced by the authorities. But then he discovered the medieval music of

Ockeghem, Obrecht and Josquin (p. 67), copying out their music by hand, and further back the wellsprings of Gregorian chant, and he underwent a revolution in his style. In that way he mirrored the discoveries of the minimalists: he pared his music down to the essentials, saying 'I have discovered that it is enough when a single note is beautifully played.' You don't sense irony in Pärt's music; you sense a purity of impulse. The piece that made the biggest impact on me was his setting of the St John Passion, in which the familiar biblical narrative is retold in ethereal, cool harmonies which have echoes of the parallel harmonies of organum in the early Middle Ages (p. 31). The beautiful *Cantus in memoriam Benjamin Britten* (*9) has a string orchestra intoning rising and falling scales, complemented only by a single bell, a perfect memorial work. Then there is a pair of smaller pieces which established his reputation internationally, *Tabula rasa* and *Fratres*, both works which exist in many different formats and scorings; they created a style for a generation of listeners, contemplative and expressive, one especially well-suited to absorbing home listening as well as the live concert. You feel as if the music is crafting a state of mind rather than tracing a development. Pärt is now one of the most performed of living contemporary composers, and he deserves to be.

From an English tradition, mixing elements of Orthodox and other religious traditions, John Tavener (1944–2013) inhabited a similar space with his succession of profoundly religious works in different traditions. His dramatic cantata *The Whale*, based on the Old Testament story of Jonah, was a hit at the Proms in 1968, and his wide-ranging pieces span the *Celtic Requiem*, using children's choir and evoking the folk tunes of his childhood, to the ambitious *Ultimos ritos*, a massive choral construction built around the writings of St John of the Cross, creating a sound-world using the *Crucifixus* from Bach's B minor Mass which emerges in a recording at the end of the piece. This is yet another homage by a contemporary composer to a great figure of the past: it is noticeable that all these composers are reaching back for inspiration to distant models, be it medieval, Renaissance or baroque, rather than, for instance, to Beethoven. Tavener shifted his religious allegiance to the Orthodox church, and a breakthrough to popular success came with *The Protecting Veil* (*6), for solo cello and strings, premiered at the BBC Proms in 1989, whose visionary intensity, with the cello playing high in its register, won it a very wide following through the recording that followed. Tavener went on to compose a vast number of religious works large and small, particularly influenced by his relationship with the Orthodox church, but also including the tiny choral setting of William Blake, *The Lamb*, which has become a classic, and the *Song of Athene*, which was heard around the world at the close of the funeral of Diana, Princess of Wales (pp. xiii–xiv), in Westminster Abbey.

One other composer belongs with these leaders of the new spiritual simplicity, and that is the enigmatic figure of the Polish composer Henryk Górecki (1933–2010). Like Pärt, he started from a position in the avant-garde, but moved towards a more minimalist style, and broke through in popular appeal when his Third Symphony was re-recorded in 1992 with the soprano Dawn Upshaw. In this 'Symphony of Sorrowful Songs', the emotional texts which reference the Holocaust are matched to slowly evolving music of impassive intensity, and the gradually building pressure of the hour-long piece gives it a devastating impact.

*

In England in the mid-twentieth century, the leading talents were neither simplistic nor minimalist, carving their own individual sound-world with great discrimination. The prodigious youthful talent of Benjamin Britten (1913–76), combined with his highly practical facility, had been evident both in his music for choir (his teenage *Hymn to the Virgin,* and later *A Boy Was Born*) and for the film unit of the General Post Office, setting poetry by W. H. Auden about the delivery by railway of the country's post in *Night Mail.* A performer as well as a composer, Britten played his own Piano Concerto at the 1938 Proms with mixed success. He travelled to America during the war, and on his return made a decisive mark with his operatic triumph, *Peter Grimes* (*16), premiered at Sadler's Wells in London in 1945. The visceral character portrayal of its anti-hero, an outsider from society who harms his apprentice boys and yet musically earns our sympathy for his plight, is set against the bustling, well-observed background of an English seaside town and the peerless evocation of the landscape in the 'Four Sea Interludes' (now famous as a concert piece, and ever more audible as a key source of postwar British music). Britten's operatic instincts flourished in *Billy Budd*, written for men's voices only, again turning on the death of its title character, this time an innocent caught up in a web of on-ship aggression. Hurt by the poor reception of the grand opera *Gloriana*, written for the 1953 Coronation, Britten turned to smaller forms. *The Turn of the Screw*, a creepily effective version of Henry James's ghost story with central parts for two children, is set for small chamber orchestra (like the earlier *Albert Herring*) so that every word can be audible.

With his partner Peter Pears, Britten skilfully adapted Shakespeare's *A Midsummer Night's Dream* for the tiny venue of Jubilee Hall in Aldeburgh, bringing the romance of the play into a twentieth-century context by the use of the ambiguous counter-tenor voice for Oberon, written for the singer Alfred Deller. The use of children's voices as the sharp-edged fairies is winning, and the opera's lilting finale 'Now until the break of day' is among Britten's most inspired ideas. Meanwhile he was assuring himself a central place in the line of English choral music with his *War Requiem* for the opening of the new Coventry Cathedral in 1962, mixing the Latin texts of the Requiem Mass with the war poetry of Wilfred Owen, conceived for three soloists of different nationalities, a sacred drama.

Britten's dramatic writing took a highly original turn away from large-scale opera in the three 'church parables' *Curlew River*, *The Burning Fiery Furnace* and *The Prodigal Son*, in which a ritualistic approach inspired by his experiences of Japanese Noh drama was brought to bear on (in the latter two) biblical stories. They represent a thoroughgoing attempt to reinvent the genre, at a time when music-theatre was gaining ground. Among his many influences, Britten heard the music of Bali, first through transcriptions for piano by the Canadian ethnomusicologist Colin McPhee; Britten later travelled to Bali and created his exotic ballet *The Prince of the Pagodas*, full of the sounds of gamelan music. These return in his last achievement in opera, *Death in Venice*, where he created an atmospherically precise sound-world to capture the mood, emotions and decay of the floating city depicted in Thomas Mann's novella. The familiarity of this story from the lush film, with its use of the Adagietto from Mahler's Fifth Symphony (p. 198), bears no relation to the sound-world of Britten's opera, which is full of bright percussion. Here the gamelan ensemble represents the innocence of the young boy Tadzio, who becomes an obsession and inspiration for the novelist Aschenbach.

The autobiographical links in the story were heightened by its being completed during Britten's final illness; it remains utterly unique in its sound-world, with a combination of weariness and aspiration.

Michael Tippett (1905–98) was much less sure than Britten technically, and did not emerge fully as a composer until the creation of his humanitarian oratorio *A Child of Our Time* with its memorable use of spirituals for choir, mirroring the chorales in the Bach Passions, and the powerful, vigorous Concerto for Double String Orchestra (*17) with its links back to the baroque. Tippett insisted on being his own librettist, not always to the benefit of his operas, yet they make a wholly characterful contribution to the landscape of the post-war scene in Britain. His characters are elemental, often symbolic figures rather than rounded personalities, and he drew inspiration from sources as varied as television drama and ancient Greek philosophy. *The Midsummer Marriage* was his first operatic score, containing some rhapsodically beautiful music (especially in the Ritual Dances) within its complex ritual framework. His second, *King Priam*, performed in the same town (Coventry) and the same year (1962) as Britten's *War Requiem*, is a really powerful, tautly scored drama of the Trojan war, and for me his best opera. There followed *The Knot Garden*, *The Ice Break* and finally *New Year* (which he finished in his eighty-third year), with their winning combination of naïve characterisation and popular references complemented by some wonderful sounds. He continued the symphonic tradition with the Vivaldi-inspired but rhythmically complex Symphony No. 2 (which suffered a famous breakdown at its first performance), the Symphony No. 3 with vocal soloist engaging with the heritage of Beethoven, and the 'life-to-death' sequence of the Symphony No. 4 with its use of a wind machine expressing birth and death. An unusual and winning work is the Triple Concerto for violin, viola and cello, with an ecstatic, Eastern-inspired central movement.

It is paradoxical to think that Britten's operatic inheritor today is Harrison Birtwistle (1934–), whose fierce, satirical *Punch and Judy* was premiered at Aldeburgh in 1968 to Britten's great displeasure, as he felt it was needlessly violent in both story and music. Birtwistle's *Gawain*, a retelling of the story of Gawain and the Green Knight, drew on powerful ancient British traditions and the finest strength of centuries of English music. Its 1994 revival at Covent Garden was the subject of a small demonstration by anti-modernist composers, though they could hardly have chosen a less suitable target than this opera so firmly rooted in the past, which enthralled its audience. It was followed by the even more ancient and mythic *The Minotaur*, and a group of smaller chamber operas. But it may well be that the most impressive opera in Birtwistle's output will turn out to be the earlier *The Mask of Orpheus*; its elaborate score involving complex electronics has made revival difficult, but it has received concert performances and a new staging at English National Opera in 2019 which reinforced both the extreme demands of the piece and its deep-rooted sonic impact.

Thomas Adès (1971–) launched his operatic career with the scandalous mini-opera *Powder Her Face* on the lurid affairs of the Duchess of Argyll, and then moved to a more traditional source for his large-scale opera *The Tempest* (*2). Although closely based on Shakespeare's play, the text was skilfully manipulated by librettist Meredith Oakes into couplets, verses and rhythms suitable for setting in the traditional forms of arias and ensembles. With virtuosity stretched to the limits in the stratospheric writing for Ariel, this exotic mix had enough recognisable elements for audiences to latch onto it immediately. Adès drew on another existing artwork in his subsequent opera *The Exterminating Angel*, based on the film by Luis Buñuel, which enjoyed huge success at the Salzburg Festival, London and New York. It is a vivid palette of character studies, brilliantly scored and executed. Adès has also flourished in the world of orchestral music with *Asyla*, one of the most widely performed of recent orchestral pieces, influenced by club music and the eclecticism of the twentieth century, later complemented by *Tevot* and *Polaris* to create a powerful trilogy; he has also become a strongly individual conductor of repertory from Beethoven to Stravinsky, and is an outstanding pianist.

George Benjamin (1960–) made a sudden international impact with his gripping and moving medieval tale *Written on Skin*, premiered in Aix-en-Provence and already the subject of different European productions (Plate 30). He followed that with *Lessons in Love and Violence*, based on the story of Edward II and his lover Piers Gaveston. Although Benjamin has made an international mark with opera, it was as a composer of instrumental music that he first had an impact; his cracklingly vivid orchestral essay *Ringed by the Flat Horizon,* completed when he was still a student, was among the most youthful works to have been performed at the Proms, and other works that have been widely performed around the world include *At First Light* and *Dance Figures.* He is a major conductor as well as a composer, and constantly uses his programmes to advance the cause of adventurous music. He has had several festivals devoted to his small but exquisitely precise output, is a supremely knowledgeable teacher, and was the consultant to BBC Radio 3's award-winning broadcast festival of a hundred years of twentieth-century music, *Sounding the Century.* Mark-Anthony Turnage (1960–) is an operatic natural: from his early brutal and iconoclastic *Greek,* retelling the story of Oedipus, to the more recent *Anna Nicole* about the doomed *Playboy* star, they pack a punch and grip an audience; along with the recently revived *The Silver Tassie* based on Seán O'Casey's play, they have assured him a place in the operatic repertory.

*

Britten's legacy dominated the post-war scene to a remarkable extent: his influence can be felt in a group of British composers who combined directness of utterance, interest in the music of the distant past, and superb craftsmanship. Equally important has been the commitment to particular performers and to writing music suited to them, rather than creating music that is purely abstract. A very personal group of selected pieces to explore among many would include music by the stunningly gifted Oliver Knussen (1952–2018), a prodigy whose composing and conducting career began at the age of fifteen when he directed his own First Symphony; later works include his *Two Organa* based on the sounds of medieval music, the Violin Concerto, a lyrical reinvention of the concerto tradition, and the beautiful and expressive Horn Concerto (*5) written for Barry Tuckwell. Inspired by Maurice Sendak's children's books (but equally appealing to adults), he composed the operas *Where the Wild Things Are* and *Higglety Pigglety Pop!* which have been widely performed.

Colin Matthews (1946–) has composed the post-minimalist *Broken Symmetry* (which was premiered by Knussen) and the orchestral *Traces Remain,* exploring relationships with the past; a work that makes an immediate impact is the ensemble piece *Suns Dance,* which later became a ballet. Matthews has been a generous supporter of other composers' work, especially through the label NMC, which has made available a huge range of contemporary repertory. Robert Saxton (1953–), directly influenced by Britten, came to attention with two orchestral works *The Ring of Eternity* and the *Concerto for Orchestra*; he later wrote an opera for radio, *The Wandering Jew*. Often drawing on and imaginatively reinventing the music of the past, especially the baroque and classical repertory, John Woolrich (1954–) has been inspired by Monteverdi in his evocative *Ulysses Awakes* and by Mozart in *The Theatre Represents a Garden: Night*, while Julian Anderson (1967–) has created in his sophisticated and scrupulous idiom at least one orchestral classic in *The Stations of the Sun*; he wrote the prize-winning choral *Heaven is Shy of Earth* and has been a noted teacher and writer.

In recent years, after the big success of his orchestral piece *The Confession of Isobel Gowdie*, the religious impulse behind the music of James MacMillan (1959–) has won audiences, especially his large-scale St John Passion and recent *Stabat Mater*. He has written practical church music for congregations to sing, contributed a new carol to King's College Cambridge, and worked with local audiences and children in his own festival, the Cumnock Tryst, in Scotland to produce music that is grounded and relevant to their concerns. In this, as in so many other cases, the connection of the composer to the community has been strengthened without in any way diminishing the quality and importance of their work.

These composers and many others have produced an outstanding era of varied new music which laid the groundwork for the thriving world of today's emerging composers. Women make up an increasing proportion of those composers – a gradual advance towards parity which is long overdue. In the field of opera alone, the Finn Kaija Saariaho (1952–) with *L'amour de loin* evokes the twelfth-century world of the troubadours in a timeless story and evocative score which has travelled widely; she and the Austrian Olga Neuwirth (1968–) with her opera *Lost Highway* are well established internationally. The music of Sally Beamish (1956–), who is a viola player, draws fruitfully on her links with Scotland and Sweden, having been composer in association to orchestras in both countries, while Tansy Davies (1973–) has written a bold opera, *Between Worlds*, based around the events of 9/11 in New York. The diverse scores of Judith Weir

(1954–) include the classic *A Night at the Chinese Opera*, the witty *King Harald's Saga*, a grand opera in under ten minutes for solo soprano, and *Storm* (*4) for young people.

Leading performance artists and creators would not want to be pigeonholed as women, or indeed as musicians; major influential figures such as Meredith Monk (1942–) and Laurie Anderson (1947–) have created wholly individual creative work across the boundaries of the art forms, and provided role models for aspiring artists. There are many examples now of female composers from diverse backgrounds who cross the bounds of classical and popular music: in Britain Anna Meredith (1978–), Emily Howard (1979–), Helen Grime (1981–) and Hannah Kendall (1984–) have all had major commissions from orchestras and festivals. Their range of influences is huge: the American Caroline Shaw (1982–), who was the youngest winner of the Pulitzer Prize for Music for her *Partita for 8 Voices*, cites her musical enthusiasms as Buxtehude, rapper Childish Gambino, Adele and spectralist composer Gérard Grisey. You could hardly devise a wider collection of models.

*

Great composers have always admired popular music of real quality. Brahms knew the famous theme of Johann Strauss's *Blue Danube* waltz, now familiar from every New Year's Day concert in Vienna, and noted down its theme, lamenting 'unfortunately not by Johannes Brahms'. Stage works using popular idioms, including the whole area of musicals, increasingly form part of the repertory. This is an observable trend: only a few decades ago classical concert seasons would rarely have included the music of Leonard Bernstein, still less Stephen Sondheim, but now they are a regular element. There have always been lighter stage pieces with huge continuing success, from Offenbach to Johann Strauss or Gilbert and Sullivan (p. 189), but George Gershwin (1898–1937) produced something different. His pioneering *Porgy and Bess*, with its all-Black cast, symphonic treatment of popular song and unforgettable melodies ('Summertime', 'It Ain't Necessarily So'), unlocked the emotions of performers and audiences. It was not an immediate success with the critics, yet has now become a landmark work, powerfully staged in opera houses today from Glyndebourne (in 1986 the pioneer, under Simon Rattle) to the Metropolitan Opera in New York (finally, in 2018). Gershwin was the absolute master of the short popular song: it is surely not unreasonable to regard 'They Can't Take That Away from Me' (*18), 'The Man I Love' and 'A Foggy Day in London Town' as the twentieth-century equivalents of Schubert and Schumann's finest miniatures. He brought his inventiveness into the classical arena with the piano concerto *Rhapsody in Blue*, scored for piano with jazz band but now usually played with full symphony orchestra, crossing the genres with ease. The influence of the blues and Black spirituals underpin Gershwin's idiom in ways that seem totally natural and integrated, broadening his appeal to the widest public. Gershwin produced a whole series of musicals with hit songs and memorable numbers, including *Girl Crazy* and *Of Thee I Sing*, but they mostly had ramshackle librettos that have to be reshaped for present-day performance. It is tragic to think what Gershwin (like Purcell, Mozart and Schubert) might have achieved had he lived longer (Plate 29).

The musical became one of the most important and popular genres of the post-war era. Richard Rodgers (1902–79) worked first with Lorenz Hart and then from 1943 with Oscar Hammerstein, a collaboration launched with *Oklahoma!* which included a string of unforgettable melodies including 'Oh What a Beautiful Morning', and then *Carousel* with 'You'll Never Walk Alone'. Today we might question the racially patronising story behind *The King and I* and even *South Pacific*, but their tunes have proved long-lasting, as even more so have the memorable numbers from *The Sound of Music*. Its film version is one of the most successful and wholesome of musicals, sanitising but not avoiding the Nazi complications of the von Trapp family story in Salzburg, with an array of unforgettable hits and a useful introduction to the rudiments of musical theory (p. 10).

From *Kiss Me, Kate* by Cole Porter (1891–1964), a racy take on Shakespeare's *The Taming of the Shrew* and full of witty numbers, to *My Fair Lady* by Frederick Loewe (1901–88), a remarkably faithful adaptation by librettist Alan Jay Lerner of Bernard Shaw's play *Pygmalion*, these musicals contain some of the most memorable tonal music of our time. The Gilbertian wit of 'Brush Up Your Shakespeare' in *Kiss Me, Kate*, and the lyrical outpouring of 'I Could Have Danced All Night' in *My Fair Lady*, have burned their way into the consciousness of a generation. The tinge of sentimentality that imbues these shows is characteristic of the form, but their orchestrations (often by other musicians) are sophisticated and the results are enjoyably compelling.

Andrew Lloyd Webber (1948–) has been the hugely successful prolific English equivalent, beginning with the exuberant children's mini-opera *Joseph and the Amazing Technicolor Dreamcoat* and the 'rock opera' *Jesus Christ Superstar* to a libretto by Tim Rice. Later, more ambitious works including *Cats*, set to a high-level libretto from the poems of T. S. Eliot, *Evita* and *Phantom of the Opera* have run constantly on the world's stages, and their combination of memorability and stylistic parody are ingeniously characterful. There have been many followers, among which is the astonishingly popular *Les Misérables* by Claude-Michel Schönberg (1944–), although for me, emotional manipulation here replaces musical distinction. Most recently the breakthrough musical has been *Hamilton* by Lin-Manuel Miranda (1980–), which uses the musical language of hip-hop and pop idioms to tell the story of one of America's founding fathers with diverse singers and actors. That truly hit the moment.

No single musical has achieved the distinction and the long-lasting life of *West Side Story* (*13) by Leonard Bernstein (1918–90), its brilliantly clever book by Stephen Sondheim (1930–) reinventing Shakespeare in modern New York combined with Bernstein's feel for melody, pungent parody and energetic exuberance. This is a one-off example of a work of genius, halfway between musical and opera. In Bernstein's sophisticated melting pot of musical influences, from fifties bebop to Puerto Rican dance music, he expands the range of his idiom to acknowledge the sources of the American tradition. Eternally eclectic, Bernstein ranged from the trendy embarrassment of *Mass* to the seriousness of *A Quiet Place*, a sequel to his much earlier *Trouble in Tahiti*. Sondheim went on to compose and write texts for some of the most ingenious musicals of the era: start with the immediately accessible *Follies, Into the Woods* or the most operatic of them all, the gruesomely entertaining *Sweeney Todd*.

Alongside the flourishing of the musical, the other entirely distinctive musical genre of the twentieth and twenty-first centuries has been music for film. This in its turn has produced a welcome development: as cinema has become ever more wide-ranging in its use of existing music and creation of new scores, it has introduced generations to music they would never think of encountering in the concert hall. Who among the audiences seeing *2001: A Space Odyssey* had previously encountered the music of Ligeti? Certainly none of us had heard it juxtaposed with Johann Strauss's *Blue Danube* and Richard Strauss's *Also sprach Zarathustra*. (There was an irony here: director Stanley Kubrick had commissioned a new score for the film, which he then casually discarded, preferring his favourite classics.) Oliver Stone's *Platoon* hugely increased the popularity of Samuel Barber's *Adagio for Strings*, while *Elvira Madigan* did the same, not very appropriately, for the slow movement of Mozart's Piano Concerto No. 21 in C.

Original music created by skilled and specialist composers has made film into a leading medium through which contemporary audiences encounter orchestral works. Lavishly scored visions by Maurice Jarre (1924–2009) and the hugely successful John Williams (1932–) used a fundamentally old-school big-orchestra sound. Jarre's sumptuous *Lawrence of Arabia* and *Doctor Zhivago*, and Williams's epic scores for the *Star Wars* trilogy of films, trod a traditional path with great panache and have proved continually popular. Nino Rota (1911–79) worked creatively with director Federico Fellini as well as Visconti and Zeffirelli, and with Francis Ford Coppola on the award-winning *The Godfather Part II*. The eclectically scored Westerns of Ennio Morricone (1928–2020), especially *The Good, the Bad and the Ugly*, were very influential on a new generation of film composers. Among leading specialist composers for film, Bernard Herrmann (1911–75) drew on a range of influences in his music for Alfred Hitchcock's *Psycho*, *Torn Curtain* and *Vertigo*: these perceptive and insightful scores have been re-recorded by symphony orchestras, with Hitchcock crediting Herrmann for his music's success in shaping the perception of the films' characters. That relationship between director and composer has not always been an easy one: the story goes that director Akira Kurosawa supplied the leading Japanese composer Tōru Takemitsu (1930–96) with classical music references for his scores for several films – but Kurosawa's desire to include a Schubert song proved too much for Takemitsu.

From Scott Bradley (1891–1977) aping twelve-note music in his scoring of the Tom and Jerry cartoons, to the minimalist scores to *Koyaanisqatsi* and *The Hours* by Philip Glass, to Michael Nyman (1944–) creating Purcell-inspired music for Peter Greenaway's period drama *The Draughtsman's Contract* and Jane

Campion's film *The Piano*, a range of diverse idioms has been accepted and celebrated by cinemagoers. An increasing trend is for orchestras to mount showings of relevant films with live music, from Disney's *Fantasia*, with its classical repertory, to Woody Allen's *Manhattan*, using Gershwin to evoke New York City, providing a new multimedia experience for the public to enjoy. But orchestras are by no means the only source of contemporary film and video-game music: advances in technology have led to increasingly electronic-inspired work by Hans Zimmer (1957–) and the Chinese-American Tan Dun (1957–) in the dazzling Oscar-winning 2000 film *Crouching Tiger, Hidden Dragon*. A huge expansion of recent years has been in the creation of sophisticated scores for video games, both original music and versions of the classics. While not originally intended to stand on their own, they have now become a popular new genre, arranged for symphony orchestras and bands, and forming the basis of shows like Video Games Live, with staging, lighting, live action and, as its website advertises, 'interactive segments creating an explosive one-of-a-kind entertainment experience'.

This is a story that will continue, as technology shapes the means of creativity and production. How will music continue to be made in the digital age? What is the future for the performance of music?

Coda
Performing the Future

Is there any way we can sum up, after this journey over a millennium and more, where the performance of music has come from and where it is going next? Across the centuries, as men and women have sung to each other, fashioned instruments, danced in rituals and shouted in celebrations, invented orchestras and conceived symphonies, built concert halls and opera houses, and now live-streamed performances across the globe, are there any common themes that might trace music's development and plot its future course?

Many in the later twentieth century yearned for this sort of continuity; as the composer and musicologist Roman Vlad wrote, 'the main problem, on the solution of which the very survival of music as a coherent form of aesthetic expression would seem to depend, is to restore to music the unity of language it had lost as a result of the post-romantic dilemma'. Vlad recognised the problem, but at least he did not prescribe a particular solution. My least favourite articulation of the way forward came from the polymath Roger Scruton in his book *The Aesthetics of Music*: 'The great task which lies before the art of sound [is] the task of recovering tonality as the imagined space of music, and of restoring the spiritual community with which that space was filled.' That yearning for the old world of exclusive tonality is pure nostalgia, as unlikely to happen as de-inventing the internet. The sense of a unified tradition of musical development has disappeared, for all the reasons this book has explored: there will be a diverse stream of different idioms stimulated by the constant, unlimited availability of music from the past which has revealed so many influences on the music of the present. That richness is surely a reason for rejoicing rather than regret. As the scholar Robert Morgan tellingly put it in *Man and Music: Modern Times*, whatever one may think about the music and art of our era, 'it reflects the world in which we live with striking fidelity . . . the pluralism of contemporary music mirrors the lack of consensus in the political, social and religious attitudes that govern how we live, work and interact'.

Those who study Western music have often tried to establish whether there are common threads that bind the language of tonal music together. Deryck Cooke, who led the completion of Mahler's Tenth Symphony, made a heroic attempt in his book *The Language of Music* to establish common melodic and harmonic devices across the centuries from Dowland to Stravinsky. The idea that common shapes, lines and textures mean similar things to people across the generations is probably limited to a single cultural tradition, and would now seem of lesser importance in a world in which so many such traditions can exist side by side. We need not yearn for unity: I would feel that what is of most interest, and what keeps us listening, is what makes different musics sound *different*, not what makes them the same. As the scholar Philip Brett wrote memorably, new approaches to performing music have 'given us a sense of difference, a sense that by exercising our imaginations we may, instead of reinforcing our own sense of ourselves by assimilating works unthinkingly to our own mode of performing and perceiving, learn to know what something different might mean and how we might ultimately delight in it'.

How do we judge what is important to us? We look around the concert and opera programmes of the world and, in spite of the diversity we have described, we see far too great a uniformity, based on the music that has become accepted as being at the heart of the Western tradition. We do not often question our understanding of what is great: what could be more central to our repertory than the symphonies of Beethoven and Brahms? They are at the core of what has become known as the canon, toured by the great international orchestras, repeated endlessly live and on record. But in truth, what has been valued at different times in our musical history has varied wildly. The expansion of our repertory in recent decades, both back to early music and forward to new contemporary music, and the growth of a variety of performing styles, has arguably turned on its head the idea of a single tradition with those Beethoven and Brahms symphonies at their heart. Yes, they have earned their place as great works that speak to succeeding generations, but that does not give them an unchanging status.

The past is full of works, from Bizet's *Carmen* to Mahler's symphonies, which have not immediately succeeded in their own time, but which have subsequently become highly esteemed. Stravinsky's *The Rite of Spring* caused a riot at its premiere, but soon became a celebrated triumph of huge influence. Our taste changes subtly and gradually. As a culture we have overlooked women composers of talent just because their music was not prominently performed; so too music by Black and minority ethnic composers. Now these are emerging into the mainstream, leading to an overdue recognition of their importance as well as their influence in creating the sounds of the twenty-first century. Recent initiatives like the founding of the Black-led Chineke! Orchestra are the beginning of a very necessary process of readjustment. There are all sorts of fluctuations in what we hear and what is performed. At one point Sibelius is valued, at others less so. Tchaikovsky represents the peak of dramatic symphonic writing for one generation, for the next it is Shostakovich. At one moment Schoenberg, Berg and Webern with their reinvention of musical language seem like the one path to the musical future; now we feel that for all we value their achievements, it was actually Stravinsky who with his magpie-like approach to tradition created the spirit of a future musical language.

The reasons for these changes in taste are complex and dynamic, to do with patronage, performers, promoters, power structures, money, musical training and audience experience, but fundamentally with the changing culture of the times. In the years of creating concerts with orchestras and conductors for the Proms and elsewhere, as programmers we attempted to balance works which would readily attract audiences with those that would expand the repertoire, persuading conductors that they did not always need to conduct pieces that audiences knew and loved, leavening the core repertoire with something more adventurous – or sometimes it was the other way round, grounding constant adventure within something more familiar. This was always a process of collaboration, balancing risk and conviction, and no doubt we made plenty of mistakes in assessing the taste of the times; we tried to suggest that Rameau had a valid place alongside Bach and Handel, that Berlioz could stand in the company of Beethoven, that Kurt Weill could be a match for Stravinsky. Some of this audiences welcomed; other experiments made little impact. In the case of many neglected composers, the jury of time is still out: for all their appeal, I regret that we never quite managed to succeed in arguing for the central place of Rameau and C. P. E. Bach in the eighteenth century, or Karol Szymanowski and Manuel de Falla in the twentieth, as part of the core mainstream repertory. On the other hand, see what has happened to Handel's operas in our lifetime: neglected for two centuries, they are now an indispensable part of our operatic landscape.

The influence of great instrumental and vocal performers in making all this happen, as in the past, is crucial, because they are the mediators with the public: the cellist Yo-Yo Ma (1955–) with his influential Silk Road Project and solo Bach played to thousands (Plate 31), the violinist Leila Josefowicz (1977–) with her advocacy of so many contemporary scores, the versatile soprano Barbara Hannigan (1971–) who now herself conducts, curates and leads ensembles (Plate 30), and the dynamic pianist Yuja Wang (1987–) among so many others have both stimulated the production of new music and have given it vividly compelling and expert performances. The Chinese pianist Lang Lang (1982–) has spread the popularity of the piano among literally millions of his compatriots and young people. Conductors Simon Rattle (1955–) at the Berlin Philharmonic and now the London Symphony Orchestra, and Esa-Pekka Salonen (1958–) at the Los Angeles Philharmonic and now the San Francisco Symphony, are advocates for new composers and have shown a continuing commitment to new work; the live-wire conductor Gustavo Dudamel (1981–), a product of the El Sistema educational movement in Venezuela, now conducts the Los Angeles Philharmonic and has created a youth orchestra for the culturally diverse young people of the city, which is helping to shape his own orchestra's future. Increasingly, inspiring role models from diverse backgrounds are widening the appeal of classical music, notably the seven members of the Kanneh-Mason family who play together, with cellist Sheku Kanneh-Mason (1999–) having wide exposure since playing at the wedding of Prince Harry and Meghan Markle (Plate 31). The long-overdue message that the experience of music is for everyone is finally being heard in a new cultural situation.

We can be sure of one thing: the music of the future in this multi-dimensional world will not grow out of a single tradition. Some signals can be seen in the mixed musical styles of the Argentinian-American Osvaldo Golijov (1960–), whose St Mark Passion is a melting pot of American genres. It is equally impossible to define the Argentinian composer Astor Piazzolla (1921–92) as classical or popular, as he grew up in the folk tradition but then studied with Nadia Boulanger in Paris; his music is immediately recognisable, his intertwining of genres magically effective. Young promise in Britain includes the quirky work of Francisco Coll (1985–), the inventive Mark Simpson (1988–), the strong profile of Tom Coult (1988–), the finely made music of Charlotte Bray (1982–), and so many others. You must choose for yourself: sample adventure through the Radio 3 programmes and the many playlists which feature the best of new music.

Thus the range of influences on today's composers broadens exponentially as our musical horizons expand. Sounds from around the world, traditional folk song or contemporary popular song, new modernism or new simplicity, post-modern eclecticism, compilations and mixes of all these genres made possible by new interactive technology: as we have emphasised, all these routes are instantly available to both composers as creators and to us as listeners. We can wonder whether this breadth makes the act of composing more difficult or more rewarding in today's world. In the end I admire each and every composer who has an imagination at which I can only wonder, who can conjure sounds from the air and formulate them, so that they transform the raw materials of the world around them into living, breathing music – as Leonardo da Vinci put it so long ago, shaping the invisible.

Looking around the world of Western classical music performance in the period just before the Covid crisis, what were the signals of the moment? There were severe economic challenges, but history demonstrates that this has frequently been the case in the past, and those organisations that suffer are the ones that have not thought radically enough about their business models and programming vision. Record companies that did not adapt to the emerging world of online file-sharing and streaming, orchestras that did not align their programmes to the changing picture of music education and audience demand, have encountered problems, especially with the large overheads that prevent rapid flexibility. Cultural diversity has been one massive area of change, arguing for greater representation of, and greater investment in, under-represented areas of our creative community. It is inspiring that so many new cultural projects – from the world's first disabled-led national youth orchestra, NOYO, to diversity champion Tomorrow's Warriors, a jazz education organisation which nurtures young multi-racial musicians from underrepresented backgrounds and uses jazz to foster greater cultural diversity in the arts – are now consciously crossing the barriers of art forms and idioms, drawing influences from different cultures and speaking of and for different identities. This undoubtedly reflects one way in which music will shift in the future, and it will imply significant positive movement in the classical music tradition and its institutions, keeping them continuously relevant in a changing world.

Alongside that challenge, there is considerable resilience. It is one of the most interesting aspects of the contemporary musical scene that the institutions of the orchestra and the opera house, after a long period of criticism and reaction against their conservatism, have regained their capacity to commission and promote new works. In the recent past it tended to be universities (especially in America) which provided the support for composers to experiment and write free of immediate commercial pressures. Now that support has shifted to the practical performing organisations, who to keep in tune with the times are treating the production of new music and the support of music education as natural core parts of their activity. It would be hugely unfortunate if the result of the economic setback caused by the pandemic were to be a return to unadventurousness, pricing out new music, young and untried voices in favour of the predictable safe bets. A far better result would be that the recovery from the pandemic accelerates the changes that are necessary.

There is one central dilemma for the classical music tradition and its institutions today. Classical music as explored in this book has moved swiftly from having a privileged position in society to one in which it is repeatedly, and in my view rightly, challenged by pop music, world music, under-represented voices and peoples, and a vast range of alternative mass entertainment; it now interacts with many other musics in our culture, which command equal status, attention, and in many cases far more market value. We need not fear classical music being a non-populist pursuit, but we do need to argue against it being written off as irrelevant. The craft, learning and benefits of a musical training are unarguably positive in terms of what they bring to the individual and society: the question is whether the base of that training can broaden sufficiently so as to reflect today's culture. Our experience of young creative musicians today is that they draw on a wide range of influences and do not distinguish between genres: they create shapes and sounds out of whatever material is to hand. In new music, the definite forms of the past dissolve in allusion and cross-reference. We live with diversity and embrace it.

This book started with an invitation to explore the music to which you most immediately respond. There can be no fixed and final menu from which to select: what I suggest on the following pages are a hundred great pieces of music, in a hundred great performances, by a hundred great composers we have met, across history, to stimulate you and enable you to make your own choices. There could be many hundreds and thousands more pieces to be encountered over a lifetime. As well as the richness of history, there is, at root, your individuality. One element of our musical reception which is critical to each of us is memory. Embedded within our brain is the music that we have heard through our lives. Each person's collection of musical data, responses, likes, dislikes and reactive emotions is unique. Yet through the communal making of music, and shared experiences of hearing music, we are united. This is one of the great miracles of live music-making, that thousands can gather to share music in a great concert hall, opera house or religious space, but we will all hear it slightly differently and react to it personally. That is why I believe that, even if interrupted by war, social change or pandemic, the communal live experience of music will endure and flourish in the future, even – and especially – in an age of technology which offers so many alternative routes to consumption.

I do not think it is an illusion that we are bound together by such live events, that they can reconcile differences and provide the perspective of unity. I believe that making and hearing music provides one of the few moments in life where the balance between the individual and the community, a single person and our linked humanity, is most profoundly achieved. That is why, whatever people describe as music, whatever music they choose to hear, the act of making music and actively participating in responding to music will never die. It is one of the essential, elemental things that make us what we are.

100 Great Works by 100 Great Composers in 100 Great Performances

We have spooled through a millennium of music from the distant past to the present. Now spool back through time with the help of this playlist and find which of these masterpieces excite and stimulate you. The great performances recommended below are all easily available via Spotify (directly linked in this book's e-book edition, or search Spotify for the playlist 'The Life of Music: New Adventures in the Western Classical Tradition – Nicholas Kenyon', non-paying subscription required), and on CD to sample or buy from www.prestoclassical.co.uk. Explore and enjoy!

1. John Adams, *Must the Devil Have All the Good Tunes?* (2019)
Yuja Wang/Los Angeles Philharmonic/Gustavo Dudamel/DG
From the great composer who gave minimalism a human face in *Nixon in China* and wrote *A Short Ride in a Fast Machine*, a pulsating new piano concerto for virtuoso Yuja Wang, conducted by the brilliant Gustavo Dudamel.

2. Thomas Adès, *The Tempest* (2004)
Soloists/Royal Opera House Chorus and Orchestra/Thomas Adès/Warner Classics
This reinvention of a Shakespearean play with an inventive libretto by Meredith Oakes is set to music of wonderful melodic range and depth by Adès. The lovers' music is eloquent, and the stratospheric sounds of Ariel are unforgettable.

3. Pierre Boulez, *Sur incises* (1998)

Ensemble Intercontemporain/Pierre Boulez/DG

The overlapping sonorities of three pianos, three harps and three percussion make this one of Boulez's most compelling, sensual and involving pieces, a superb window into his distinctively French colouristic sound-world.

4. Judith Weir, *Storm* (1997)

BBC Singers, Temple Church Choristers/Endymion/David Hill/Signum Classics

Weir's transparent soundscapes inspired by the past have a great resonance in the present: here she creates music for young people in the *Tempest*-inspired *Storm*, and echoes Pérotin in *All the Ends of the Earth.*

5. Oliver Knussen, Horn Concerto (1994)

Barry Tuckwell, Lucy Shelton/London Sinfonietta/Oliver Knussen/DG

Supreme horn virtuoso Barry Tuckwell makes light work of Knussen's lyrical, beautiful concerto on a disc including his expressive settings of Walt Whitman and the chiming, medieval-inspired *Two Organa*.

6. John Tavener, *The Protecting Veil* (1987)

Steven Isserlis/London Symphony Orchestra/Gennadi Rozhdestvensky/Erato

An immediate triumph at the BBC Proms in 1989, John Tavener's keening, lamenting hymn to the Mother of God summed up the new spirituality in Steven Isserlis's intense performance; the recording was a major hit.

7. György Ligeti, *Études* for Piano (1985–2000)

Pierre-Laurent Aimard/Sony

There's no greater piano music from the end of the twentieth century than these dazzling and inventive studies drawing on African rhythms and vivid descriptions to create wonderful webs of chiming sequences.

8. Hans Werner Henze, Symphony No. 7 (1984)

City of Birmingham Symphony Orchestra/Simon Rattle/Warner Classics

Henze was a master of orchestral sounds, putting him firmly in the symphonic tradition. The atmospheric power of the Seventh Symphony, alongside the extrovert *Barcarola*, makes a perfect introduction.

9. Arvo Pärt, *Cantus in memoriam Benjamin Britten* (1977)
Soloists/Hungarian State Opera Orchestra/Tamás Benedek/Naxos
In a fine Naxos compilation of the Estonian composer's finest work from the modernist First Symphony, this peerless tribute from one great composer to another stands out, eloquent and serene, for strings with a single bell.

10. Philip Glass, *Einstein on the Beach* (1976)
Philip Glass Ensemble/Philip Glass/Sony
This collaboration with Robert Wilson was one of Glass's finest and longest-lasting achievements, its hypnotic progress across five hours mapped out with precision and alluring ritual. Listen at leisure!

11. Steve Reich, *Music for 18 Musicians* (1974–6)
Steve Reich and Musicians/ECM New Series
Minimalism at its finest, the tapestry-like intricacy of shifting chords and gradually morphing harmonies are perfectly captured by Reich's supple, flexible but rhythmic musicians, their art concealing art.

12. Luciano Berio, *Sinfonia* (1968)
Jard van Nes/Concertgebouw Orchestra/Swingle Singers/Riccardo Chailly/Decca
A classic 1960s work of allusion to music's past, Berio's surreal *Sinfonia* echoes Mahler, Debussy and a host of earlier music. Explore also his folk-song arrangements, songs of the earth, and the abstract *Formazioni*.

13. Leonard Bernstein, *West Side Story* (1957)
Soloists/San Francisco Symphony/Michael Tilson Thomas/SFS Media
Film purists may want the original soundtrack, but for modern sound this version of Bernstein's classic, pulsating musical triumphs – beating the composer's own regrettably operatic version – and reinforces its classic status.

14. Dmitry Shostakovich, Symphony No. 10 (1953)

Royal Liverpool Philharmonic Orchestra/Vassily Petrenko/Naxos

Of all the twentieth-century symphonies which have grabbed audiences' attention, those by Shostakovich stand out for their often brutal force. The Tenth from 1953 is utterly compelling with its fiercely percussive Scherzo.

15. Francis Poulenc, *Stabat mater* (1950)

Marlis Petersen/NDR Chorus/Stuttgart RSO/Stéphane Denève/Hänssler

Too often thought of as lightweight, Poulenc's finest music has a religious fervour: this setting of the Marian hymn *Stabat mater* is here effectively contrasted with his witty ballet score *Les biches.*

16. Benjamin Britten, *Peter Grimes* (1945)

Stuart Skelton/Soloists/Bergen Philharmonic/Edward Gardner/Chandos

This was the opera that reignited British music after the Second World War, here in a new and gripping account under Edward Gardner. The sea interludes are ever more impressive as a source for our new music.

17. Michael Tippett, Concerto for Double String Orchestra (1938–9)

Academy of St Martin in the Fields/Neville Marriner/Decca

Tippett's music overflows with warmth and communicative fervour, and this baroque-inspired Concerto is coupled here with other successful string-based works like the Corelli Fantasia in the classic rich Academy sound.

18. George Gershwin, 'They Can't Take That Away from Me' (1937)

Fred Astaire/Soloists/Orchestras/Classique Perfecto

Although his *Rhapsody in Blue* has become a concert classic, Gershwin's real skill was creating perfect songs, and here is an ideal selection in historic recordings by singers including Fred Astaire.

19. Béla Bartók, *Music for Strings, Percussion and Celesta* (1936)

Oslo Philharmonic Orchestra/Mariss Jansons/Warner Classics

Growing from a dark, winding fugue, and conjuring up unearthly night music before the final folk dance, Bartók's double-orchestra layout, linked by a prominent piano, creates antiphonal sounds of punch and pungency.

20. Olivier Messiaen, *La nativité du Seigneur* (1935)
Jennifer Bate/Treasure Island
A key figure of the twentieth century as composer and teacher, the heart of Messiaen's output is his religiously committed organ music: from these sacred cycles, try the terrific finale 'Dieu parmi nous' to blow the roof off!

21. Alban Berg, Violin Concerto (1935)
Isabelle Faust/Orchestra Mozart/Claudio Abbado/Harmonia Mundi
This concerto in 'memory of an angel' (Manon Gropius) is the most Romantic and affecting of twelve-tone pieces, drawing in a Bach chorale. A beautiful performance, coupled with Beethoven's concerto.

22. Karol Szymanowski, Violin Concerto No. 2 (1933)
Frank Peter Zimmermann/Warsaw Philharmonic/Antoni Wit/Sony
The gorgeous textures of Szymanowski's two violin concertos make a perfect introduction to his folk-inspired music, here idiomatically realised by a Polish orchestra with Frank Peter Zimmermann, coupled with Britten's concerto.

23. Kurt Weill, *The Threepenny Opera* (1928)
Soloists/Marek Weber and his Orchestra/Otto Klemperer/Capriccio
The smoky haze of Berlin cabaret is evident in these archive recordings from 1928–31 by Weill's wife Lotte Lenya and others, at the end of a Weimar culture soon to be extinguished by the Nazis.

24. Leoš Janáček, Sinfonietta (1926)
Vienna Philharmonic Orchestra/Charles Mackerras/Decca
Janáček was a late-flowering composer of great originality; the windswept fanfares of his Sinfonietta are among the most thrilling sounds of the twentieth century, here under the master who led his revival, Charles Mackerras.

25. Jean Sibelius, Symphony No. 5 (1922)

City of Birmingham Symphony Orchestra/Simon Rattle/Warner Classics

The symphonies of Sibelius have veered in and out of fashion, but Rattle has constantly performed them; No. 5 features dramatic pauses at the end. Also here is the famous recording of the Violin Concerto by Nigel Kennedy.

26. Sergey Prokofiev, Piano Concerto No. 3 (1921)

Martha Argerich/Berlin Philharmonic Orchestra/Claudio Abbado/DG

Drifting onstage as if looking for a cup of coffee, Argerich always seemed distracted but never failed to deliver stupendous performances of this showy piece, hard-hitting yet warm. She adds Ravel's virtuosic *Gaspard de la nuit.*

27. Maurice Ravel, *La valse* (1919–20)

Rotterdam Philharmonic Orchestra/Yannick Nézet-Séguin/Warner Classics

On a superb disc which proclaimed a new talent in Nézet-Séguin, Ravel's eerie, turbulent deconstruction of the waltz marks the collapse of a civilisation, alongside the glorious suite from the ballet *Daphnis et Chloé.*

28. Edward Elgar, Cello Concerto (1919)

Jacqueline du Pré/London Symphony Orchestra/John Barbirolli/Warner Classics

It was this work, which I heard played by du Pré at a Prom rehearsal when I was thirteen, that led me to so much music, and her account still retains its phenomenal depth and intensity, at once tragic and assertive.

29. Gustav Holst, *The Planets* (1918–20)

BBC Symphony Orchestra/Andrew Davis/Warner Classics

These planetary portraits are a perfect introduction to the drama of twentieth-century orchestral music, complete with the great melody of 'I vow to thee my country', and a close that evaporates into space.

30. Giacomo Puccini, *Gianni Schicchi* (1917–18)

Angela Gheorghiu/Soloists/London Symphony Orchestra/Antonio Pappano/Warner Classics

The wittiest and sharpest of Puccini's operas, this marvellously hilarious comedy is among Pappano's finest recordings, and features one of Puccini's most famous arias. It is coupled here with the other two one-act operas of *Il Trittico*.

31. Carl Nielsen, Symphony No. 4 'Inextinguishable' (1916)
San Francisco Symphony/Herbert Blomstedt/Decca
More eccentric and extrovert than Sibelius, Nielsen's symphonies have a wild imagination that in the Fourth results in a battle to the death between two sets of timpani, releasing the orchestra's raw power. Blomstedt is here unsurpassed.

32. Igor Stravinsky, *The Rite of Spring* (1913)
Kirov Orchestra/Valery Gergiev/Philips
It is surely impossible to choose the greatest performance of this central work, but Gergiev's pulverising account searches to the earthy roots of the music, and places it at the heart of the Russian tradition.

33. Ralph Vaughan Williams, *Fantasia on a Theme by Thomas Tallis* (1910)
Sinfonia of London/John Barbirolli/Warner Classics
This reworking of an Elizabethan hymn-tune by Tallis, serene and calm in a classic performance under John Barbirolli, seals the ancestry of English music across the centuries. The evocative pastoral of *The Lark Ascending* is also included.

34. Sergey Rachmaninov, Piano Concerto No. 3 (1910)
Vladimir Horowitz/RCA Victor Symphony Orchestra/Fritz Reiner/RCA
In this famous disc of the Third Concerto, Vladimir Horowitz outdoes even the composer's pianism, the late-Romantic idiom and the virtuosic demands fearlessly tamed from the first artless melody.

35. Anton Webern, Six Pieces for Large Orchestra Op. 6 (1909/28)
Berlin Philharmonic Orchestra/Pierre Boulez/DG
The sternest of the Second Viennese School, Webern created sounds that could not be anyone else's, and in Pierre Boulez they found their ideal, clarifying advocate, warm yet precise: he enabled this music to make sense.

36. Arnold Schoenberg, *Erwartung* (1909)

Jessye Norman/Metropolitan Opera Orchestra/James Levine/Philips

This dense, atmospheric portrayal of a woman wandering through a forest is peerlessly realised by Jessye Norman in superb voice, with the detailed support of the Metropolitan Orchestra and James Levine.

37. Scott Joplin, *Piano Rags* (1906–17)

Joshua Rifkin/Nonesuch

Absorbing the ragtime idiom into piano music, Joplin had huge success which was not quite matched by his one opera *Treemonisha*; his music was revived by scholar-pianist Joshua Rifkin and later featured in the film *The Sting*.

38. Claude Debussy, *La mer* (1905)

Concertgebouw Orchestra/Bernard Haitink/Philips

Haitink's always exquisite, scrupulous music-making had a deep resonance with French tradition, and here with the orchestra he led for many years is a gloriously turbulent portrait of the sea.

39. Charles Ives, *Three Places in New England* (1903–14)

St Louis Symphony Orchestra/Leonard Slatkin/RCA

'Are my ears on right?' Ives used to ask: he was one of the most original recreators of the world around him, as revealed by these three multilayered portraits of the music he heard, from marching bands to overheard songs.

40. Gustav Mahler, Symphony No. 5 (1901–2)

Berlin Philharmonic Orchestra/Simon Rattle/Warner Classics

This is the live performance with which Rattle inaugurated his tenure of this great orchestra, fantastically focused and with his trademark rhythmic energy and bite, showing Mahler at his supreme best.

41. Richard Strauss, *Till Eulenspiegels lustige Streiche* (1894–5)

Berlin Philharmonic Orchestra/Herbert von Karajan/DG

For me, it's best to avoid Richard Strauss's more overblown pieces, but the perfect characterisation of Till Eulenspiegel and his story is brilliantly delivered by Karajan's crack orchestra.

42. Giuseppe Verdi, *Falstaff* (1893)
Tito Gobbi/Soloists/Philharmonia Orchestra/Herbert von Karajan/Warner Classics
The most humane of all Verdi's operas, his last essay in the form breathes a warm-hearted lyricism and culminates in an exuberant fugue. Karajan with Tito Gobbi as Falstaff is peerless, with a great cast.

43. Johannes Brahms, Intermezzo in B minor Op. 119 (1892)
Jeremy Denk/Nonesuch
In this collection Denk places Brahms's ethereal, late Intermezzo in B minor in the context of music sweeping across seven centuries from 1300 to 2000: it could well be a signature disc for this book!

44. Antonín Dvořák, Symphony No. 8 (1889)
Czech Philharmonic Orchestra/Jiří Bělohlávek/Decca
It is difficult to have a top symphony, but ever since I played this in my youth orchestra, it's been a favourite for its swinging rhythms and melodic warmth: the Czech players under Bělohlávek capture its idiom perfectly.

45. Arthur Sullivan, *The Gondoliers* (1889)
Soloists/Glyndebourne Chorus/Pro Arte Orchestra/Sir Malcolm Sargent/Warner Classics
For fantasy and charm with a clever whiff of social criticism, the verve of *The Gondoliers* with its long opening scene is totally sunny, here with top singers including Elsie Morison and Geraint Evans, driven by Sargent's sprightly rhythms.

46. Camille Saint-Saëns, *The Carnival of the Animals* (1886)
Martha Argerich, Antonio Pappano/Santa Cecilia Orchestra/Antonio Pappano/ Warner Classics
Saint-Saëns came to dislike his most popular piece, but we can revel in its wit when so well played by two musical geniuses as here; Pappano also conducts the big 'Organ' Symphony with his Roman orchestra.

47. Anton Bruckner, Symphony No. 7 (1881–3)

Concertgebouw Orchestra/Bernard Haitink/Philips

It is so difficult to choose between the recordings that Bernard Haitink has made of this great symphony: here the sonorities are rounded and humane, the immense flow of sound naturally controlled.

48. Gabriel Fauré, Requiem (1877–90)

Soloists/Collegium Vocale Gent/Orchestre des Champs-Élysées/Philippe Herreweghe/ Harmonia Mundi

Fauré's serene and unassertive Requiem has surely never been equalled for its understated beauty, and Philippe Herreweghe sculpts its melodies with gentle skill, adding Cesar Franck's underrated Symphony.

49. Piotr Tchaikovsky, *Swan Lake* (1875–6)

London Symphony Orchestra/Pierre Monteux/Decca Eloquence

Here are sounds from a past orchestral world, under a conductor I heard as a youngster and always admired; the colours of the score deftly shaped and Tchaikovsky's fine instrumentation revealed.

50. Georges Bizet, *Carmen* (1875)

Teresa Berganza, Plácido Domingo, Sherrill Milnes/London Symphony Orchestra/ Claudio Abbado/DG

It is remarkable to think that Bizet's *Carmen* was initially a failure, especially given its huge subsequent success, for the melodies are unforgettable, its story powerful. An outstanding cast here brings the scorching drama to life.

51. Modest Mussorgsky, *Pictures at an Exhibition* (1874)

Vienna Philharmonic Orchestra/Gustavo Dudamel/DG

Ravel's extravagant orchestration of Mussorgsky's vivid character pieces are skilfully coloured in this virtuoso performance under Gustavo Dudamel, linked to extensive education work inspired by his El Sistema project.

52. Richard Wagner, *Die Walküre*, Act 1 (1856)

Stuart Skelton, Heidi Melton/Soloists/Hong Kong Philharmonic/Jaap van Zweden/Naxos

Maybe don't start with a whole Wagner opera! Act 1 of *Die Walküre* is gripping and powerful, with Stuart Skelton and Heidi Melton as Siegmund and Sieglinde. You'll soon be drawn into the engrossing drama.

53. Franz Liszt, Sonata in B minor (1853)
Alfred Brendel/Philips
Realised by a pianist who is able to convey complete structural understanding of great music in his performances, this superb account of the Sonata is in one breath from the first note to the last – an epic human drama.

54. Felix Mendelssohn, *A Midsummer Night's Dream* Overture (1842)
Budapest Festival Orchestra/Pro Musica/Iván Fischer/Channel Classics
The miracle of the seventeen-year-old Mendelssohn's Overture is eternally fresh; Iván Fischer's precise orchestra captures all its elfin grace, and adds songs by Felix's sister Fanny Mendelssohn.

55. Robert Schumann, *Liederkreis* Op. 39 (1840)
Wolfgang Holzmair/Imogen Cooper/Wigmore Hall
Holzmair's lightness of touch and Cooper's gentle eloquence are perfectly paired in this selection of Schumann's songs on the course of love, with the achingly bittersweet 'Mondnacht' a highlight.

56. Frédéric Chopin, Ballade No. 1 in G minor (1835)
Arturo Benedetti Michelangeli/DG
Surely one of the best recordings of anything ever! The imperious Michelangeli's total grip of Chopin's marvellous structure, climaxing in a torrential transition to the frantic coda, is unforgettable.

57. Clara Schumann, Piano Concerto (1835)
Isata Kanneh-Mason/Royal Liverpool Philharmonic/Holly Mathieson/Decca
Clara was rather better known than her husband as a performer, and now her own music receives its due with a striking performance of her Piano Concerto by this talented pianist, leading the way for an overdue revival.

58. Gaetano Donizetti, *L'elisir d'amore* (1832)

Kathleen Battle, Luciano Pavarotti/Soloists/Metropolitan Opera Orchestra and Chorus/James Levine/DG

Some may prefer Donizetti's many serious operas, but this classic comic piece bubbles with fun, and features Pavarotti's trademark *bel canto* aria 'Una furtiva lagrima' alongside a host of memorable melodies.

59. Vincenzo Bellini, *Norma* (1831)

Maria Callas/Soloists/Orchestra and Chorus of La Scala Milan/Tullio Serafin/ Warner Classics

The *bel canto* style features the eloquent Maria Callas at full stretch, supported by Christa Ludwig and Franco Corelli in a recording that captures perfectly an old-school operatic tradition of flexible grace.

60. Hector Berlioz, *Symphonie fantastique* (1830)

London Classical Players/Roger Norrington/Erato

The fantastic visions and original sounds of Berlioz's truly revolutionary narrative symphony are here revealed on the instruments of the time, under Roger Norrington's vivid direction in a now- historic recording.

61. Franz Schubert, String Quintet in C (1828)

Amadeus Quartet/William Pleeth/DG

The sublime slow movement of this quintet never fails to lift the soul, here in a classic version by the Amadeus Quartet joined by cellist William Pleeth, which makes the most of the poised lyricism.

62. Gioachino Rossini, *La Cenerentola* (1817)

Cecilia Bartoli/Soloists/Chorus and Orchestra of Teatro Comunale di Bologna/ Riccardo Chailly/Decca

Cecilia Bartoli's joyously brilliant coloratura singing is art at the service of high emotion, and the whole performance of this ever-fresh masterpiece fizzes with Italianate energy under Riccardo Chailly.

63. Carl Maria von Weber, Two Clarinet Concertos (1811)

Andrew Marriner/Academy of St Martin in the Fields/Neville Marriner/Philips

The family firm of clarinettist Andrew and his father conductor Neville Marriner bring virtuosic sparkle to these demonstrative pieces which unusually for the time treat the clarinet as a brilliant soloist.

64. Ludwig van Beethoven, Symphony No. 5 (1807–8)

Vienna Philharmonic Orchestra/Carlos Kleiber/DG

One of the greatest classics of the recording era, Kleiber's terrifyingly intense Beethoven Fifth is a must-listen. Try also the Seventh, recorded on DVD with the Concertgebouw, for another electrifying experience.

65. Wolfgang Amadeus Mozart, *Le Nozze di Figaro* (1786)

Soloists/Drottningholm Opera Orchestra/Arnold Östman/Decca Florilegium

Others may prefer classic Erich Kleiber or high-tension Georg Solti, but I love the woody and transparent sounds from the Drottningholm Opera ensemble which I saw in their tiny court theatre in Sweden.

66. C. P. E. Bach, Symphonies (*c.* 1780)

English Concert/Trevor Pinnock/DG Archiv

Quirky and individual, the symphonies by J. S. Bach's highly original second son are full of dramatic surprises, which the pungency of Pinnock's period instruments captures with style and flair.

67. Joseph Haydn, Symphony No. 44 'Trauer' (1772)

English Concert/Trevor Pinnock/DG Archiv

Among Haydn's supremely inventive symphonies, this stormy middle-period work, with a slow movement that Haydn wanted to be played at his funeral, has a canonic minuet and a finale that hits home hard.

68. J. S. Bach, *Goldberg Variations* (1741)

András Schiff/ECM New Series

For those who prefer the modern piano to the harpsichord in Bach's music, this luminous, meditative and tranquil traversal of Bach's great variation set is the finest in modern times, beautifully recorded.

69. George Frideric Handel, *Ariodante* (1735)
Joyce di Donato/Soloists/Il Complesso Barocco/Alan Curtis/Erato
Of all Handel's many operas, *Ariodante* has some of the greatest music, vivid dances, and with Joyce di Donato at the helm, two gloriously contrasted showpiece
arias in 'Scherza infida' and 'Dopo notte'.

70. Jean-Philippe Rameau, *Hippolyte et Aricie*: dances (1733)
La Petite Bande/Sigiswald Kuijken/Deutsche Harmonia Mundi
What fantastically varied and inventive colours sound through this sequence of
dances! The French baroque idiom is here at its exotic best, animated by a fine
Dutch ensemble of period instruments.

71. Georg Philipp Telemann, *Tafelmusik* (1733)
Musica Antiqua Köln/Reinhard Goebel/DG Archiv
The amazingly prolific Telemann produced acres of operas and cantatas, and
his instrumental music is wonderfully effective, even as 'table' (i.e. background)
music, as played by Goebel's fiery ensemble.

72. Domenico Scarlatti, Keyboard sonatas (1720s–1750s)
Pierre Hantaï/Mirare
The percussive attack of the harpsichord brings these sonatas to life, with their
biting dissonances and sharp edges that often sound inspired by the guitar, here
played with great rhythmic freedom.

73. Jan Dismas Zelenka, Trio sonatas (*c.* 1721–2)
Heinz Holliger/Soloists/DG Archiv
Few recordings have made such an impact on me as this astonishing collection
of six trio sonatas with virtuoso bassoon, by a contemporary Bach knew: bold,
eccentric music superbly realised by Holliger and friends.

74. Antonio Vivaldi, Concerto for four violins in B minor (1711)
Rachel Podger/Brecon Baroque/Channel Classics

The composer of endless concertos, here making four violins sing in diverse harmony, glittering like the Venetian sea: a work Bach later arranged for four harpsichords, for him and his sons to play.

75. Arcangelo Corelli, Violin Sonatas Op. 5 (1700)
Pavlo Beznosiuk/Avison Ensemble/Linn
At the start of the eighteenth century, Corelli published these famous sonatas which demanded considerable elaboration of the Adagios by the soloist, here deftly and beautifully realised by Pavlo Beznosiuk.

76. Jean-Baptiste Lully, *Armide* (1686)
Soloists/Les talens lyriques/Christophe Rousset/Aparté
It is remarkable that in recent years more than ten Lully operas have been recorded; this is his most famous, skilfully guided by Christophe Rousset, with idiomatic soloists, a fine chorus and glorious sound.

77. Henry Purcell, *Dido and Aeneas* (*c.* 1683–8)
Sarah Connolly/Soloists/Choir and Orchestra of the Age of Enlightenment/Steven Devine and Elizabeth Kenny/Chandos Chaconne
The most affecting hour of baroque drama, a rare English opera from surely our finest composer: superb music brought to life by a stylish cast led by Sarah Connolly's magnificent and moving Dido.

78. Marc-Antoine Charpentier, *Le reniement de St Pierre* (*c.* 1680–1700)
Les Arts Florissants/William Christie/Harmonia Mundi France
An expressive mini-Passion telling the story of St Peter's betrayal and his subsequent grief, with a deeply affecting final chorus sung by the group who have made this fine composer's music their own.

79. Heinrich Biber, *Battalia* (1673)
Musica Antiqua Köln/Reinhard Goebel/DG Archiv

The violinistic adventures of Biber in his Rosary Sonatas should be explored, but start with this hilarious miniature depicting the noisy stages of a chaotic battle, both funny and tragic, in a collection of baroque miniatures.

80. Barbara Strozzi, Arias and cantatas Op. 8 (1664)
Emanuela Galli/La Risonanza/ Fabio Bonizzoni/Glossa
One of the most important women composers of the Italian baroque, her lyrical arias and passionate cantatas now rediscovered and stylishly performed by Galli and Bonizzoni's Italian forces.

81. Claudio Monteverdi, *Beatus vir* (1641)
Cantus Cölln/Concerto Palatino/Konrad Junghänel/Harmonia Mundi
From his wide-ranging sacred collection the *Selva morale e spirituale*, Monteverdi's classic setting of the psalm *Beatus vir* dances with life, its music is shared with the secular madrigal, *Chiome d'oro*.

82. Heinrich Schütz, *Musikalische Exequien* (1636)
Vox Luminis/Lionel Meunier/Ricercar
One of the most underrated of great composers, Schütz's grave and serious setting of German Requiem texts is sung here by a superb recent arrival on the scene, the Belgian-based ensemble Vox Luminis.

83. Gregorio Allegri, *Miserere* (1630s)
Roy Goodman/Choir of King's College Cambridge/David Willcocks/Decca
A famous old recording by the King's College Choir features a young treble soaring effortlessly in the decorations to Allegri's psalm setting, which Mozart heard in Rome and wrote down from memory.

84. Orlando Gibbons, 'See, see, the Word is incarnate' (*c.* 1620)
Choir of New College Oxford/Edward Higginbottom/CRD
Best known for his madrigal 'The Silver Swan', Gibbons wrote glorious church music, including this remarkable telling of Christ's life story from birth to resurrection and ascension, condensed into a few eloquent minutes.

85. Carlo Gesualdo, Madrigals, Book Five (1611)

La Venexiana/Glossa

The eccentric and wholly original music of Gesualdo is forever coloured by his murder of his first wife and her lover. Here his harmonic twists and turns are captured with passionate clarity by La Venexiana.

86. Tomás Luis de Victoria, Requiem (1605)

The Sixteen/Harry Christophers/Coro

The sombre but sensual Requiem Mass by the Spanish master of polyphony, sung with fervour by one of our leading choirs which has taken its programmes of sacred music around Britain's churches.

87. John Dowland, 'Can she excuse my wrongs' (1597)

Emma Kirkby/Anthony Rooley/Erato

Among Dowland's songs of genius are many derived from dances: the lively tread of 'Can she excuse my wrongs', also a Galliard, is captured by the famous early music duo of Emma Kirkby and Anthony Rooley.

88. Orlande de Lassus, *Lagrime di San Pietro* (1594)

Ensemble Vocal Européen/Philippe Herreweghe/Harmonia Mundi

Lassus was perhaps the first truly European composer, and this final set of sacred madrigals of St Peter has a powerful emotionalism, beautifully delivered by Herreweghe's young voices.

89. William Byrd, Mass for Four Voices (1592–3)

The Cardinall's Music/Andrew Carwood/ASV

Byrd wrote three Catholic Masses, probably for private performance, at a time in Elizabeth I's reign when he could have been prosecuted; they are wonderful examples of their form, full of drama and yearning for peace.

90. Thomas Tallis, *Spem in alium nunquam habui* (c. 1570)

ORA Singers/Suzi Digby/Harmonia Mundi

The great forty-part motet by Tallis, for eight choirs of five voices, was perhaps performed in Nonsuch Palace, and is recorded here alongside a new forty-part commission from James MacMillan.

91. Giovanni Pierluigi da Palestrina, *Missa Papae Marcelli* (1567)
Odhecaton/Paolo Da Col/Arcana
The classic Mass which expressed the ideals of the Council of Trent for intelligibility in polyphony, sung by an ensemble which places it carefully in the context of the Roman liturgy of the time.

92. Josquin des Prez, *Missa 'Pange lingua'* (c. 1515)
Tallis Scholars/Peter Phillips/Gimell
From one of the great British ensembles who have done so much to revive Renaissance sacred music, a serene account of Josquin's eloquent Mass that lets his polyphonic lines emerge with warmth and focus.

93. Johannes Ockeghem, Requiem (1461)
The Clerk's Group/Edward Wickham/ASV
Death was often featured by medieval composers: Ockeghem wrote a moving tribute to his fellow composer Gilles Binchois, and here composes a Requiem probably for the King of France, Charles VII.

94. Guillaume Dufay, *Missa 'Se la face ay pale'* (1434–5)
Diabolus in Musica/Antoine Guerber/Alpha
Dufay's most famous Mass, in his typical lyrical style, beautifully performed with one singer to a part and no extraneous instrumental decoration, by a fine French early music ensemble.

95. John Dunstaple, *Quam pulchra es* (c. 1425)
Hilliard Ensemble/Erato
Dunstaple led the way in Europe during the period of Ars Nova with his consonant, appealing music, here precisely realised by the superb Hilliard Ensemble in one of their many classic recordings.

96. Guillaume de Machaut, *Messe de Notre Dame* (*c.* 1360)
Taverner Choir and Consort/Andrew Parrott/Erato
A pathbreaking recording, this all-vocal performance of Machaut's great setting of the Ordinary of the Mass was among the first ever of its kind, and packs a punch with every detail captured.

97. Pérotin, *Viderunt omnes* (*c.* 1200)
Early Music Consort of London/David Munrow/DG Archiv
At the end of the twelfth century, a flourishing of the arts at Notre Dame in Paris produced this four-part organum lasting a full twelve minutes in this superbly sung realisation by Munrow's Consort.

98. Anon, *The Play of Daniel (Ludus Danielis)* (*c.* 1180)
The Dufay Collective/William Lyons/Harmonia Mundi
'Anon' surely counts as a great composer, so many are the works attributed to her/him! This medieval music-drama kickstarted the American early music revival; here it receives a colourful reworking.

99. Hildegard of Bingen, *Ordo virtutum* (*c.* 1151)
Sequentia/Barbara Thornton/Benjamin Bagby/Deutsche Harmonia Mundi
We know little about medieval composers, but the achievements of the abbess Hildegard of Bingen are amazing: this miracle 'Play of the Virtues' is a true drama, compellingly realised by Sequentia.

100. *Dies irae, dies illa* (12th century)
Capella Antiqua München/Konrad Ruhland/Sony
The most famous of all ancient plainchant antiphons, the hymn-like Sequence from the Requiem Mass, which resounds through the ages of music, right up to Berlioz and Rachmaninov.

Further Reading

I cannot hope to match Alfred Einstein, who introduced his Short History of Music *of 1917 by saying disarmingly that 'it was written in a few weeks, at a time and place that precluded resort to any books of reference'. On the contrary, this book is dependent on the work of many authors: here is a brief selection of books that have provided valuable information, quotations and background for this volume: all contain further bibliographies and useful reading lists.*

History

Burkholder, J. Peter, Donald Jay Grout and Claude V. Palisca, *A History of Western Music*, fifth edition (Norton, 1996)

Elkin, Robert, *The Old Concert Halls of London* (Arnold, 1955)

Elkin, Robert, *Royal Philharmonic* (Rider, 1946)

Fenlon, Iain, ed., *Man and Music: The Renaissance, from the 1470s to the End of the 16th Century* (Macmillan, 1989)

Gioia, Ted, *Music: A Subversive History* (Basic Books, 2019)

Goodall, Howard, *Big Bangs* (Chatto & Windus/Vintage, 2000)

Goodall, Howard, *The Story of Music* (Chatto & Windus, 2013)

Griffiths, Paul, *A Concise History of Western Music* (Cambridge University Press, 2006)

Griffiths, Paul, *Modern Music: The Avant-Garde since 1945* (Dent/Braziller, 1981)

Hanning, Barbara Russano, *A Concise History of Western Music*, fifth edition (based on *A History of Western Music*, ninth edition) (Norton, 2014)

Hogwood, Christopher, *Music at Court* (Folio Society, 1977)

Horowitz, Joseph, *Classical Music in America: A History of its Rise and Fall* (Norton, 2005)

Hughes, Meirion and Robert Stradling, *The English Musical Renaissance 1840–1940* (Manchester University Press, 1993/2001)

Knighton, Tess and David Fallows, eds, *A Companion to Medieval and Renaissance Music* (Orion/Schirmer, 1992)

Morgan, Robert P., ed., *Man and Music: Modern Times, from World War I to the Present* (Macmillan, 1993)

Paxman, Jon, *Classical Music: A Chronology* (Overlook Omnibus, 2015)

Price, Curtis, ed., *Man and Music: The Early Baroque Era, from the Late 16th Century to the 1660s* (Macmillan, 1993)

Ross, Alex, *The Rest Is Noise: Listening to the Twentieth Century* (Farrar, Straus and Giroux, 2007)

Rushton, Julian, *Classical Music: A Concise History from Gluck to Beethoven* (Thames & Hudson, 1986)

Samson, Jim, ed., *The Cambridge History of Nineteenth-Century Music* (Cambridge University Press, 2002)

Taruskin, Richard, *The Oxford History of Western Music*, six volumes (Oxford University Press, 2003)

Taruskin, Richard and Christopher Gibbs, *The Oxford History of Western Music*, College edition, one volume (Oxford University Press, 2013)

Treitler, Leo and Oliver Strunk, eds, *Source Readings in Music History*, revised edition (Norton, 1998)

Whittall, Arnold, *Musical Composition in the Twentieth Century* (Oxford University Press, 1999)

Witt, Stephen, *How Music Got Free: A Story of Obsession and Invention* (Penguin, 2016)

Zaslaw, Neal, *Man and Music: The Classical Era from the 1740s to the end of the 18th century* (Macmillan, 1989)

Performance

Bowen, José Antonio, ed., *The Cambridge Companion to Conducting* (Cambridge University Press, 2003)

Brown, Howard Mayer and Stanley Sadie, eds, *The Norton/Grove Companions in Music: Performance Practice*: Vol. 1, *Music before 1600*; Vol. 2, *Music after 1600* (Norton/Macmillan, 1989)

Cook, Nicholas, Eric Clarke, Daniel Leech-Wilkinson and John Rink, eds, *The Cambridge Companion to Recorded Music* (Cambridge University Press, 2009)

Day, Timothy, *A Century of Recorded Music: Listening to Musical History* (Yale University Press, 2000)

Dorian, Frederick, *The History of Music in Performance: The Art of Musical Interpretation from the Renaissance to Our Day* (Norton, 1942)

Ehrlich, Cyril, *The Music Profession in Britain since the Eighteenth Century: A Social History* (Oxford University Press, 1985)

Kelly, Thomas Forrest, *First Nights: Five Musical Premieres* (Yale University Press, 2000)

Lawson, Colin and Robin Stowell, eds, *The Cambridge Encyclopaedia of Historical Performance in Music* (Cambridge University Press, 2018)

Lawson, Colin and Robin Stowell, eds, *The Cambridge History of Musical Performance* (Cambridge University Press, 2012)

MacClintock, Carol, ed. and trans., *Readings in the History of Music in Performance* (Indiana University Press, 1989)

Parrott, Andrew, *Composers' Intentions? Lost Traditions of Musical Performance* (Boydell, 2015)

Philip, Robert, *Early Recordings and Musical Style: Changing Tastes in Instrumental Performance 1900–1950* (Oxford University Press, 1992)

Philip, Robert, *Performing Music in the Age of Recording* (Yale University Press, 2004)

Rink, John, ed., *Musical Performance: A Guide to Understanding* (Cambridge University Press, 2002)

Spitzer, John and Neal Zaslaw, *The Birth of the Orchestra: History of an Institution, 1650–1815* (Oxford University Press, 2004)

Vinquist, Mary and Neal Zaslaw, *Performance Practice: A Bibliography* (Norton, 1970)

Weber, William, *The Rise of Musical Classics in Eighteenth-Century England* (Oxford University Press, 1992)

Young, Percy M., *The Concert Tradition* (Routledge, 1965)

Works

Everist, Mark, ed., *The Cambridge Companion to Medieval Music* (Cambridge University Press, 2011)

Hiley, David, *Gregorian Chant* (Cambridge University Press, 2009)

Holden, Amanda, ed., *The New Penguin Opera Guide* (Penguin, 2001)

Horton, Julian, ed., *The Cambridge Companion to the Symphony* (Cambridge University Press, 2013)

Kalinak, Kathryn, *Film Music, a Very Short Introduction* (Oxford University Press, 2010)

Kenyon, Nicholas, ed., *The BBC Proms Guide to Great Choral Works* (Faber, 2004)

Kenyon, Nicholas, ed., *The BBC Proms Guide to Great Concertos* (Faber, 2003)

Kenyon, Nicholas, ed., *The BBC Proms Guide to Great Orchestral Works* (Faber, 2004)

Kenyon, Nicholas, ed., *The BBC Proms Guide to Great Symphonies* (Faber, 2003)

Maddocks, Fiona, *Music for Life: 100 Works to Carry You Through* (Faber, 2016)

Philip, Robert, *The Classical Music Lover's Guide to Orchestral Music* (Yale University Press, 2019)

Staines, Joe, ed., *The Rough Guide to Classical Music*, fifth edition (Rough Guides, 2010)

Instruments

Gill, Dominic, ed., *The Book of the Piano* (Phaidon, 1981)

Gill, Dominic, ed., *The Book of the Violin* (Phaidon, 1984)

Montagu, Jeremy, *The World of Baroque and Classical Musical Instruments* (Overlook Press, 1979)

Montagu, Jeremy, *The World of Medieval and Renaissance Musical Instruments* (Overlook Press, 1976)

Montagu, Jeremy, *The World of Romantic and Modern Musical Instruments* (David & Charles, 1981)

Munrow, David, *Instruments of the Middle Ages and Renaissance* (Oxford University Press, 1976)

Thought

Blanning, Tim, *The Triumph of Music* (Allen Lane, 2008)

Butt, John, *Playing with History: The Historical Approach to Musical Performance* (Cambridge University Press, 2002)

Clayton, Martin, Trevor Herbert and Richard Middleton, eds, *The Cultural Study of Music: A Critical Introduction* (Routledge, 2003)

Cook, Nicholas, *Music: A Very Short Introduction* (Oxford University Press, 1998)

Cook, Nicholas and Mark Everist, eds, *Rethinking Music* (Oxford University Press, 1999)

Fulcher, Jane F., ed., *The Oxford Handbook of the New Cultural History of Music* (Oxford University Press, 2011)

Kenyon, Nicholas, ed., *Authenticity and Early Music* (Oxford University Press, 1986)

Lang, Paul Henry, *Musicology and Performance*, eds Alfred Mann and George J. Buelow (Yale University Press, 1997)

Taruskin, Richard, *Cursed Questions: On Music and Its Social Practices* (California University Press, 2020)

Taruskin, Richard, *The Danger of Music and Other Anti-Utopian Essays* (California University Press, 2009)

Taruskin, Richard, *Text and Act: Essays on Music and Performance* (Oxford University Press, 1995)

Treitler, Leo, *Music and the Historical Imagination* (Harvard University Press, 1989)

Walls, Peter, *History, Imagination and the Performance of Music* (Boydell, 2003)

White, Avron Levine, ed., *Lost in Music: Culture, Style, and the Musical Event* (Routledge, 1987)

Science

Ball, Philip, *The Music Instinct* (Vintage, 2010)

Blacking, John, *Music, Culture and Experience* (Chicago University Press, 1995)

Honing, Henkjan, ed., *The Origins of Musicality* (MIT, 2018)

Levitin, Daniel J., *This is Your Brain on Music: The Science of a Human Obsession* (Penguin/Plume, 2007)

Pinker, Steven, *How the Mind Works* (Norton, 1997)

Powell, John, *How Music Works* (Penguin, 2010)

Powell, John, *Why We Love Music* (John Murray, 2016)

Sloboda, John, *Exploring the Musical Mind* (Oxford University Press, 2005)

Dictionaries

Blom, Eric, rev. David Cummings, *The New Everyman Dictionary of Music* (Oxford University Press, 1988)

Griffiths, Paul, *The Thames and Hudson Encyclopaedia of 20th-Century Music* (Thames & Hudson, 1988)

Jacobs, Arthur, *The Penguin Dictionary of Musical Performers* (Penguin, 1990)

Kennedy, Michael, *The Oxford Dictionary of Music*, revised edition (Oxford University Press, 1994)

Latham, Alison, *The Oxford Companion to Music* (Oxford University Press, 2002)

Lawson, Colin and Robin Stowell, eds, *The Cambridge Encyclopaedia of Historical Performance in Music* (Cambridge University Press, 2018)

Oxford Music Online (incorporating *The New Grove Dictionary of Music and Musicians*, second edition, eds, Stanley Sadie and John Tyrrell, Macmillan/Grove 2001)

Randel, Don Michael, ed., *The New Harvard Dictionary of Music* (Harvard University Press, 1986)

Samuel, Rhian and Julie Anne Sadie, eds, *The New Grove Dictionary of Women Composers* (Macmillan, 1994)

Classics

Abraham, Gerald, *The Tradition of Western Music* (Oxford University Press, 1974)

Allen, Warren Dwight, *Philosophies of Music History* (Dover, 1939/62)

Copland, Aaron, *What to Listen For in Music* (Signet/Penguin, 2011)

Dart, Thurston, *The Interpretation of Music* (Hutchinson, 1954/67)

Kerman, Joseph, *Opera as Drama* (Faber, 1956/88)

Lambert, Constant, *Music Ho!* (Penguin, 1933/48)

Mitchell, Donald, *The Language of Modern Music* (Faber, 1976)

Rosen, Charles, *The Classical Style* (Faber, 1971/76, new edition 1997)

Rosen, Charles, *Critical Entertainments: Music Old and New* (Harvard University Press, 2000)

Westrup, Jack, *An Introduction to Musical History* (Hutchinson, 1955/67)

Index

Page numbers in italics refer to the list of 100 Great Works.